AN AFFAIR OF THE HEART

INSPIRED BY THE LETTERS OF LOUIS UNTERMEYER

Mildred Marshall Maiorino

Writer's Showcase
San Jose New York Lincoln Shanghai

AN AFFAIR OF THE HEART
Inspired by the letters of Louis Untermeyer

Writer's Showcase
an imprint of iUniverse.com, Inc.

For information address:
iUniverse.com, Inc.
5220 S 16th, Ste. 200
Lincoln, NE 68512
www.iuniverse.com

ISBN: 0-595-19033-2

Printed in the United States of America

To my family: First to my Husband, Salvatore, whose support has always been unfailing, and especially to our sons, Nick and Anthony, who have helped me to "grow up."

Contents

POETRY

Foreword

Mildred Marshall Maiorino has a rare and exceptional quality to her writing and her spirituality further illumines her work.

An Affair of the Heart is a book you will not want to put down. Fate conspired that Mildred would decide to take a different ship than she had originally booked to go to Italy to further her operatic career. On the new ship she met a dashing and handsome young Italian. The consequences ended as a fairy-tale romance come true.

Her brief encounter with Louis Untermeyer, America's most renowned literary critic of that era, initiated a twenty-four year correspondence regarding Mildred's prose and poetry. It makes fascinating reading apropos the history of that period.

—Daphne Huntington

Author's Note: Daphne Huntington is herself a poet and writer whose poetry has appeared in several national and international anthologies. She studied art at the London School of Arts and Crafts, UK and E'cole de Louvre, Paris, France. She and her sister Venetia Epler have distinguished themselves as mosaicists having created one of the world's largest mosaic murals for the facade of the Christian Heritage Mausoleum, Forest Lawn, Covina, California, measuring 30 x 180 feet.

Acknowledgements

Louis Untermeyer, my long-time mentor and friend, had offered many times over the years to write the foreword for my first book of poems. Since his death intervened, I can only take this opportunity to express my gratitude for the invaluable criticism and encouragement he gave so generously during the years of our association.

Just as my family helped me to "grow up" in a personal sense, Mr. Untermeyer aided in the growth and flowering of my creative expression until, hopefully, I grew up in that direction. Though he had left this physical plane of existence when *"An Affair of the Heart"* was written, I feel he hasn't really gone –that his voice can still be heard with the ears of my heart–those ears that listen and understand.

The entire book could be devoted to expressions of gratitude to all those "others" within the range of my awareness for the lessons, both pleasant and difficult, filling the textbook of life, but will conclude with a big "thank you" to my life-long friends, Lucilla Udovick and her sister Anne for their love, support, and inspiration.

PREFACE:
POETS ARE BORN, NOT MADE

Yesterday I gave a lecture at a regional meeting of the "National League of American Pen Women" on how I became a poet after spending fifteen years studying music, opera in particular. Following my talk a lady in the audience suggested that in addition to the nearly one hundred and fifty books of poetry and prose I've written I should do a volume on the letters I'd received from Louis Untermeyer while working with him. Everyone who knows me is aware of the special literary friendship we shared, one that continued for twenty-four years until his death in 1977. Oddly enough this was so gratifying to me that I felt no need to share my work with the rest of the world and get into the hassle of a literary career, although frequently urged to do so by Louis Untermeyer.

"You'll receive rejection before your work is accepted," he cautioned, "and the **better** your work is the more likely it is to be rejected!"

That certainly sounded like a catch twenty-two, as we say these days, and I must have told myself I didn't want to know the answer to it, not at that time anyway, so it wasn't until almost twenty years after Louis Untermeyer's death that I became serious about bringing my work out. I soon discovered it must be in the **good** category, because so far it has been rejected by publishers all over the place. It's a good thing, though, that my mentor had informed me of the possibility that what I'd written might be "good" otherwise I'd think I'm a very bad poet, turning out stuff no one wants to read. Well, editors anyway!

After composing poems for many years I had at last run the gamut of poetic inspiration in around fifty books. Later I decided to add a running prose commentary to each volume and writing these turned out to be such fun I switched to this medium altogether.

I suppose many people would insist that I'm still a poet, "moonlighting" and doing prose on the side. Here I can only agree, since once you're a poet you're always one, and there just isn't much you can do to cure this incredibly wonderful "disease" except to use the antidote of writing! Louis Untermeyer once told me that in his youth he'd been interested in music, which might have been why he was so sympathetic when he learned I was a student of opera in Italy at the time I started writing.

Oddly enough, it was this interest in opera which led me to seek further study abroad where I was destined to discover my affinity for poetry. But before I get into that story, I must explain why I chose the title "Poets Are Born, Not Made" for my opening chapter. I truly believe that inside everyone a poet is waiting to be born, although not many folks ever probe deeply enough to become aware of its presence. This is something like finding out who you are as a soul and not many people have done that either, or we'd be living in a totally different world.

Once you discover the beauty of writing poetry, it becomes a kind of obsession. You might find yourself chewing over the idea for a poem like people get embroiled in a sexual fantasy and look around for someone with whom to share their feeling. A real poem comes from the same deep place inside yourself so in a sense writing, especially poetry, might be compared to a sexual-cerebral "affair of the heart" that often proves astounding to the poet, as well as self-revelatory to the reader.

Well now, I guess I have to explain that! Over the years a curious fact has emerged: I've personally learned more from my own writing than any reader ever could, so in that regard I'm teaching myself. It's said that the teacher is the taught, student and teacher being one. Taken a bit further I'd say the soul and the essence of its experience are one, also. I really don't think you could have anyone else's orgasm for them, although you might have your own at the same time, and as most participants would agree, that's the best way to do it. Sexual expression then becomes a shared thing of being alone **together**, which is what poetry is, too. When the poet makes a deep connection with the reader it partakes of all the above in a very special sense.

Of course this is seen while you're looking from a higher perspective which doesn't normally enter physical expression or people would be reading poetry so they could engage in intercourse with a poem instead of their favorite person. If it actually worked that way, I can tell you poetry books would be enjoying tremendous popularity instead of remaining at the bottom of the list as they presently are.

I've heard that this whole scene will soon change as people become more aware of life's continued expression in other dimensions and are able to connect with it there, as well as here. Reading, and or writing poetry, is one of the best ways I know of to expand our awareness so we can connect with various levels on those invisible planes. I'd even go so far as to say that reading poetry ranks right up there with the appreciation of nature as a key to unlock the doors of other dimensions, both psychic **and** spiritual.

You may be wondering what the difference is between psychic and spiritual. For me "psychic" is like receiving information **about** someone, while "spiritual" is actually seeing and talking with them, just as the best poetry pulls you into communion with the author right away. I suppose you might say it's like falling in love which has its own inexplicable expression and rapport.

This only substantiates what was implied earlier about everyone being a poet, since obviously the reader's tuning into the same source the author has, or he wouldn't find anything very interesting in those silly looking squiggles on the page. Words are just words until the soul opens your eyes and gives meaning to them. So keeping all of this clearly in mind I'll continue with my saga of how I became a poet.

Maybe I should clarify that a little and tell you how a poet rather thinly disguised as a writer of prose is finding her medium in the work I'm doing at the present time...

ITALY:
A VOYAGE
OF DISCOVERY

A CHANGE IN PLANS

I'd already devoted some fifteen years of my life to music, opera mainly, when I was given a marvelous opportunity to continue my work abroad for at least a year, possibly more. This was certainly an offer I couldn't refuse, since not long before this I'd had a long talk with God about the mess I'd made of my life and appealed to him for help in finding a new direction.

Now as most people know, if they've ever done what I did, God always answers prayer. This is a good point to remember: there's **no unanswered prayer.**

"What!" I heard a friend once say, like I'd lost it, "I asked God for a new car and he gave me that beat up old Chevy."

"But you got a car, didn't you?" I reminded him. "You should have been more specific about the one you wanted!"

The truth is, I've discovered that God answers prayer in his own way and in his own time, since time isn't something God goes by, not in the sense we do.

"But what if God says 'No'?" he asked.

"Then 'No' was his answer."

Actually I'm getting into all of this to illustrate the fact that God's response regarding the outcome of any situation is highly unpredictable. For instance, after I'd had that big conversation with God he proceeded to do very little about it except get me to a performance of "Aida" in which a famous opera singer of that era, "Renata Tebaldi" sang the starring role. Afterwards while attending a crowded reception for her back stage, I had the privilege of meeting her and asking who she'd studied with. She complied graciously, highly recommending the teacher she worked with in Milano, Italy, who was her coach for many of the operas in her repertoire.

I carefully wrote her teacher's name and address on a slip of paper and got a letter off to Italy the following week. When "Madame Carmen Melis" replied, she said she'd be pleased to accept me as a student, so the foster family who was sponsoring my career decided a trip to Italy was definitely the next step I must take to complete my operatic studies. Subsequently I opted to make the journey on a freighter sailing out of "New Orleans" which would give me a lot of free time to work on my scores and relax in the sun with nothing in particular to do for a month or so.

Now pretty soon you'll begin to see how God does things. About a week before my scheduled departure I fell seriously ill with a high fever caused by a chronic infection I suffered from at that time, which made me so sick nothing short of a miracle could have gotten me aboard that freighter. Since no miracle was forthcoming, the whole thing had to be canceled. Perhaps you, along with myself, will detect the seemingly cruel irony in what took place after that, when I joined the company of many other spiritual neophytes, scoffing at God big time along with the myth of answered prayer and all such benighted nonsense!

By way of offering some comfort in my disappointment, I was informed that when my health was fully restored, passage would be booked again, but this time on a liner sailing from New York. I'd begun feeling, in view of all that was happening, that perhaps I wasn't destined to study in Italy after all. However, God proceeded to overturn all such negative assumptions, and I was re-scheduled to leave during the latter part of August on an Italian liner, the "Conte Biancamano." Our ship would dock in Naples for a day, then continue on for a cruise, stopping at several points of interest in Sicily before terminating the voyage in Genoa.

Are you beginning to see the handiwork of God in all of this? As I stated earlier, God has his own way of doing things so if you've asked for his help you might as well toss out your version of how you expect that help to arrive. Then after closing the window of your expectation you can open the door of your heart to what God has in mind. Right here at the beginning of my story I must tell you that I've never been a religious person, although I have been, and still am working on becoming "spiritual."

Just what that quality is will hopefully be revealed as my book unfolds, or perhaps I should say **our** book, since as pointed out earlier, I truly think that inside everyone a poet waits to be born. I might also add that the execution of any form of art assists the fulfillment of this inner discovery, since you can live a spiritual life even when you're not much interested in following a particular religious path, here or somewhere else in the world.

While you may have been trained and brought up in any of the world's religions whether Buddhist, Hindu, Jewish, Mohammedan or one of the many Christian sects, becoming spiritual is like doing graduate study and going a step beyond all of these paths. Would this be like a trip to Italy to study opera? I do believe it's something like that, although you could stay right in your own home town and become God's gift to opera.

Like his poets, God doesn't care where his singers grow and develop their skill, or if they ever become famous and applauded by others for what they do. Sometimes this happens only after a poet has departed to continue his existence on the "other side," a term I'll be using now and then throughout this book.

It was said that the great poet, Emily Dickinson, wrote mostly for the personal fulfillment it gave **her**, completely ignoring any thought of recognition and fame. I can only say that being recognized posthumously didn't make her poetry any greater than it already was! Quite possibly, though, she escaped the criticism leveled at her for not writing as other poets did. Her experiments in the use of an innovative and sometimes startling poetic technique upset many traditionalists of her day who failed to appreciate the mystical depths of her writing.

I discovered that Louis Untermeyer truly understood where Emily Dickinson was coming from, and since I knew how much he admired her work, this "hooked" me into writing several poems in which I imitated her style. All of this will be revealed in the correspondence I later had with him.

But now, let me get back to my life-changing voyage to Italy, which I personally feel was instituted by God. On the "Conte Biancamano" I had the good fortune to meet another singer with a marvelous voice, fortunately quite different from my own! After encountering one another in several social get-togethers in the Lounge, Lucilla informed me one evening that she had also changed her passage from another ship so she could sail on the "Conte Biancamano," hoping as I had to improve her knowledge of Italian.

One evening Lucilla decided to tell me an amusing story about a friend of hers in New York who had gone to a party and the moment she entered the room caught the eye of a man there playing the piano. "My friend was engaged to another man, but she suddenly stared at the pianist and said to her companion, 'That's the man I'm going to marry,' and it happened just that way."

"You know something, Lucilla," I retorted, "that's an unbelievable story, as silly as if I were to say I'm going to marry that handsome man dancing over there, and I don't even know him!"

Lucilla laughed. "I guess you're not very romantic."

During the voyage, Lucilla had sung for the Catholic Mass each morning, which another passenger who loved music told me about. Subsequently she'd introduced me to Lucilla and before I knew what was happening had arranged for both of us to sing as featured soloists for the "Captain's Dinner," a gala affair topped off with a caviar and champagne supper given especially for us following the concert. We were both so well received that for the remainder of the voyage we were treated like visiting royalty. In retrospect I must say this is preferable to being royalty and treated like something else!

A couple of nights after the concert, Lucilla and I went out on deck, and bumped right into one of the handsomest men on this Earth, sitting alone in a deck chair and looking at the full moon. I noted immediately that he was the same man I'd seen dancing in the Lounge when Lucilla had related the story about her friend attending a party in New York and I'd ridiculed it!

"I'm sorry I had to miss the concert," he said. He introduced himself and told us that although his name was Salvatore everyone called him Sal. "I heard from some friends that your singing was tremendous. Would you girls allow me to buy you a drink?"

Lucilla and I accepted his offer, and ordered lemonade. Then after a few minutes of small talk about the ship, travel and sea sickness, which several passengers suffered from, Lucilla excused herself saying she was tired and had a big day ahead of her the next morning since she planned to explore Naples.

It seems superfluous to say that I really didn't mind being left alone with a modern-day Valentino, so I opted to accept Sal's invitation and have another drink. More lemonade I might add, since I've never been at all attracted to alcohol.

During our conversation I discovered Sal was interested in poetry. He'd read "The Prophet" by Kahlil Gibran, which I never had, having spent so many years with my head in an opera score memorizing roles for various performances at the "Opera Lab" where I studied with Vladimir Rosing, a gifted stage director of operas as well as musical segments in certain films. He'd also staged the "California Story" at the well known Hollywood Bowl in Los Angeles. In addition to opera, I was busy rehearsing and singing as a paid soloist for All Saints Episcopal church in Beverly Hills.

"I find Gibran expresses truth in a non-sectarian way," Sal went on to explain. "People who aren't especially religious can learn a lot from his writings."

"When I get to Milano and settled somewhere, I'll see if I can find Gibran's book," I promised. "I suspect it will be an Italian translation over here. As you can see, my Italian's not too great yet. Lucilla speaks much better than I do."

Sal laughed and told me his parents had been born in Italy so he'd grown up speaking Italian. After we finished our drinks, he asked if I'd like to go for a stroll around the deck and I consented rather quickly. It was an August night made in Heaven with a full moon on the horizon that was breath-taking if you're into full moon appreciation like I've always been. There was something magical in the air that night, filled with what I would now call an "aura of predestination" which may have been why we stayed up until three A.M. completely losing track of time.

As we walked around the deck looking at the dazzling reflection of moonlight on the ocean, Sal said, "And to think I almost missed being on the Conte Biancamano! At the last minute I canceled my ticket on an American ship so I could take this one."

"Something like that happened to me, also," I said, laughing. "Oddly enough Lucilla told me she'd had the same experience! Could this be the hand of fate arranging things for all of us to meet?"

"That might very well be," Sal said, giving me a strange look.

"I really must get to bed," I said a bit reluctantly at last, "since I'm planning to go ashore tomorrow with Lucilla."

"I'm getting off in Naples, too," Sal said, "and meet my relatives. Then we'll all go to Avellino where my father's family lives."

"Do you plan to remain in Avellino?"

"I expect to stay there for a while before leaving for Perugia where I'll attend college for a year or so."

After a moment, he said, "May I ask what your plans are?"

"I'm disembarking at Genoa and then go on to Milano."

"Do you know where you'll be staying?"

"Not yet. The only contact I have there now is with 'Madame Carmen Melis' who will be my voice teacher."

"Would you give me her address?" Sal asked.

"Of course. Maybe you'll send me a postcard!" I hinted.

"I expect to be traveling through Milano later this year on my way to visit relatives in Turino," Sal confided. "Maybe I can call your teacher and she'll tell me where to contact you," he added with what seemed more than a casual interest.

"If anyone knows where I am, it will be my teacher," I said.

Shortly after that Sal escorted me to my second-class cabin where we said good-night. Although he only kissed me lightly on the lips I sensed the tremendous chemistry between us, something I found quite intriguing. I must confess that although I got very little sleep that night, I did go ashore as scheduled the next morning, accompanying Lucilla and a few other passengers who wanted to go sightseeing, then before boarding the ship again stop at a little "ristorante" somewhere to eat.

Sal had disappeared with members of his family, and as I would later learn, went home with them to Avellino, located thirty-five miles or so from Naples. Post-war Italy was going through a painful time of readjustment following the second World War, especially economically, and as yet there was a lot of poverty and uncertainty regarding the future. I can still see the sad faces of pedestrians walking past the windows of the "ristorante" while we were having lunch, which we soon learned is "dinner" in Italy.

The long parade of people asking for money in the streets had been quite disturbing, also, making us feel more than a little guilty as we stuffed ourselves on that marvelous Italian food and attempted to forget the poverty around us. It was almost as much of a "downer" as the feeling people had in America during the depression in 1929, which I remember only vaguely.

After returning to the ship, we sailed on to dock at "Messina" where we took a bus up to "Taormina" and joined a guided tour of a marvelous ancient temple looming with immortal grace on top of a high cliff overlooking "Mount Etna." The waters of the incredibly blue Mediterranean lapping the shore, painted one of the most unforgettable vistas of nature that can be seen anywhere.

The next day we continued our cruise along the seacoast until arriving in Genoa, the birthplace of Columbus. In Genoa Lucilla and I stuck together like two magnets who hadn't yet found a way to separate from one another, or were perhaps discovering they didn't want to! A group of American sailors on leave in Genoa immediately took us over, offering refreshments, which we accepted figuring there was safety in numbers. After we finished, our exuberant sailor friends, delighted with the company of American girls again, helped get our luggage on the train for Milano.

Since Lucilla had brought a rather cumbersome trunk with her this proved quite a task! When all of our stuff was safely aboard we leaned from the open windows of the train before it pulled out, smiling and blowing kisses to our gallant "knights" in their cute white sailor uniforms.

During the ride to Milano Lucilla invited me to accompany her to the "Grand Hotel" where she planned to stay, and share a room with her. "We can get a bigger room and pay less," she said, taking a practical view of our situation.

"That's true," I agreed, a decision that would pave the way for our emerging friendship throughout the months to come. It wasn't long before we decided to share an apartment, fully furnished on the seventh floor of what would be called a "condo" here in America, overlooking the busy piazza below where noisy street cars whizzed by day and night.

In the months to come we'd also discover that this fortuitous joining of our lives and our finances would save the day for us many times there in that strange country where we'd be living what often turned out to be a life style far removed from anything either of us had been accustomed to in America...

U.S. Sailors to the Rescue

Refreshments with Rescuers

Departure for Milano

Mildred in Operatic Costume

Sal in Service

LIFE IN ITALY

As time passed Lucilla and I became very close friends, and although we studied with different teachers, we enjoyed discussing some of the fine points of what we were learning with one another, even singing "The Letter Duet" from "The Marriage of Figaro," an opera I'd performed for the Opera Lab in Los Angeles as well as on television, singing the role of Suzanna. Our sharing extended to the household chores such as shopping and laundry, although Lucilla did most of the cooking, since she loved good food and I was a lousy cook, never having had much practice.

As I stated previously, Lucilla's Italian was considerably beyond the point mine had reached, and at that time "beyond" didn't have to be very far! I went around the streets posing questions to pedestrians lifted straight out of Mozart's "Marriage of Figaro," asking some unsuspecting stranger: "Wouldst thou direct me to the next bus arrival?"

Although I'd been studying Hugo's book on Italian for some time, the only phrase I recall now was, "Quale delle ciliege matureranno prima: le bianche o le nere?" Translated this means "Which of the cherries will get ripe first: the white or the black?" To tell the truth I never found an opportunity to use the above sentence throughout my nearly two-year stay in Italy!

At first I had a really great gift for getting similar Italian words mixed up, like "uova" the word for eggs, and "uva" meaning grapes. Can you picture going into one of those little markets and asking for a dozen grapes or a bunch of eggs as I frequently did? Another duo that drove me slightly crazy was "aglio" the Italian for garlic and "oglio" their word for oil. Requesting a bottle of garlic or a piece of oil drew the same response of laughter as the previous mixer-uppers.

At that time, instead of supermarkets, there were numerous small establishments selling their own specialties, so a lot of people looked forward to having a good laugh on the days it was my turn to shop. On one memorable occasion Lucilla had asked me to do the marketing for her. Although it was her "turn" she had an afternoon lesson with the Maestro and wanted to cook a chicken for dinner. As usual, I agreed since I loved her cooking. I was doing great with finding everything she'd asked me to buy until it came to the chicken and I couldn't remember the Italian word for the critter. Finally in desperation I asked the owner of the store, "Dove si compra la madre di un ouvo?"

Translated this means, "Where can you buy the mother of an egg?" At first she gave me an astounded look, then disappeared laughing into a little room at the rear of the store, returning with a chicken, its head and feet attached, and as usual all its inner organs still inside.

The signora we rented our apartment from had once made a kind of "ragu" for dinner, using the cleansed and chopped intestines of the chicken. If you didn't know what was in it, you'd probably have thought it was delicious. But then I suppose that's the way it is with a lot of things in this world, and not just "ragu!" Anyway the chicken cacciatore Lucilla made for dinner that night was marvelous, and for as long as I live someone will be telling that story again of how I asked for a chicken when I couldn't remember the name for it in Italian...

I really must record for posterity that the climate in Milano made the city then, and still would make it one of my least favorite places to live, being extremely damp and enclosed in fog throughout much of the winter. I'm sure the Milanese climate, so different from that of sunny California, might be directly blamed for many of the colds Lucilla and I experienced that first year. On one occasion after I came down with a bronchial infection that just wouldn't quit, Lucilla decided to delve into that big "trunk" she'd brought with her and find a few books for me to read.

"Honey, here are some anthologies of poems compiled by Louis Untermeyer and they're just great."

At the risk of seeming ignorant, if not downright stupid, I asked, "**Who** is Louis Untermeyer?"

"He's only the foremost literary critic in America. Don't you remember, he discovered Robert Frost and promoted his work."

"Oh yes," I mumbled, "I do recall reading some of Frost's poems in High School."

"Well, you'll know a lot more about Robert Frost as well as Louis Untermeyer after reading these books." Surprisingly I really enjoyed them, sharing some of the poems with Lucilla.

"This stuff's terrific!" I said. Lucilla seeing the spark of interest she'd aroused suggested I write a poem myself just to try my hand at it.

"I don't know anything about writing poetry," I replied. "I'm a singer, remember?"

"Well, you're not able to sing right now so why not do something else? How about writing a poem for **me**? I always wished someone would do that and no one ever has." With mock pathos, Lucilla put her hand on her heart, and rolled her eyes upward.

"Not even one of those boy friends of yours in New York?" I asked, teasing her, knowing she didn't like socializing much, being totally dedicated to her career just as anyone who wants to be successful must be.

"Not even them," she admitted.

Although at first I felt silly writing a poem to someone who was sitting right there beside me, I did come up with a couple of trite stanzas about Lucilla and our friendship which she loved, or pretended to, for the sake of creative encouragement.

"Great," she said, "now that you've gotten started, keep it going, honey. Write something else."

"About what?" I asked, between fits of coughing.

"Italy. You should have a lot of good stuff written by the time you get back to America"...

Lucilla was sure right about that! When I returned to New York over a year and a half later I would have a notebook filled with personal observations, along with my response to the Italian culture we were slowly becoming part of. I can't imagine a more beautiful setting for the birth of a poet than Italy, so filled with the aura of antiquity and the breath-taking beauty of nature which Lucilla and I would learn to appreciate quite fully during our travels in the coming months. Add to this the incredible intensity of the potential romance both Sal and I were involved with on inner levels, and a poet couldn't help being born!

That first year in Milano, Lucilla and I shared a lot of memorable experiences. I recall the time her agent got seats for us at the famous "La Scala" Opera House where portions of the third act of "Aida" were being filmed for the first "Cinerama" movie in which three cameras were used to photograph the scene. Later these tracks were spliced together to create one wide-screen picture, which wasn't all that gratifying since you could clearly detect visible lines where they'd been joined.

The seats Lucilla and I, along with her agent, happened to have that night were right down front, and when the cameras were turned on the audience, guess who showed up very prominently for the folks back home when the first "Cinerama" film was premiered in Los Angeles, dressed in our most elegant attire? That was certainly an exciting evening, especially when the American director, "Mike Todd," who was in charge of the filming, strode up and down the isle impatiently, waiting for the Italian stage director to O.K. the scene for the first take.

"Will somebody please tie up the Maestro, so we can get on with the show?" he called out in English, which possibly only Lucilla and I appreciated since in those days there didn't seem to be many Italians who spoke English. Anyway, they finally got ready to film the scene and the "Aida" segment was magnificent.

In the fall Lucilla and I, along with her agent, were invited to have dinner at the home of the foremost tailor in Italy. It was said that he'd once made a suit for one of our American presidents. I forget which one, but it was something he was quite proud of. I must say that the elegant "pranzo" he and his Signora served us was really first class all the way. There were so many courses that even before the roast lamb seasoned with garlic and rosemary appeared, I was stuffed and could only sample it.

The dinner had started at one o'clock with antipasto and at five we were still seated around the table, our host playing the guitar while we all sang. Lucilla and I did our share of the singing, everyone joining in to render quartets and choruses from various operas. Italians really knew their operas then and probably still do!

This exciting relationship with Lucilla's agent came to a crashing halt just before Christmas, when he developed an overly possessive attitude towards his two young American protegees who definitely knew their way around, and had no need of a chaperon to manage their lives, as well as their careers. Lucilla's anyway, since at that time I was definitely flying alone regarding my own future. Lucilla had a truly magnificent voice even then, and in future years would become quite famous throughout Italy, applauded for her rendition of sixty or more operatic roles, not only in Italy but in many countries around the world.

Meanwhile, in early spring Lucilla and I were planning a short vacation and sightseeing tour of nearby Nervi. Just before we were scheduled to depart I said, "I can't possibly leave with you today, Lucilla! We'll have to postpone our plans until tomorrow." Of course she was more than a little put out with my sudden decision, although neither of us guessed the reason for my belligerence until that afternoon when the phone rang and Sal's voice came over loud and clear.

"Good, I'm glad I found you at home. While passing through Milano on my way to Turino I decided to call your teacher, hoping the number you gave me on the ship was correct. Since I'm talking to you, it must be!" he said, laughing.

Needless to say I was delighted, especially when Sal invited me to have dinner with him that evening. Lucilla and her date joined us for one of those marvelous Italian feasts so affordable in Milano's restaurants then, and for only pennies compared to what you'd pay these days. The outcome of all this was that the four of us decided to make the trip to Nervi-Genoa together and spend a few days there before Sal continued on his way to Turino. During the afternoon we had an absolutely incredible time sightseeing on the boardwalk at Nervi, then later we all spent the evening at a little night spot where we had a couple of soft drinks and danced while a trio of musicians played. I was devastated to have Sal find out I'd never learned to dance well, especially the tango, which I hadn't even attempted.

He said, "Well, it definitely takes two to tango, so right now you're going to learn the tango!" As it turned out, Sal was a great teacher of the tango as well as the rhumba, dances I'd somehow managed to miss in my zeal to set the world on fire as an opera singer. The truth is, I never did learn to tango, not even with Sal leading me through it quite expertly, nor to rhumba with the abandon he displayed. But the chemistry was there anyway.

As we danced he said, "You know I could sweep you off your feet if I wanted to!" Now wouldn't you know I got angry with him for saying that? It was the part "if I wanted to" that struck me as a "put down." So after that we were off to our first lover's quarrel until about three months later when Sal decided to return to Milano and put things in their proper perspective.

After a few days of sightseeing around Milano showing him some of the things Lucilla and I had already seen, like Da Vinci's "Last Supper" which had been miraculously preserved during the bombing of Milano, and also the famous "Duomo" cathedral, the four of us planned another trip together to the Island of Capri. On the way there a few days later we made a brief stopover in Rome for a quick sightseeing jaunt through the "Vatican," promising to return later and do justice to this magnificent Basilica, then a springtime tour of some old Roman ruins, their ancient columns crumbling in the immortal grass growing around them...

On Capri everything was so green and filled with the mystery of spring. Actually a poem I later wrote about our stay there tells the story better than any words of prose I could come up with now. Oddly enough a poem can say more in a few lines than pages and pages of prose, since it captures the inner essence of what took place right along with its poetic description.

VISTAS OF BLUE MIST AND FLAME

Was it the wonder of our new-found love
or the burgeoning spring on the Island
that each time I think of it
enchanted bells begin to ring,
recalling that day on the balcony
when we saw in the distance so far below
those vistas of blue mist and flame…

Or is it that eyes and ears of love
make jewels of ordinary things
which those merely physical
trample underfoot in the dust of thought,
or crush with the hammer of words?
            I wonder…

Like the blue-diamond silence we felt
the day we explored the famed Blue Grotto,
its shimmering hue of a sunlit sky
diffused with luminous silver fire
then confined in a white-domed cave…

Ringing once more with rhythmic joy
the sound of the bells is fused again
in walks we took along Island paths
ecstatic with springtime flowers,
while people sang their blithe canzoni
winged with love and laughter…

And now the bells' enchantment
ascends to a pandemonium of bliss
as I think of the day it rained and rained
and we didn't go out at all…

You're free at this point to draw your own conclusions as to what happened the day it rained! That's just about as much of a "kiss and tell" author you can expect me to be in this book. After Capri, I think Sal and I were both pretty sure our future would be spent together, not only during our remaining time in Italy but for the rest of our lives when we returned to America. Since this wouldn't take place for some time yet, we decided to do a lot of sightseeing and traveling to well known tourist spots in various parts of Italy, each one made more marvelous because we were there together…

That second Christmas in Milano Sal and I became officially engaged, exchanging lovely gold rings he'd had especially made with my name engraved inside his, and his in mine. For that occasion he invited me to attend Christmas Eve Mass with him. Although I'm not a Catholic, I'd frequently attended Mass with Lucilla who was. After the Mass, Sal and I knelt at a little altar devoted to Mary, the mother of Jesus and he presented me with his gift. We decided to wear the bands on our right hands as engagement rings in Italy and when we got married switch them to the left.

Although that was a great idea, tourists from Germany thought we were already married, since many people from there wore wedding rings on their right hand. I'm sure people everywhere caught on pretty fast that Sal and I were really serious about how we felt, and regarded us as "fidanzati," or engaged, wherever we went.

Often Sal was mistaken for one of our popular movie stars from that era and asked for his autograph. I suppose they looked on me as his "lady" and I was accepted in that role anyway, if not for having any movie-star status of my own. Now and then passengers on buses would line up outside as we got off and simply stare at us, like fans do at stars arriving for the Academy Awards in Hollywood. I'll never forget Sal dressed in his powder blue suit, nor the feeling of pride I had while wearing my strapless off the shoulder paisley print sundress in kind of a burnished red color.

I guess it never occurred to the Italians in those post-war days that if Sal really were a movie star we wouldn't have found it necessary, nor even desirable to travel by bus or tram, but would have had our own private "limo" driven by a uniformed chauffeur!

Lucilla & Abramo

Sal & Lucilla in Rome

Springtime in Rome

The Night I Learned to Tango

A Café in Rome

Along the Boardwalk in Nervi

A Wonderful Day in Nervi

Sal & Mildred on Capri

ESCAPE TO
THE ISLAND OF ISCHIA

In early spring that first year, I'd decided to study with Lucilla's teacher, "Maestro Montesanto," who lived in an apartment just across the piazza from us. He had been a well known singer at La Scala at one time and since then had found great success teaching his art to a large number of students. With the advent of the muggy, unpleasant summer weather in Milano, Maestro opted to relocate his studio on the "Island of Ischia" for a couple of months. Ischia is in the same general territory as the better known and more popular "Island of Capri," so Lucilla and I were really looking forward to seeing another of Italy's scenic wonders.

During the weeks we stayed on Ischia I discovered there was something spooky about that whole atmosphere on the Island, which inspired a lot of strange feelings, as though I'd been there before in some former lifetime. I latched onto that idea anyway and wrote a poem about it, which was later praised by Louis Untermeyer as having expressed the mood of my inner thoughts and feelings, whether they'd been inspired by some faraway incarnation or something closer at hand, like being in love.

But now let me return to Rome for a moment and tell you about an interesting experience I had there on our way to Ischia. Before leaving for Italy, I'd sung at a luncheon in a guest appearance for a business men's organization my sponsor supported. During lunch we got to talking to someone who was a friend of "Herbert Coleman" the producer of the movie "Roman Holiday" scheduled for filming in Rome that summer with "William Wyler" directing.

The gentleman at the luncheon had been so impressed with my singing, that he sent a letter right away to Mr. Coleman asking him to see me, when and if I should be traveling to Rome during the filming. Sal and I were already on our way to Ischia before I remembered to get in touch with Mr. Coleman, although we thought it best if I kept my appointment with him alone, without disclosing that I was in Rome with a "companion," a bit of a subterfuge I must admit in looking back on it now! After I'd called Mr. Coleman he invited me to have dinner with himself and "William Wyler" at a popular restaurant in Piazza Navona called "Tre Scalini."

Can you believe, I would have preferred spending the evening with Sal, although I did keep the appointment with Mr. Coleman so I could send a full report to my sponsor back in Los Angeles. After all, it isn't everyone who has the opportunity to meet the producer as well as the director of what would later become a film classic! Although I had no way of knowing this at the time, I got myself into a glamorous cocktail dress and went out to meet these two lions of the movie industry.

Surprisingly we had a marvelous time and after dinner, both Mr. Coleman and Mr. Wyler wanting to extend the evening, took me to one of those little night clubs Rome was famous for so we could dance and continue our talk together. Mr. Coleman decided his friend "Billy" should do the honors dancing with me. "Billy's a better dancer than I am," he said with a grin.

After I'd told Mr. Coleman about an audition I'd done at Paramount Studio the previous year, he said, "Young lady when you return to America I want you to get in touch with me. I'm the one who can help you get started in films."

The experience I related to him had taken place not long before I left for Italy when I auditioned for "Roy Fiesta," head of the music department at Paramount. I'd taken my own accompanist along since I planned to sing the entire aria from the first act of La Traviata: "Ah forse lui" followed by the difficult "Sempre Libera," still a tour de force for me on a bad day!

Not only did the whole thing go remarkably well, but I decided to zoom up and knock off a high "E flat" at the end of the aria instead of my usual high "C" which was easier, especially if you were nervous, and I certainly was! Later I learned from the friend who had arranged for the audition, that "Roy Fiesta" had remained to hear the entire aria, saying at the end of it, "I'd rather listen to that voice than Lily Pons." Perhaps you recall that Lily Pons was a leading coloratura "diva" of that era.

After being told I'd soon be leaving for Italy and further operatic study, he said, "When your friend returns tell her to come see me right away." Although I wasn't destined to do that, I've always felt happy that he liked my voice anyway.

Both Mr. Coleman and Mr. Wyler asked if I could remain in Rome for a few days since the cast and crew of "Roman Holiday" were out of town on location. When they returned to shoot further scenes in Rome I'd be there to meet "Audrey Hepburn" and "Gregory Peck," the well-known stars of the film at work on the set. I declined with what I now realize was a phony show of regret, saying I must continue on my way to "Ischia" where my teacher was waiting to begin our work together on several operas.

The truth is I wanted to be with Sal and spend some time with him on the Island before he returned to Avellino and that, of course, was exactly what we did! Our teacher, and several students who had accompanied him, including Lucilla and myself, were staying at one of those enchanting old villas located on the hillside overlooking the Mediterranean. Not far from us were the famous mud and mineral baths, which we also visited now and then during the six weeks or more we were there. It was said that the world-renowned conductor, "Arturo Toscanini," came every summer to stay at a villa on the hillside just below us, paying frequent visits to the mud baths. However, as fate would have it, he wasn't in Italy that year due to career commitments, so we never had the good fortune of bumping into him at the baths!

On the ceiling of the room Lucilla and I shared, were hand painted frescos that might have graced a museum. They were seemingly in the villa just for us to enjoy during the day, and some of the nights as well when the moon was full and we were lying in bed sharing "girl" talk. Our room opened out onto a lovely terrace, surrounded by flowers and citrus trees loaded with fruit.

A few sonorous Pine trees reposed on the hillside, sighing in the wind and showering peace over the garden. Each day I'd sit looking at a bed of daisies nodding in the breeze from the sea, as it blew intermittently over their heads, while I composed poetry about Italy and the Island, feeling all the while those indefinable emotions I soon came to associate with Ischia. So you'll get an idea of the feeling I was experiencing at that time I'll add one of my poems about it here. I do think it captures my mood better than any prose ever could...

DRY STORM AT MIDNIGHT

Midnight, and the storm came,
a strange dry storm in the dry season
        on the Island,
awaking us to a sense of foreboding
that defied all logic and reason.

Through the shuttered window panes
        bars of lightning beat:
now bright, then black again,
like primordial neon lights
from the ruins of a buried street.
Overhead dried branches moved,
fitfully scrawling in the wind
their dusty hieroglyphics
over red tile slates on the roof.

Spellbound, in close embrace—
motionless as a double statue,
we stared at the moon
sitting stoically like a stunned
          bright sibyl
in the ruined temple of her sky.
Fine white dust rained bitter and dry
on ghostly flowers and trees,
while around our feet a desiccated
skirl of leaves spun spasmodically...

Abruptly the cord of the spell
was severed in a momentary lull—
releasing us to the shelter of our room
the storm hurling after us
a final, shuddering feral cry,
then a long dissatisfied sigh
as it moved away over the sea
leaving one lone shutter swinging
          slowly in the wind—
back and forth like a troubled breath,
back and forth in the wind...

If while reading this poem, a similar response is born in your heart, then you're one with the poet, along with that fellow who resides within myself. When you succeed in synchronizing your feeling with that of the writer, and read without letting the critical, judgmental observer of the mind take over, you may enter the spirit of the author's work. I truly believe that when you connect deeply with any form of art, whether it's painting, writing, or music then you've tapped into a form of universal creativity we all share. For me the substance of something sacred is revealed in this discovery, and not in what is created outside ourselves, and then defined as such.

One day while Lucilla and I were seated on the terrace after lunch, which as you know by now is "dinner" in Italy, Lucilla mentioned how she was having trouble getting the feeling the Maestro wanted her to have when Tosca kills Scarpia in the well known Puccini opera "Tosca" which she was studying that summer.

Suddenly, right out of the blue a little bat emerged from under the bushes with a high terrified squeaking. I think he'd been hurt. Lucilla expressed her dislike for all bat creatures, and I couldn't whip up much enthusiasm for them either right then as we both pulled our feet up on the reclining chairs where we sat. Pretty soon the maid came running out of the villa in a pair of wooden soled zocoletti like a lot of people wore on the Island.

"Odio quelle bestie! I hate those beasts," she screamed, and then to our horror began stomping on the frightened baby bat until all that remained of it was a bloody pulp on the "terrazzo." All this commotion had brought our "padrona" outside to investigate, right at the close of the uneven conflict.

"Basta, Norina," she called in a loud voice. "Now clean up this mess!" We sat in total silence as Norina attempted to remove the blood stains but without much success.

When everything quieted down again, Lucilla said, "You know, honey, after seeing what happened here I think I can do that scene from Tosca now and sing it the way the Maestro wants it."

"You're right," I said wryly. "Killing's killing!"

I couldn't help wishing that Norina had chased the little bat into the shrubbery and let it live. I think it was there on the "Island of Ischia" that I first became aware of a certain mysterious light within myself, opening the way for future investigation along this line after Sal and I were married in California. I've discovered that no matter how happy we may think we are in this world there's always a new horizon to explore. Attempting to remain isolated at any point in a charmed circle of existence is to invite its decay...

I could go on and on writing about Italy, particularly Ischia, but by the end of August Sal and I had decided to leave Italy and travel to Paris for a couple of months so I could explore the background of several French operas, particularly "La Bohème." Now that I think back, though, I'd say that our trip to Paris was mostly a great excuse to be together in that intriguing city.

For a long time in Italy I'd retained a rather weird tendency to speak Italian with a French accent, which I'd studied in college, although my fiancé coming from an Italian family background, was at times more than a little frustrated by the intricacies of the French language while we were in Paris. I still laugh remembering the difficulty he had one morning trying to order two hard boiled eggs: "deux oeuf dure" and coffee with sugar. For him at that time "toute suite" meant with sugar.

Actually we had a glorious time in Paris, although I didn't study much French opera while I was there! We did go to visit "Versailles" and "Fountainbleau" as well as "Chartres," and even the Pigalle and Moulin Rouge. At the Pigalle we saw naked girls dancing in a rather bored fashion, while a group of American soldiers on leave tried not to fall asleep. Following this experience I had to admit that clothes do make a woman more attractive, as well as desirable! I've found that when you come to the "naked truth" of anything you tap into its vulnerability, and you have to be ready for that or it can really shake you up!

After a few glorious weeks in Paris Sal returned to Italy, promising to come back and escort me to Milano later where I would again share the apartment with Lucilla, just as we'd done since our arrival there. The next week I received a postcard from Sal's sister, Irma, who was visiting Italy, saying that our Maestro's wife had died quite suddenly of a massive heart attack on Ischia later the same day Sal and I took off for Paris.

I was so shocked on hearing this news that I couldn't rest until I'd gotten my feelings down on paper. I've discovered that writing about something painful helps bring a kind of "clearing" of those emotions...

DEATH ON ISCHIA

The view from the terrace
rose shimmering out of the sea—
a hazy blue pearl of beauty
cupped in the palm of the August afternoon
and we laughed to see Arno, that
        amiable cur,
sprawled comically in the cool, torn earth
        beneath the trellis...
Now she is dead.
God, this heat has gone to my head!

This hideous bloated corpse—all that
        remains of her,
is driving those busy swarms of flies insane
as they light with carnivorous glee
on the blue hand-painted basin
someone placed beneath the casket
when drops began seeping through its wood:
now half-filled with her blood.
How much blood can one small body contain?
The mattress of her bed was soaked clear
        through
and had to be buried, too...

That sweaty smell of unwashed humanity
and sickening fetor of death
made me so weak I crept outside

for fear I should faint, to wait exiled
on the steps like a naughty child:

"Requiem aeternam donna etis
Domini: et lux perpetua luceat eis."

The voice of the priest drones on
while I stare at a crimson bougainvillea
     gone riot on a nearby wall
surrounding a garden of fig trees,
heavy with hot green figs lolling plumply
beneath the broad green umbrellas
of their dusty, sheltering leaves…

Far below is another world where the sky
     meets the sea
in a cool, clean sweep of blue
that goes on and on past seeing,
while little white clouds go reeling by
as though newly transfigured in ecstasy
fleeing before the mischievous wind
as he plays at launching his toy ships,
then abruptly runs away to teeter
precariously on long fence rows
     of grape vines…

A wandering minstrel breeze,
blowing down from the shadow of Mount Epomeo,
sings with the fragrance of ripening grapes
     and robusto burgundy wines
before entering the open windows
     of the church,

to emerge dissonant with the smell of death,
and all of the grapes gone rotten...

Sick again I walk down the powdery
        descent of the road
toward the coolness of the sea,
the choir still chanting lugubriously
the Libera Me for the dead...

"Libera me Domini morte
Aeterna in die illa tremenda
Quando caeli movendi sunt et
Terra: Dum veneris judicare
Saeculum per ignem"...

This rather morbid poem might be written off as merely the product of my depression and the feeling of separation I felt after Sal left me alone in Paris if it weren't for the fact that on my return to Milano, I showed the poem to Lucilla.

After reading it she said it made her hair stand on end. "How could you describe this whole terrible scene so clearly when I know for a fact that you weren't there?"

"I can't say, Lucilla. It was just as though I'd tuned into everything that went on."

"Well, there's no way you could have known about that hand-painted basin they placed under the casket to catch drops of blood when it seeped through. Did anyone mention that to you?"

"Who?" I asked. "The postcard I received later from Sal's sister in Avellino only informed me of the Signora's death later that day, after we left for Paris. In a way I'm glad we left early and missed all of that!"

"Somehow," Lucilla said, with a strange look, "I don't think you missed a thing! Maybe you were right there beside me sitting on the church steps and feeling like I'd throw up at any minute!"

Actually this poem proved to me anyway, that consciousness can be in two places at the same time, although this wasn't done through any method of "astral projection" to a certain spot, like I've heard many psychics can do...

In Paris, when Sal returned from Italy, we'd gone to meet an artist friend of his at the "Deux Magots" restaurant, frequented by many famous artists in the past. Then on another evening we joined Peter and his German room mate for dinner served in their attic apartment, furnished mostly with packing boxes and filled with canvasses both finished and unfinished, stacked everywhere around the room. Perhaps the poem I wrote about the evening we spent with Peter, who would later become a rather well known artist, his work applauded and displayed in various museums, will describe what happened better than any of my prose can do now.

A SCENE FROM LA BOHÈME

You and I, a Paris night
and that artist friend of yours
who lived in an attic—
    though seldom alone!
And you carrying under your arm
    all the way
a two-foot long loaf of bread
that you flourished about like a sword
    or a cane
at several passing pedestrians
who only smiled indulgently
at two crazy people in love!

Then all of us sitting on the floor—
our table some wooden crates,
and waiting so long for dinner
while Peter finished his latest painting
of a dozen sweet red peppers
carefully arranged in a bowl,
feeling afterwards a bit sacrilegious
when he insisted we eat them—
although as he pointed out,
they'd just been immortalized
on a twelve-by-sixteen canvas...

Later that night the two of us
got to giggling about it,
saying we thought that evenings like this
only happened in La Bohème...
Right in the middle of all that laughing
I became the frail Mimi
and you a wooing Rodolfo
falling in love all over again
in a Paris of long ago...

While Sal and I had a lot of fascinating experiences in Paris, for the sake of this account I'll return once more to Milano, and relate a few highlights from the rest of our stay in Italy. By then we'd decided that since returning home and getting married had become the top priority in our lives, we wanted to enjoy seeing as much of Italy as we could while there.

Perhaps, as Sal and I often said, we wouldn't be passing that way again, not in this lifetime anyway...

Early Morning on the Isle of Ischia

Antonio's Carozza on Ischia

WHILE TRAVELING TOGETHER

In January Sal and I decided to visit the charming city of Venice which strangely enough keeps its magic even in the middle of winter. Riding in a gondola might not have been as romantic then as it was in the summer, but the cold only gave us a great excuse to cuddle up closer while sightseeing on the Grand Canal.

We discovered that pigeons get hungry in winter as well as summer so we had a lot of fun feeding them. I'm not quite sure who decided it should be two P.M. when the huge flocks arrive for their feast of grain in the "Piazza San Marco" but the pigeons sure caught on to that a long time ago!

The truth is, we found them hanging out in the square most of the time, since tourists are always passing by...

PIGEONS IN THE SQUARE OF SAN MARCO

Every day in the crowded square
when the great bell tolls two o'clock,
they arrive in a rushing flurry of wings
to their feast of golden grain...

From distant markets and courtyards,
over winding canals and rooftops,
past the oriental turrets of San Marco,
sweeping swift and sure they fly—
the sky filling fast with an urgent cloud
of palpitant grey wings descending,
tiny creatures ignorant of time,

yet drawn by some irresistible force:
greater than knowing,
    filling all space,
        and transcending all time
they come...

In moments of exaltation our hearts
    soar inexplicably away
to explore an inner world of bliss,
drawn by that same mysterious force,
as swift and sure as those eager wings
above the rooftops of Venice.
Greater than knowing,
    filling all space,
        and transcending all time,
love comes...

By now it has probably become apparent that my poems were taking on mystical overtones even before I knew what that meant! This quality develops when one has a deeply inquiring nature, something of great assistance for the "birthing" of a poet. I truly believe this comes as we experience life from its depths, and not by polishing up our technique for writing a perfect sonnet to impress the intelligentsia of poetry.

During what remained of our stay in Italy Sal and I made several trips to various tourist spots. In between our adventures he returned to his grandmother's home in "Avellino" while I continued my singing lessons, although not with as much enthusiasm as I had during the early months in Italy. I found myself doing more and more writing, although most of these poems about the places we visited, were written after the fact. At the time something interesting is taking place we're usually so absorbed in what's happening that to write about it then would be tantamount to making love and stopping in the middle of it to write down a few notes on how things are progressing. Frankly I don't know anyone who could do that, and I certainly wouldn't want him making love to me!

The next poem I'll record for you was actually written in Rome after Sal set sail for New York in February. I planned to join him there sometime in June a few months later, but before he left we stored up a lot of memories on trips we made together, and it was these that I drew upon later for poetic inspiration.

A short weekend trip to "Camoglie" where we watched a group of fishermen as they came ashore at sunset to hang their nets to dry, inspired the following poem.

FISHERMEN OF CAMOGLIE

It is sunset when the last of the
    fishing boats come in,
and we watch the men as they move
    in rhythmic silhouette:
dominant arm and dark brown net
drawn taut against the music of the sky.
The corky mesh lies wet,sea wet
and salty on the pier,
where a symphony of fingers lifts it high,
each gaping new-made tear exposed
    to critical eye
before it is hung to dry…

As they work the men begin to sing—
first one and then another joins in
    until they all are caught
in a pulsing, swelling net of melody
pulled from an unplumbed sea of
    camaraderie.

Then arm in arm they drift to a little
    café for a draught
of wine or spumy beer, or set their
    steps toward home—
the surge of love running swift,
as swift through the tides of thought
as the pull of the sea through the net:
this eternal net of pain and joy
in which our lives are caught,
like fish from the boundless sea
of a vast, unplumbed Infinity…

Often Sal would decide to remain in Milano for a week or so, staying at a nearby "pensione" and we'd take off to explore some of the scenic wonders not far from there. I especially remember nearby "Bellagio" where we toured the "Villa Carlotta" which had been the home of "Benito Mussolini" Italy's former premier.

While I could devote a whole chapter to the day we spent in Bellagio, I do think the following poem written later in Rome will say everything I'd want to in prose. It not only describes the day we toured the villa and the grounds, but also brings up thoughts about our lives and how we're spending them in this kaleidoscopic world. Whenever I wrote a poem I seemed to bump right into the spirit behind it which somehow led to thoughts about that as well. This was true not only then, but would become deeper throughout my life as a writer…

THE VILLA CARLOTTA

The haunting sculpture,
"Amore and Psyche"
is the single exotic bloom
of the Villa's interior—
enchanting lovers and non-lovers alike
with equal facility…

Lovers, as we were then, when not
creating their own "Amore and Psyche"
love wandering in gardens like those
      surrounding the Villa,
where slopes of amorous azaleas
      sunbathe beside the lake
and thickets of blue hydrangeas
are encircled by stern-limbed trees:
dark eunuchs guarding a harem,
then at last to discover along the way
in an ivy-entwined pergola
a cool retreat for kisses warm
      with evening promise...

Walking through the bee-filled sweetness
      of the Jasmine Arbor,
you may feel as we did, the restless
      spirit of "Il Duce"
pacing beside you up and down
      the gravel paths,
and wonder, too, why the blue flame
of love is smothered and lost so soon
in the acrid smoke of bitterness,
that darkens the vision and destroys
      all life
until ashes, only ashes remain...

When things slowed down a little before Sal left, we went to visit "Firenze" where we toured the museum there filled with priceless treasures of art. We even visited one of those old monasteries Italy's famous for, but the idea of living a celibate life at that time seemed a superfluous discipline for finding the path to the joy Sal and I already knew!

One day we went for a walk, pausing on an old bridge called "Ponte Vecchio" which actually means Old Bridge! As we stood overlooking the Florentine countryside, I softly sang a favorite aria, "Oh, Mio Babbino Caro" from the opera "Gianni Schicchi," which I'd studied in America and also in Italy. I'd never sung it with so much feeling, though, as I did that day while a few curious pedestrians listened for a few minutes, then continued on their way, smiling at two goofy Americans clowning around in Florence...

THE PONTE VECCHIO

Spanning the river Arno,
this fourteenth century bridge,
arched beneath Florentine skies,
intermingles the grace of antiquity
with the sprawling commercialism
of smart new shops for tourists...

In Florence began the Renaissance,
here was the cradle of Dante,
Michelangelo, Da Vinci and Galileo,
and here the Medici family reigned...

Hovering around Ponte Vecchio
in the misty swirl of morning light,
these ghosts of ancient grandeur
hold our hearts entranced by the past
until overhead the roar of a plane
recalls our hearts to love's immediacy
and the timeless thrill of a kiss,
as below the bridge on a country road,
a cart drawn by oxen makes its way
following the custom of centuries...

One day we walked through the Town Square in Florence looking at a memorial placque inscribed to the Dominican monk "Savonarola," a reformer who had lived there during the seventeenth century and incurred the wrath of Pope Alexander, the second. He was later excommunicated, then ultimately tortured and executed on that very spot where he was burned to death by a slow process, kept alive with cold compresses placed on his body so the torture could continue longer and "purge him of his sins." After all these centuries, I'd be inclined to ask only one question: "**Whose** sins?"

I can't help wondering why a few self-righteous people ever felt they'd been appointed by God to do this "purging" when HE has all the earthquakes, hurricanes and tornadoes at his disposal here, along with the present-day slaughter on our modern freeways...

Later that month my fiancé and I made a trip to nearby Como, and of course went rowing on the lake in the light of a full moon. While there we were so entranced with one another and the beauty of "Lago di Como" that on three successive evenings Sal forgot to pay the waiter for our after-dinner coffee. Somehow I felt the waiter understood, and even in post-war Italy would have forgotten to ask for payment if he could have afforded to do so!

This next poem describes our enchanted evening of rowing.

LOVE'S TIMELESS WORLD

Our hearts were so young,
winged with the never-known-before
    innocence of love
and we laughed at all those foolish
    little things
out-of-love people never see
that night in June when we bargained
    with Antonio
to take us rowing on the "Lago di Como."

He smiled behind his postcard mustache
curled like a picture in rotogravure,
then tying his jaunty red sash a bit tighter
we drifted silently away in the moonlight.

Our boat glided smoothly through
shimmering Monet reflections
of shore lights on the water,
while we listened to the fading beat
     of popular music
from the lake-side dance pavilion.

As we neared the center of the lake,
sounds from the shore receded
to velvet echoes in the distance,
and the silken splash of water
     around the boat
became the only sound remaining
to pervade our timeless world of love...

In the darkness our whispers mingled
     with the water's caress,
eluding the ears of Antonio
who only stared with discreet attention
toward the arc of his poised left oar,
sharply etched against the moon...

One morning we were up early walking beside the lake, after having our usual "colazione," or breakfast of café-latte, bread and jam, and while we paused, almost as if on cue Sal threw a pebble far out into the lake, creating not only a memory but the setting for my next poem written after he left for New York.

DAWN ON THE LAKE

At dawn today we walked beside
the still perfection of the sleeping lake,
a fragrance drifting on the windless air
borne lightly as a dream floats into
   the mind...
Suddenly, impulsively you hurled a small
   round pebble
far into the lake and called aloud—
   though no one heard.

With scarcely a sound your tiny pebble
sank into the water's depths,
yet how strange to see arising
from such an insignificant source
ever-expanding circles moving wider
   and wider still,
until the eye could no longer contain them,
though sight if clear enough
might follow their course to
   another dimension...

Then silently as perfume is lifted
   on the air
came a moment of understanding—
timeless, complete, more volatile than
   thought or word,
revealing how all of life is linked
in ever-widening circles of perception:
a timeless movement caught in the eyes
   of Time...

So frequently since the morning I observed those circles moving outward when Sal tossed his pebble into "Lake Como" I've used this symbol of expanding circles to convey a lot of the Truth that I was then, and still am attempting to express.

I've often thought about how even those circles that continue moving past the visible ones, are circling outward into their own reality, merging with invisible worlds on land, or in the heavens. Life itself goes on beyond the ability of our earthly eyes to perceive those mysterious circles through which it moves in an endless progression, circles that continue spiraling outward, then upward into countless invisible dimensions, on and on throughout eternity...

As a teacher of modern times has said, "There just isn't any top to the upward movement of spirit!"

ALL ROADS
LEAD TO ROME...

Several times while living in Italy, we passed through Rome on various occasions. Whether we were on the way to Capri or Ischia, coming back from there, heading for Naples, or making the return trip to Milano, we usually stopped in Rome, either briefly or for a couple of days. There's something so central about this city that the old saying in my title here seems especially true.

A couple of months or so before I left for America Lucilla decided to move to Rome where she'd chosen to remain, and I of course opted to stay with her until the time came for my own departure in June. For the trip home I would sail from Naples on the "Andrea Doria" that beautiful Italian liner which later sank, not as dramatically as the "Titanic" but just as final in the outcome. Fortunately this didn't happen on my trip to New York!

While staying in Rome those two months, I wrote a lot of poetry, recalling many of my travels with Sal and the beauty of Italy. Two or three times during our trips, we'd gone to visit the "Colosseum." Once we were there rather late at night with a full moon peering down at us just as it has for centuries, observing all the changes humanity has gone through while creating new settings for life's unfoldment on the surface of this planet.

Later I recorded a number of these observations in a book of poems entitled "What The Moon Sees." Some of the feelings I had on our visits to the "Colosseum" may be found in this book, along with a lot of profound realizations I've experienced since then.

Below is the poem I wrote in Rome after Sal left...

WHISPERS OF LOVERS

The day we went to the Colosseum
sightseeing with a group of tourists,
you whispered to me:
      "There's something here—
      I don't know what it is,
      something felt and yet unseen
      that hovers everywhere"...
Yet the sunshine's caress on those
      crumbling walls,
and the echo of bird calls from
      springtime skies
belied the words you spoke!

Later one night we were walking—
      aimlessly as lovers do,
and found ourselves again at the Colosseum.
Hesitantly we tip-toed inside,
into the brooding silence that pervades
      this lonely place,
and suddenly I sensed it, too,
      just as you had...

An ambience of sadness floats
in the ghostly atmosphere,
filling its dark arena of strife
with the anguished cries of martyrs
whose presence roams there still,
yet smiling now in benediction
as from the darkness of ancient archways

> rise no longer those piercing screams
> and moans of pain
> but only the whispers of lovers...

The trip described here was made after our stay on Capri. No other visit there has ever quite equaled this one, when I was seeing everything with the eyes of my new-born love, along with the deep insight this often bestows. Later one night after having "cena" at one of those charming and inexpensive little Roman restaurants with tables set up under an outdoor arbor, we went for a walk, ending up beneath this marvelous tree. Perhaps it was a Chestnut, since these seemed to be growing everywhere in Italy.

SPRING ETERNITY

After the Spanish Steps
and Fontana Trevi's nostalgia,
we left the crowds to explore
an anonymous little street—
coming suddenly upon a tree,
whose budding green innocence
crowned with the candle halo
of a golden street lamp,
called our hearts to share
a moment of communion with her...

Concealed in her sibilant depths
gleamed an iridescent emerald,
pulsing with light and joy,
and as we stood before
our tree's Druidic shrine,
fluttering in the wind,
we pledged eternal love,

taking with us in our hearts
an ever-living treasure
beyond all price or measure!

Another time while we were spending a few days in Rome we went to see an underground "Capuchin" cemetery right in the middle of the city on "Via Veneto" where the bones of deceased monks had been used to decorate various rooms. It was actually quite interesting, although I couldn't get used to a certain musty odor pervading the air inside the place, nor the strange vibrations still hovering all around the area.

I couldn't help thinking that most of the monks who had contributed their "bones" for the architecture, had gone on to reside for a while in one or another of those invisible dimensions on the other side. I truly hope they found the peace and joy they yearned for during their sojourn here on Earth.

Somehow I felt that Sal and I had already come to the end of our search regarding that. The only cloud on the horizon was the thought that we must be separated for a while before I joined him in New York...

The previous summer, I'd taken a couple of days off from my stay on Ischia to meet Sal in Naples and attend an opera given in an outdoor theatre. It reminded me of concerts I'd attended at the "Hollywood Bowl" in Los Angeles, although not as large and showy as those had been. The same full moon shines over either theater, lending enchantment to the scene. The opera that night became one of my all-time favorites, never forgotten.

ON HEARING THE OPERA "TURANDOT"

I think of it and my heart spins back
on uncontrollable wings of love
to that warm August night we attended
    the "mostra"—

so intimately beneath the stars,
and once again I succumb to the spell
of that weirdly beautiful opera,
"Turandôt"...

He looked and performed like a
            visiting god
in his glorious blue costume with
            a white plumed hat,
and while singing the aria, "Nessun Dorma,"
he lifted his eyes to the star-filled sky,
as the naked music of his heart
was revealed before us totally
unashamed...

Moments like this are rarely given
when the wings of the soul soar away
            in the night—
and two hearts in love join Earth to Heaven
while the mind in a daze cannot decide
whether Heaven has been transported to Earth,
or if Earth has somehow miraculously flown
to Heaven!

After the opera was over Sal and I went for coffee, then a long slow walk beside the "Bay of Naples" bathed in the light of the moon, trying somehow to escape the advances of a driver in a horse-drawn "carozza" who seemed determined to have us ride with him. Actually we preferred walking, and to savor the night before retiring to our not very glamorous room **without** a view. In a nearby café we heard someone with a beautiful natural voice singing "Santa Lucia" and creating a soul memory that will last forever...

From the window of her apartment in Rome Lucilla and I could look over the wall into someone's garden next door. Although I'd never know who the garden belonged to, nor what its history was, I created my own story about it for this next poem.

VIEW OF A ROMAN GARDEN

The colubrine coils of the clouds
writhe and twist through the sky
like some gigantic serpent,
while from its cavernous "maw"
tongues of lightning flick hypnotically,
raping the soft and yielding wetness
    of the rain,
reversing the Hindu's serpentine ritual
    meretriciously to Eve,
and I attendant again at a window
    that looks on an Apple tree
        that grows in a well-kept garden
that is called "Priapus" paradise…

After Sal left, I had a lot of time to read and study Lucilla's books, thereby increasing my vocabulary as well as my knowledge of the work a few other poets have done. My natural bent, though, had been from the beginning to create as uniquely as possible, letting my inner "voice" say what it wants to. Although my writing may have reflected certain impressions stored from my reading, the way I put them together was definitely my own…

One of the deepest impressions I brought back from Italy is the love of music in the hearts of her people. Often in the early morning hours during our stay in Milano I'd wake, hearing a horse-drawn cart going by in the street, the driver singing on his way to deliver fresh vegetables and fruit to some of the small markets in Milano. I'm sure there aren't many people here in America who could, or who would care to sing like that while doing their jobs in our busy offices, or even a factory somewhere.

On one memorable occasion that first winter we woke in the middle of the night, hearing the sound of singing drifting upward from a little bar on the street below. A chorus of voices rose on the wings of song, until it reached the seventh floor apartment we occupied, enchanting our ears and our hearts with another memory. While the men were obviously in various stages of inebriation, that only seemed to improve the intensity of their singing.

In Italy at that time you could hear many incredible natural voices in the street, in cafés, or even in someone's home where a party might be in progress. Perhaps the language itself with its open vowel sounds contributes to this phenomenon...

A VOICE IN THE WINTER NIGHT

One dreary winter Milano night,
while dense fog webbed the sleeping city
in November cold and gloom,
we woke as though summoned by a dream
to the shore of a sunlit paradise
where a young man's haunting tenor voice
lifted its vibrant bel canto tones
to fill our darkened room...

One by one his café companions
added their random harmonies
to create a luxuriant bloom of sound
whose ever-ascending crescendos of warmth
unfolded at last to expose its heart,
although in the heat of too much wine
its petals soon wilted and fell apart
like blossoms to the ground...

At dawn the café, deserted, silent
lay concealed in veils of fog,
yet the song continued to flow
from the haunting depths of the soul
where barriers of race and tongue
are consumed with thought's divisive mist
like the shrouding layers of Milano's fog
burn away in the sun's morning glow...

As mentioned previously, we'd all made a trip to nearby Genoa and Nervi that first year, where during the day as well as at night the four of us strolled along the boardwalk, eventually separating to be alone, which is the way of lovers all over the world. After Sal left for New York, I revived the memory of our three-day stay there to write a poem about it.

THE COAST OF NERVI

Imagine this the pinnacle of a gigantic
cascade of black and torturous rock
spiraling upward toward the shore,
with a wild eldritch cry arising
           from the heart
of this captive eyre of the sea!
This cliff—dark spawn of sea and shore,
sneers contemptuously at the many-footed
           dominion of the sea walk,
winding like a cobbled crown along its
           arrogant acclivity...

Its unconquerable imperturbability
waits stoically through the cyclic
           attenuation
of baby steps, the centaur thunder of youth,

or the eager pause and coupled waiting
of lover's indeterminate going,
listening to the measured stop-and-go
    of perambulators,
then the slow rheumatic tread of age
    upon the scuffled stone…

At last, in the velvet sibilance of the night,
passing kaleidoscopically beneath the scrutiny
    of the moon,
the long black cliff again resigns itself
    to the sea—
to the intermittent bite and roar
of her waves' erosive nibbling on the shore…

Perhaps you've seen the tendency I was developing toward "wordiness" here, something Louis Untermeyer picked up on rather quickly, indicating that simplicity of expression touches the heart at a deeper level.

Actually I'd already decided on my own that it really wasn't necessary to show off my whole vocabulary of newly acquired words to express the emotion I felt, and that the complexity of form I sometimes chose might even be running interference to this.

At the time Sal left for New York, Lucilla and I were in the throes of getting ready to close up our apartment in Milano and make the move to Rome, so I wasn't able to see him off on the American liner, the "Independence," when it sailed from Naples. His family in Avellino did the honors then, and when I left Italy in June, Lucilla took time off to come to Naples and bid me "Bon Voyage" on the spectacular new ship, the "Andrea Doria." The last thing I recall seeing was her smiling face as she waved good-bye.

Nearby a woman was nursing her baby quite oblivious of the crowd around her, while the strains of "Santa Lucia," a haunting Italian "canzone" resounded from somewhere on the pier, as though reminding me of all I was leaving behind. After the boat had sailed, I realized that without Sal most of the magic of Italy had mysteriously disappeared, and I could hardly wait to see him again! From what I remembered of New York, though, I wasn't looking forward to a prolonged stay there either, certainly not the year and a half it turned out to be!

On the "Andrea Doria" I enjoyed a very pleasant and relaxing voyage. At breakfast the morning after we sailed, I was chattering in Italian, having finally gotten pretty good at speaking it during my stay in Italy. While conversing, I said to the woman seated next to me, "I'm certainly looking forward to getting back to America!" This was delivered of course in my most perfect Italian.

She replied, "Oh, have you been there before?"

I said, "Oh yes, I'm from California." Everyone at the table was sincerely amazed.

"You speak so well we thought you were Italian!" they said. Although I found their remarks flattering at the time, they soon had to admit that if I were Italian I wouldn't be asking the names of things I wasn't familiar with like I was continually doing. That was fun though, and while I met a lot of interesting people during the trip home, there was no one I related to with any degree of closeness. All I could think of was my fiancé and how happy I'd be to see him again in New York after our long separation.

How different this voyage was from the one I'd started out with on the "Conte Biancamano" nearly two years prior to this! I couldn't help wondering, since God had taken control of my life, what he had in store for me in the future.

Lucilla had previously made all the arrangements for me to move in with her sister, Anne, and share the expenses of her "East Side" apartment in New York. Since apartments weren't easy to find, not at the price I could afford to pay, I accepted her offer gratefully. At least I'd have a place to stay.

At this point the future seemed uncertain at best, and I soon began wishing there were some way Sal and I could have remained in Italy for a long, long time instead of having to return to what would seem at first only a dreary and unattractive way of life, compared to the haunting beauty we'd known in Italy...

Fishermen of Camoglie

Rowing on Lago di Como

Venezia

NEW YORK:
I MEET LOUIS
UNTERMEYER

RETURN TO MY HOMELAND

My return to America, after an absence of almost two years, was somewhat shocking at best, and if it hadn't been for being reunited with Sal, I'd have found it more disturbing than it was.

Holding me in his arms for a long time to console me, he said, "Honey, I know just how you feel. I went through the same thing when I got back and I'm just now getting 'Americanized' again!"

As soon as I was settled in the apartment I'd be sharing with Anne, Sal invited me for dinner at his family home in New Jersey. I had no idea what to expect, but nothing could have prepared me for the crowd of people gathered around the huge dining room table, laden with food that was astoundingly reminiscent of Italy. Sal's father owned and operated a delicatessen, so there was never any lack of special goodies for parties, or the Sunday dinners I attended regularly for the year and a half I remained in New York.

Sal and I soon eased into our new life style together, although we often spoke longingly of Italy and wished we were rich enough to return, even for a short visit. I couldn't believe I was actually **homesick** for Italy, after all the complaining I'd often done! I guess there's just no satisfying anyone in this human state, something that soon sets us thinking, erroneously I admit, that Heaven must be somewhere other than here in our own hearts.

Sal's family were all wonderful to me. This included his sister, Irma, and two brothers along with his father and stepmother. Everyone welcomed me with open arms and open hearts, which is more important than anything else we may find in this life. Anne and I soon became good friends as well, although she was so close to Lucilla they were like "twins" in the love and understanding they shared. Anne's apartment was on the fourth floor of our "East Side" dwelling, and since there was no elevator, going out for one reason or another, then returning to climb those four flights of stairs kept us in good shape physically! After the beauty we'd seen and been part of in Italy, I found life in New York drab and colorless, not only on the outside, but inside myself as well.

Sal and I planned to be married in California and live there afterwards, so I could hardly wait to get the show on the road and travel west. In the meantime we enjoyed a lot of sightseeing in New York and New Jersey. One day Sal gave me a book written about many different species of trees. He knew how much I loved nature, and on weekends we'd go "tree scouting" as we called it, looking for some of the varieties described in my book. I was so excited every time we discovered one of them, it was almost like saying hello to an old friend!

That whole summer in New York was long and terribly hot. On weekends Sal and I drove to the shore in New Jersey and my experiences on these jaunts soon found their way into new poems. That included some of our drives through the countryside. I jumped at anything that offered an escape from seeing the sad living conditions of many people on the "East Side" sitting on their front steps, or little porches to get a breath of cool air. All of this was so different from the life I'd led in Los Angeles that I found it nothing short of depressing. Only my love for Sal kept me looking forward to our future together in California.

In July, not long after I arrived, I remembered that Lucilla had told me "Louis Untermeyer" lived in New York. So one day, without much enthusiasm I must say, I looked his name up in the phone directory and decided that at some indefinite time in the future I'd call him. Then one afternoon a few days later, while lying down to rest, I heard an inner voice saying, "Call him."

I replied, also inwardly, "Some other time." After that I settled down to take my nap, but that voice prodded me again, "Call him." I promised to do so the next day for sure. That wasn't good enough to satisfy the nagging voice which reiterated, "Call him," and then added for greater clarification, "**now!**"

I decided that if I were going to get any rest at all I better make the call. "Maybe he won't be home," I mumbled to myself, but such was not to be the case, however, because a woman with a pleasant sounding voice answered the phone. I knew that Louis Untermeyer was married so I figured this must be his wife. I asked to speak to Mr. Untermeyer, hoping maybe I had the wrong number.

To my surprise she said, "Just a moment," and then called him to the phone.

I told Louis Untermeyer my name and he asked, "How did you get my phone number?"

I answered truthfully, wondering why that mattered. "Out of the phone book, Mr. Untermeyer."

"Oh," he said, as though he'd forgotten people could do that.

Following this he asked a question about something which I felt was beginning to intrigue him. "But how did you know I'd be home? Usually I'm not, but today I had to return for something."

"Maybe this sounds silly, Mr. Untermeyer, but I heard an inner voice telling me to call you. I ignored the first two times this happened, then the third time the voice said '**now**' so I thought I better do it."

I could see this whole thing had aroused his curiosity about me. "What was it you wanted to discuss with me?"

"Poetry," I replied. "You see I'm an opera singer and while I was in Italy studying, I started writing just for the fun of it. Now I have a whole notebook full of poems, and I really would like to know if my poetry has any merit before I abandon my aspiration for an operatic career. There's no one I could think of who knows more about poetry than you do."

I went on to explain, "You see, while I was living in Milano I read a couple of your anthologies which my room mate had brought with her to Italy. I must tell you that I really enjoyed those books, and also writing my own poems after that. Everywhere we went I wrote about it, afterwards you know, because at the time something's happening you really don't have any inclination to write, but only to enjoy whatever's going on."

"That's quite true," he agreed, then after a moment of silence as though he were checking his appointment book, he said, "I could see you this coming Friday at eleven o'clock before I go to lunch. Could you come to the 'Decca Records' building at that time?"

After I'd said I could, he proceeded to give me the address and even added some directions for the transportation I could take to get there from where I lived.

As you can imagine I was tremendously excited about this new development, since the appointment had been made about a week before I was to meet him. I decided to take my whole notebook and show him everything I'd written while in Italy. Actually I hadn't been doing too much writing since my return to New York where I was occupied getting acquainted with my fiancé's family and becoming oriented to the new-old environment of my homeland."

By the time that fateful Friday came, I was dealing with more than butterfly nerves, since I'd begun doubting the outcome of the whole venture. I couldn't stand the thought of having the work into which I'd poured my heart and soul ridiculed, even by the foremost critic in the country! If I could only have known then that throughout the twenty-four years I was to work with Louis Untermeyer, he would never give me any instruction in the form of ridicule, that might have made my ordeal easier.

When I arrived at the "Decca Records" building, I paced up and down in front of it for some time, since I'd gotten there a bit early. I began berating myself, tempted to forget about the whole thing and return home. What saved the day was the courage I've had to display all my life in the face of enormous difficulties. Believe me there have been plenty of those to deal with during my youth in Alabama, as well as after we moved to Michigan when I was nine, and in the years that followed. Even after I moved to Los Angeles as a young adult, all kinds of new challenges arose, right up to the time I left for Italy.

So now as I remembered all of this, there was no way I could back away from this present one! So without wasting any further thought on it I got into the elevator and ascended several floors, probably to the third as I recall, and entered the door of Louis Untermeyer's not too impressive office. There were some other people around, working at their desks which didn't bother me, since Mr. Untermeyer moved forward immediately to greet me, taking my hand and introducing himself.

At first I was somewhat shocked to see the short physical stature of this man of letters who had such a respected reputation in the literary world, along with a hundred books or so credited to his own name. I noted that he wasn't much taller than I was, and would probably be unimpressive if you happened to pass him in the street without knowing who he was.

"Come over here, my dear. Sit down beside my desk and show me your work." While I got my notebook out of its case, he asked where I was from and I told him Los Angeles, since I truly consider California my home. He then revealed the depth of his knowledge about voice inflections.

"Have you ever lived somewhere in the Middle West?" he asked, with an enigmatic smile.

"Michigan," I said, "in a small town near Detroit."

Satisfied that he'd verified this, he said, "I also detect a bit of a southern accent playing hide-and-seek here and there."

"That could be because I was born in Alabama and lived there until the age of nine when we moved to Michigan." I later realized he was engaging me in this conversation about my background simply to put me at ease before he read my work.

After flipping through my notebook for a while, he fixed his eyes on mine and looked at me intently. "This is pretty good work, you know." He paused for a while as he read a few more poems, then said, "Perhaps I shouldn't ask this, but what about your singing career? Do you plan to continue with that?"

"Possibly," I said, "but at the moment I'm waiting for my fiancé to complete his preparations for moving to California where we plan to be married. But this will take a while," I added. That didn't seem to surprise him, and he continued reading, turning the pages of my notebook quickly and glancing with a practiced eye at things he found particularly interesting.

"You have a natural gift for unusual metaphors and finding the right similes to create the mood you want to express."

This whole exchange was music to my ears, since I hadn't expected him to relate as deeply to my work as he seemed to be doing. An hour went by so quickly I could hardly believe it. When he'd finished, Mr. Untermeyer reminded me that he had a luncheon appointment. Then he asked if I'd continue with my writing for the next two weeks and after that come to see him again, bringing everything I'd written.

By that time I was so at ease with him, I felt as though I'd known him sometime, somewhere before. Throughout our long association he never seemed to be a stranger to me at any time, yet there was no physical contact with him except when he occasionally took my hand in greeting, or to say good-bye while I was in his office. When I saw him for the last time before we left for California, a year and a half after I started working with him, he only held my hand a bit longer than usual and said he'd enjoyed working with me.

As you can imagine, I was really turned on with writing some more poems after that first meeting! Everything I saw, or new place Sal and I explored in New York or New Jersey became the subject of a poem, or notes for writing one in the future. Near the end of the two weeks I called Mr. Untermeyer and made another appointment on Friday, which seemed to be a good day for him, When I returned to the "Decca Records" building this time, it was with a totally different feeling in my heart than on the previous occasion. I couldn't believe that had been only two weeks earlier.

In the interim Sal had taken me to "Greenwich Village" and to see the "Brooklyn Bridge," to lie in the sands of South Beach on Staten Island, and Jones Beach on Long Island. Even walking together in the park doing our "tree scouting" was an exhilarating adventure, because now I had an objective. After all, I was writing for Louis Untermeyer, and not for a few friends who might read my work, or only listen politely while I read it to them.

Now here I was two weeks later, standing in front of that same building with such a happy feeling inside, instead of apprehension. This had to be a good thing that was happening to me!

When I got to his office, Mr. Untermeyer came forward like an old friend and shook my hand, appearing eager to read what I'd brought him. Sometimes he chuckled with a certain delight, and at other times simply nodded his head in acknowledgment of something he felt the same way about. At the end of the session, he closed my notebook and handed it back to me.

"These poems are getting to be professional now. You've made amazing progress this last two weeks." After a few minutes he asked, rather curiously I thought, "Are you doing anything with your music now? I mean, are you still planning a career in opera?"

I replied that I really wasn't doing much because we didn't have a piano where I was staying, and I felt sure the neighboring tenants wouldn't appreciate warm-up scales, which I'd have to do in order to get my voice back in shape, let alone sing an operatic aria. In some mysterious way I realized I was transferring the artistic fulfillment I'd found in music to the more visual art of writing poetry, which perhaps no one but Mr. Untermeyer would read!

He then asked if I'd studied literature in college, or taken any related courses somewhere.

"Actually I haven't," I confessed. "I was mainly interested in pursuing my musical studies and learning French, which came in handy while I was staying in Paris."

"Well then, my dear," he said, "I believe it's time for you to begin a reading program that might be helpful to you. Have you ever heard of Thomas Wolfe?" I admitted that I really hadn't, feeling somewhat stupid, since I didn't know if Thomas Wolf was a poet or a politician. Mr. Untermeyer chuckled, noting the puzzled look I gave him.

"You can go to any library and take out copies of his books. Start with 'Look Homeward Angel' or 'You Can't Go Home Again'. Wolf was a prodigious modern writer turning out a lot of material before he died at the age of thirty-nine. There's something in your work that reminds me of him," Mr. Untermeyer continued, "like a diamond that hasn't yet been fully cut and faceted."

"I'll pick up those books this weekend and get started," I promised, realizing I was now becoming quite excited about everything that was happening. Then I ventured to ask which of the poems I'd brought him that he liked especially.

"The one called 'Walk In The Park' strikes a new note, filled with unusual imagery, sensuous and warm. This is a quality I see playing hide-and-seek in most of the work you've shown me so far. At times it seems reminiscent of a young D.H. Lawrence."

Not wanting to appear ignorant **again**, I concluded on my own that "D.H." must have been a poet like myself, and decided to look him up at the library.

For the record I'll include in this section some of those poems I wrote in New York while working with Louis Untermeyer personally, so you can formulate your own ideas about what I was doing, and perhaps see the progress that was made in my work over the years as I moved from a beginner's concern with writing "poetry-poetry" to finding a way to express my growing interest in mystical ideas, which would later become a life-long commitment.

WALK IN THE PARK

Since early this morning the flutes
     of spring
have been calling through every
     open window
with invitations to come outdoors,
and in the magic of afternoon
we go walking together in the park—
so carefree through the budding wood,
the feeling of Sunday everywhere
in its domed cathedral atmosphere…

The April breeze turning cool,
darts with shivery, silver freshness
in and out among the trees
where flocks of gossipy swallows—
usurping the prayerful trees,
are perched like twittery-fluttery fruit
on all their branches, starkly mute,
awaiting the evening chorale…

Now and then the swallows rise
with a crescendo whir and stir of wings
into the darkening skies,
and night begins to resound her lute
softly plucked by soft black fingers
in twilight arpeggios of peace,

> while the sun goes down with a shout,
> goes down with a red-throated shout!

I recall Mr. Untermeyer saying he particularly liked the ending here with its emphasis on the sun going down with a shout which was repeated in the last line. He called all of these things the expression of your own "voice" and it soon became evident that he would go to any lengths to help you preserve that quality, staying away from imitations of anyone else, no matter how great they were. He never taught me **how** to write, but only planted new seeds of inspiration to stimulate the flow of inner creativity, allowing my abilities to expand in their own way and in their own time as I grew artistically.

Although he seemed to have a few preferences among poets, some still living then, as well as those from the past, he said this was personal and not necessarily an indication of their recognition by the world. He mentioned the simple depth of Robert Frost's poems and asked me to pay particular attention to those, as well as the work of Emily Dickinson. Most people who've read his anthologies are certainly aware of the interest Mr. Untermeyer had in the achievements of Robert Frost, and all he'd done to promote the work of this wonderful poet at the beginning of his career.

In retrospect I'd say that Robert Frost was certainly lucky to have had such a keen mentor and friend. Only now after all the years that have gone by since the death of Louis Untermeyer do I truly appreciate how lucky I was, too!

LIFE ON THE EAST SIDE

Although I was grateful to have a place to live in New York, sharing an apartment with Lucilla's sister, Anne, I couldn't help missing my home in California, nor even the peripatetic existence I'd enjoyed previously in Italy and France. Being with the one you love is something almost anyone longs for, yet the poet in me also yearned for the beauty left behind. Sal felt pretty much the same way and was looking forward to our future together in California.

Life on the "East Side" was certainly a far cry from Milano, "la nebbia" or the fog, included! My stay in New York, however, inspired several poems which Louis Untermeyer read and enjoyed. When he liked something he took time to point out the things he considered special about it, seldom getting into any technical analysis nor even suggesting a specific expression to work with. I suppose he felt that as I developed my skills, some particular form would emerge, or I'd simply discover my own. Ultimately I decided to use Japanese forms like the "tanka" and "sedoka" for most of the nature volumes I wrote later. These poems, as you may know adhere to a strict **syllabic** count instead of rhyme and meter.

But to get back to the "East Side," especially that first summer I spent there, enduring almost unbearable humidity and heat. This was something I'd rarely experienced in California where the climate is more on the dry side. On the street where Anne and I lived in New York most of the people came from a very modest background and often many foreign countries as well. This included a large group of Italians, and one of the highlights in my day was going shopping at the neighborhood stores looking for fresh fruit and vegetables to prepare for the evening meal, which I usually shared with Sal when he came to see me after work.

Most of the time Lucilla's sister spent the evening with a friend who lived nearby, returning later for the night. This gave Sal and me some welcome time alone for dinner together and "other things." Sometimes we'd take off to see a movie. It seemed that just about every major film that's ever been made was playing somewhere in New York. Any favorite movie I'd seen in the past and wanted to share again with Sal became accessible.

We'd gone to see "An American in Paris" while staying in Paris, then on our return to Italy had seen the film in Italian. Of course in Paris, there was a sound track for the dialogue in French. In Italy, converting the voices of American actors and actresses to the Italian language was expertly done, where "doppiagio" had become a fine art. When you heard Gene Kelly or Gregory Peck, or any other star, the same timber and inflection was in the Italian voice, making it a new and exciting experience.

One evening in New York we took off to see "An American in Paris" in English, having dinner on the way at a little cheapie restaurant we could afford. At least we'd be cool for a while. Often we'd turn on the fan in my apartment and lie in front of it, pretending the wind was blowing under the Pine tree on Ischia.

Now and then we'd go out for ice cream somewhere in the neighborhood, looking at people along the way seated despondently on their balconies fanning themselves and talking, possibly about how unpleasant the weather was, just as we were! Seeing all of this on so many occasions awakened great empathy in my heart, and inspired the following poem.

PASTORAL OF THE EAST SIDE

A solitary tree, remote and aloof
    as a goddess in green
shimmers in her squalid setting
like a priceless emerald
pinned to the breast of a whore!

The sun goes down, but heat only flows
more thickly through the air,
as everywhere people begin blooming
in the steel gardens of fire escapes,
or sprouting from concrete hothouses
on steps or sidewalk—waiting listlessly...
For what: a breath of cool air?
Or for joy to descend like rain
bringing renewal outer and inner.

Only the children cavort and leap
        like springtime lambs
in the meadow of the street.
A few bold urchins unloosing
a torrential mountain stream
from the gaping mouth of a fire hydrant,
run and scream with shrill delight
when cars and trucks go roaring by:
fierce tigers and elephants
        and charging lions,
their great eyes glowing in the dark!

Evening at last settles wearily down
in her crumpled bed of night,
while the stars emerge to beam
their celestial benediction...
Then capriciously from the hidden depths
of a murmurous forest of sound
comes a laugh, and a husky thrill-noted coda:
"God damn you, Mae, but I love you!"

From the time he first read my work until he left this world twenty-four years later, Louis Untermeyer marveled at the way I alternated from exalted expressions to using the common vernacular with such ease. This I believe he concluded was part of my own unique "voice" and made no attempt **ever**, to push me in one direction or the other, hoping to create a more polished poet.

I've come to realize that it's actually this ability to incorporate the sacred and the profane that brings us to the brink of spiritual realization. "Holier than thou" may turn out to be holy as that term is understood, but it will never encompass the **whole** of what God is. I long ago decided that God must be everything or he's nothing, and maybe both of these! Joining a private club of belief up there in the sky has never been my aspiration. I suppose after I'd read the work of poet, "Walt Whitman" when directed to do so by Louis Untermeyer as one of his reading assignments, an ongoing activity while I was in New York, I had at last stumbled over a kindred spirit in poetry.

"Spiritual" and "religious" aren't exactly soul mates as I see it, since the practice of any religion ultimately leads to the discovery of what true spirituality is, unless like a dog with a bone we refuse to let go and move to a new expression. This must be something like Jacob's ladder in the Bible…

Often I'd lie awake at night after Sal left for New Jersey, dreaming about our future life together in California and listening to all the sounds rising upward out of the stillness of the night. On one such occasion I turned on the light in the kitchen so as not to disturb Anne, and wrote a poem about all of that.

NIGHT SOUNDS IN NEW YORK

Night settles over the city,
brooding through long paragraphs
of stillness punctuated by familiar sounds,

while the fingers of a breeze
toy absent-mindedly with the window shade…

In the street an old car sputters,
dies, and then starts again
as two voices emerge, argue in
brief crescendo then slowly blend
into the scattered network of sound,
held together by the thunderous
ticking of the clock.

The courting cries of an alley cat
rend the darkness, and on the curb
the clicking of dice in a crap game
    goes on interminably…
Overhead the newly-weds in their
    creaking bed
play their nightly game of pleasure,
    pleasure and sorrow,
both sides of the coin coming up
    in a game…

Silence at last descends with its peace
in which all these sounds merge
and blend, but in no way disturb,
nor bring its blessing to an end…

It became obvious to me after re-reading these earlier poems that my work would inevitably move in a spiritual direction, especially when the door for that opened later in California. Perhaps you might conclude, as I did, that I was ripe for this development and it presented itself in just about the same way everything else has in my life. Looking back on all of this now I can see how that was part of what God had in mind for me all along, since his objective doesn't appear to be making us rich and famous, but only that we return "home" again to him.

I think most people would say that since we're all going to die anyway, maybe I'm thinking of something else when I use the word "home." For me physical death, whether it happens fast or becomes prolonged, isn't what I mean by returning home. Our home in spirit is where we reside in the oneness again, no longer caught in a life of separation, as most of us still are, engaged in endless conflict not only with others but within ourselves. Many friends have reminded me that a lot of people do become rich and famous along with carrying on what might be called a religious life, so there must be some kind of paradox in what I'm saying now.

The truth is, I really don't think so! Being rich or poor doesn't affect the realization of spiritual truth, although if you're poor you may be more anxious to find a way out of that situation. Being attached, whether it's to a huge bank account or a favorite "pot" and here I mean one to cook in, only contributes to keeping us bound to life here on Earth. I've discovered that freedom is to have little, or much and still be able to remain centered inwardly...

It seemed that the longer I lived in New York the more philosophical I became. This quality, which may be seen emerging in the following poem, greatly intrigued Mr. Untermeyer and I think he was aware, long before I was, that this would be the direction my work would eventually take.

"HOMECOMING"

Grattaciele, gratte-ciel, skyscrapers,
often seen in the rotogravure of newspapers:
what do they mean to my love and me
just home from France and Italy?

A forest of lonely, mechanical trees
erupting from concrete hills,
within whose steely web of leaves
life waits prowling hungrily,
concealed and crouched like a
      great carnivore
to spring upon and devour
from the daily carrion of misery
a succulent moment of joy…

Walking together through the park
in the depths of a strange
      insomniac night,
we see those sleepless eyes alight
      unseeing in the dark,
then speechless we stand in the green
      desolation
vibrating to shocking wounds of sensation
like an aching thought amputated from mind
or eyes gone suddenly blind…

In the darkness a sleek, black serpent
      goes by
intoning its ancient litany
to sell in the market what Eve got for free
from the same ever-flourishing apple tree!

Certainly the time my fiancé and I spent together in New York, or at his family home in New Jersey was totally happy. Just being with one another was sufficient to cancel out most of the negative aspects of the "waiting game" we were playing.

Later in the summer we went to "Atlantic City" which I saw for the first time, and realized that the Atlantic Ocean is almost as impressive as our own marvelous Pacific, although a different atmosphere pervades everything. Wherever you go you'll find this to be true, and I suppose this accounts for our choice of a place to live, when we have a choice that is. Sometimes it's made for us. I've found that many people who don't like the word "karma" accept the Biblical law of cause and effect with the added advice, "Cast your bread on the water and it shall return to you tenfold."

As for myself, I see that what happens **HAPPENS**, and it doesn't much matter what you call it. As we realize the truth of this, we understand that the name we give to God doesn't have much significance either, since HE goes on being what HE is anyway. Whether I call lightning a phenomenon of nature, a space ship searching for a landing, or the vengeance of the Lord, doesn't change the real nature of those flashes of light I see up there in the sky, sometimes benign and at other times destructive!

As the months passed I continued following the reading program Mr. Untermeyer outlined for me, gleaning a great deal of knowledge about literature in general and what other poets had written. Oddly enough I felt no inclination to copy, nor imitate anyone, although I had great admiration for work that had been done in the past. Mr. Untermeyer's own poetry I found enchanting and also incisive in its wisdom. In some strange way he was like a father to me creatively, and perhaps this accounts for the close bond continually being forged between his spirit and mine.

Certainly over the years he has encouraged and fostered far greater poets than I could ever hope to be, yet I think he sensed from the beginning another quality beyond the literary, or even the development of a poet that intrigued him. In retrospect, I'd say this was the spiritual direction I would take later in Los Angeles when I became a student in an esoteric group and began seriously investigating these matters. After that occurred he blatantly encouraged me to follow that inner voice wherever it led.

This "voice" has fortunately been endowed with an outrageous sense of humor, which emerges at times and saves me from the scourge of false pride, poetically as well as spiritually. When the creator bestows a sense of humor, I consider this one of the most significant of his gifts.

It appears that life itself is a "Divine Comedy" which we turn into a tragedy by refusing to see the truth of what's going on. Mr. Untermeyer was tremendously delighted when he first saw this humorous view taking shape in my writing, like in the poem which follows. In post war Italy maid service was inexpensive, gauged by American standards, so my roommate and I indulged ourselves by having our apartment cleaned once a week. One day our maid related the following amusing story about her little nephew…

A SHY BAMBINO

At two he knew only to flirt
with the folds of her skirt,
and the shadow of his taciturnity
was all they could see.
A whispered "Va bene" an inaudible "Ciao"
made her volubly vow
to spank the poor baby
for his shameful timidity…

"He's afraid to speak," she told everyone
as with cooing adulation
they tried to draw him out
to join them in the fun,
but his answer was only a pout.
So that day in the crowded station
where they met his Uncle Mattia,

what devil could have made him shout
      to his aunt stentoriously:
"But look, Oh look, dear Zia,
the train is making pee-pee!"

FLYING ON
THE WINGS OF PASSION

While living in Italy I'd written a group of poems, looking from the male side of myself, like a glimpse into the future when people have become androgynous. By that term I mean where both masculine and feminine polarities are balanced within ourselves.

You may wonder if this has something to do with the blending of masculine will and feminine feeling, and I'd say that it does. Don't we do that now while merging our two physical forms? In the coming "New Millennium" I feel sure this will take place inwardly in a more inclusive sense. The light of the soul itself is neither masculine nor feminine, but the perfected union of both.

Perhaps you'll enjoy a few of these turn-about poems just as Mr. Untermeyer did. The setting for the first was under the Pine tree growing on the hillside near the villa on Ischia. Sal and I would often spread a huge beach towel beneath it and just lie there for a long time listening to the song it sang to our hearts. Perhaps you're aware that Pine trees, especially Deodars, exude tremendous energy, a good thing to remember if you ever need it.

MY PRISONER!
Your hair,
tawny, electric
is caught in a carpet
of pine needles—
pierced with the pungence of them

and filled with the warm
mystery of their sighs...

Teasing
you cover my face
with the fragrant cloud of it
and I must strive
frantically
to gather all of it
in my hands,
to free your mouth
and kiss the veiled passion
of your lips as I hold you
bound by your hair:
my prisoner!

In the next poem of this genre I return to Italy and the "Island of Ischia" once more to create a lover's quarrel between Sal and myself. Of course the best thing about a quarrel, as you probably know, is making up!

Actually Sal and I seldom had then, or even now, a serious argument or misunderstanding...

THE "STORM"

Midnight. The storm has forced itself
      into my room
awaking me to the bitter memory
      of our quarrel...
I think of her, angry, unyielding
and of how she locked the door
to her kingdom of satin and lace.

But… There are other ways!
I remember the broken shutter latch
as I leap into the thrashing wind—
down the terrace and into her room,
filled with ribbons of lightning
flashing through shuttered window panes,
and playing grotesquely over her
        sleeping face.

I seize the warm sleep softness of her,
        whispering:
"The storm in our hearts separated us,
now another storm has brought me to you
and I must have you, possess you,
love you until that storm, too, has
        spent itself
and made you mine once more!"

Mr. Untermeyer often said that although many poets wrote with feeling, I wrote with passion. My guess would be that he meant passion of the heart, and only someone who understands that language can respond to it completely! And here again I must say that we bump right into what I call "spiritual."

For the following poem I returned to Michigan, remembering a river where I used to go swimming with my first love. Although I had a bathing suit on then, when I wrote the poem I took it off! Well, it was my poem after all, wasn't it?

WHERE THE REEDS WAIT STILL…

And there were reeds
growing in the river:
I remember there were reeds

that grew tall and still
waiting for "Pan"…

And there was a girl—
I could never forget
that there was a girl,
like you, my love,
who swam and called to me
      from the river,
nude and slim and pliant as
      a reed—
waiting for me where the reeds
      wait still…

The next poem is another of those imaginary scenes that quite possibly might have taken place at some time in one of my past lives. I have a feeling I've done everything and plenty of it! I made mistakes then, and I'm still doing so, although I suspect we learn a great deal more while making all these mistakes, than when we do everything right!

Doesn't what we now look upon as "right" only reflect what we learned in the process of making mistakes? So I've found that ultimately there are no mistakes at all but only learning!

THE "ELOPEMENT"

Everyone sleeps, undisturbed
by the breathless whispering,
and our flying secret footsteps,
as we gain the darkness of the
      carriage, undetected!

Only the pause of a suspended
      heartbeat

to remember, to reflect, to realize
that the future is risked, all
> else lost!

All is clutched in these palms of
> the present,
this moment of madness at midnight
as the speeding horses plunge onward
> into the night…

That first autumn we spent together in New York and New Jersey was a season of total delight for Sal and me. On weekends we drove through the woods for a feast of flaming trees. In retrospect now I'd say that some of them were reminiscent of the Maples we'd see years later in Maine. I've always found something so special in trees, a kinship I can in no way explain. Mr. Untermeyer really enjoyed this next poem, saying he particularly liked the imagery I used in it, like "swollen exultance" of trees for example…

CORNUCOPIA OF DELIGHTS

You are still the spring, my love,
a spring that fulfilled her promise:
rich with the first ripe fruits of October
lush and mellow and pungent,
piquant as a saucy apple,
opulent as taut-skinned grapes
heady with purple, and heavy with many
> libations to love…

Sated as a pumpkin, indolent as
> Indian Summer,
you purr in the sun, sheathing the frost

in the folds of your flaming cloak.
Supine on the hills you loll on your
    multi-hued couch
and laugh with a corn leaf rustle
breathless, inchoate as the first kiss
    at a Saturnalian feast...

A Cornucopia of delights
you bring the swollen exultance
    of trees
and the harvest—the harvest
    of singing fields:
my love, you are October!

Although roses fulfil their role as "Queen of the Flowers" daisies play another part entirely. When I was a young girl in Michigan I recall seeing fields of white wild daisies blooming in exquisite purity, like the soul. Why I should choose this serene setting for the somewhat turbulent passion expressed in the next poem seems strange to me now, since I've come to regard daisies as being like the soul itself in this world of violence, always pure and lovely no matter what might be happening. There's never been a time when this wasn't true, but perhaps only now I see it...

A FIELD OF WHITE DAISIES

I am lost in a woodland
field
a field of white daisies—
daisies nodding in the August heat,
that shimmers and flashes
in the sunlight...
Breathless

I stand in a sea of a hundred
eyes
that follow me as I
dart
this way and that,
clutching the torn white ruffle
of my skirt.

Then suddenly I am falling,
fainting, reeling into the blackness
of closed eyes
where all the daisies
are taller than I am
except the pungent breath
of those that lie crushed
beneath me…

Panting
my senses leap up to a world of
blue,
the flash of a bluebird's wing
into the bottomless blue depths of the
sky
holding your eyes as they narrow,
merge,
change into two pinpoints of blue
descending…

Although this whole poem was a fantasy, it's one that's easy to partic-
ipate in through the poet inside yourself! Again I have to say that this
isn't related to Earth, but what I call spirit!

I don't know about you, but since I was a child I've loved the wind. I could never say I love tornados or hurricanes, but I'm a pushover for gentle breezes blowing anywhere. I feel certain that there must be a Heaven where the wind blows with special sentience, and like the soul itself moves in an invisible, yet tangible form to gather all things into the heart of oneness.

I find this especially true when I'm in a deep contemplative mood, walking in the wind along the ocean, or perhaps down a quiet street somewhere lined with trees, whether it's California, Michigan or any point in between. I've also discovered that the view from the top of a hill, whether on Earth or in those invisible dimensions on the heights within oneself, brings a certain expansion of awareness. Mr. Untermeyer liked this next poem, also, especially its mood of exultance and the feeling of oneness with nature expressed in my own sensuous imagery...

MOOD ON A HILLTOP

Today, my love, you fill my heart
and the whole wide Earth as well,
while I alone, and secretly exultant
     lie on top of the hill,
knees drawn up, cupping the sky
on my knees like a flowing
     blue satin coverlet
filled with handfuls of cloud fluff...

Intimate and warm as the touch
     of a hand
the sun surrounds me as I lie
with the myriad green thrust of the grass
     beneath my back,
lifting my body in a long-held shiver

of poplar leaves in the wind
that has come by unexpectedly,
  to nuzzle my face,
drawing me up to all my height
tall and free on the hill!

Teasing through my hair,
and blowing it into bold disarray,
he molds my dress with impudent fingers
around my breasts and thighs,
pulling the flimsy muslin stuff
  tight against my body
until weightless and free I rise
to touch the floating skies:
a golden goddess deified!

Then suddenly he runs away like
  a baffling lover
leaving me poised breathless
  as an incomplete statue,
awaiting the return of my sculptor wind—
motionless and ecstatic still
standing on top of a soaring hill...

Recently I read how a teacher of modern times had stated that women in particular have a natural affinity with the wind. I can only agree with him, since I also feel, as he did, that women are able to commune with the wind from a very deep level within themselves, and learn many mystical things in their contact with this aspect of nature...

Can men do this? I haven't figured that out as yet, but I only know that I can, and have.

ELFIN LAUGH...

My life in New York soon settled into a daily regime of writing, reading and waiting to see Sal after work each evening. We often talked about the time when we'd leave for California, driving across the country sometime in November during my second year there, then after arriving in Los Angeles about ten days later be married on December 19th. This wonderful time of year just before Christmas has always been a special favorite of mine. I know that June is the traditional month for weddings, but I wasn't at all unhappy when we let it pass, and continued building our mood of anticipation until November.

In the meantime, there were a lot of fascinating things to do in New York. We attended a performance of "La Bohème" at the Metropolitan Opera House in which an old friend was singing the role of Musetta. Then one day we toured the "Metropolitan Museum of Art" and even went to see the famed Rockettes at "Radio City Music Hall." There never seemed to be a dull moment in our lives, since our love gave a special meaning to everything we did together, in addition to the loving, that is...

On weekends we frequently drove to the home of family members who lived in Keansburg on the New Jersey shore. While I've always found being with other people tremendously interesting, the inner life I was discovering in my work with Louis Untermeyer was far more meaningful to my awakening and process of self discovery than any form of socializing could ever be. All my experiences at that time became a potential source of poetic inspiration.

One night on our way to the Jersey shore we drove past an old cemetery. On previous trips I'd only glanced at it, but on this particular night there was a full moon looking down with that special sentience I've often noted emanating from the moon. The realization of how long that same moon has been gazing down at humanity's doings here on the planet, seeing all the dreadful things that have taken place, as well as the passions tasted beneath its light, spooks me more than any "spooks" wandering around a cemetery ever could. These days the presence we feel lurking in a cemetery might only be that of a mugger!

The morning after seeing that old cemetery in the moonlight, I got busy and wrote a poem about the unforgettable feelings it had inspired. I recall Mr. Untermeyer saying after he read it, that he particularly relished "orange impertinence."

AN ELFIN LAUGH

One must first dispel fear:
the only occupant here
is a long held pause of silence.
These sleepers have flown beyond
Earth's seething sphere of violence...

Docile as dried petals blown
       in the wind
Or a dead leaf crumbled in the hand
the inhabitants of this closed land
of spectral cinematography
are content to spend
their time in dreaming,
the present seeming only the bright
unbearable cenotaph of the past:
its elfin laugh forever resounds
through the halls of another place...

In this lone field there is nothing
>> to dread
but the bright full face of the moon
>> overhead
peering with orange impertinence
on the epitaphs of the dead...

The reading program I was involved with under Louis Untermeyer's direction kept me busy, also. Not only the task of going to the library and taking out the books, but getting them read before my next visit with him. Usually these meetings took place weekly, although when he was out of town on lecture trips, or vacationing, I had to wait until he returned. Often this seemed like a much longer time than it actually was!

Although my personal life was totally satisfying in my relationship with Sal, my artistic and poetic longings reached their fulfillment in the association I had with Mr. Untermeyer. Over the years people have laughed at me, asking why I insisted on calling Louis Untermeyer, **Mr.** Untermeyer instead of Louis, and although I'm sure he wouldn't have minded if I'd called him Louis, I never thought of doing so! Perhaps addressing him formally was my way of showing the profound respect I had for him.

Then again, maybe it goes back to my childhood. I remember my mother always calling my father "Mr. Marshall" instead of using his first name. Of course, the fact that my father was seventy years old when I was born while my mother was in her early twenties may have been a factor there. I really can't say, and since my mother died while I was still quite young, my father having died when I was seven, I never had a chance to discuss this with her. I'd be inclined to wonder now if when my parents made love she ever called out "Joe" to him, or continued the Mr. Marshall formality. Since I was so used to hearing her speak of him in that way, even after his death, my guess would be that she did.

Or maybe she just said, "Oh God" and that would cover the whole field! You've probably noticed by now that I'm not at all a person you'd think of as being religious, although for a long time I've considered myself a spiritual seeker. By "seeker" I mean wanting to find out the truth behind this fleeting earthly existence. There has to be more to it than the seemingly senseless play of events in our lives, or like the handsome priest, who had befriended Lucilla and myself in Milano, said one day, when asked how he felt about renouncing the sensual side of this life: "Se no, ho sbagliato molto!" Translated this means, "If not, I've made a huge mistake!" I've often thought about him and wondered if God requires the state of celibacy or if we haven't come up with that idea in our attempts to learn more about our own inner self…

I certainly never felt the need to eliminate sexual expression from my personal life nor to demand it from anyone else either. If this turns me into some kind of a "New Age" freak, then I'm perhaps one of the oldest members in that group! I truly feel that spiritual unfoldment takes place when we enter the very depths of whatever we're experiencing, and go **through** it completely until we reach the other side where we'll encounter a new level.

I once wrote a poem on the presence of desire within myself and what that implies…

DRUMS

Desire is the beating of drums,
beating
     and beating
      and beating,
forever beating in my flesh:
   sometimes far,
      sometimes near—
a savage tom-tom
beating in my blood.

Perhaps, my love,
      I could be good
if it weren't for the drums—
        those drums beating
in my flesh...

Desire, as various sages point out, becomes our biggest obstacle on the path to enlightenment. This isn't necessarily our desire for sex, but the desire for all kinds of things like winning the lottery, or a beauty contest, and wanting to keep up with the Johanns, the Schmidts or the neighbors, whoever they might be! They also point out that the desire for God is not to be counted among these earthly ones.

Here you can lump all of those desires together, and give the whole package to God. I suppose this might be compared to people who are over their heads in debt solving the problem with one big loan from the bank with which to pay off all the others! If you don't believe in God you may have a problem with this, but the good news here is that if you don't like any of the available models you can create one for yourself that nobody knows about. Invisible, formless spirit can easily move in and make itself at home in any form. Even a rock, a crystal, or anything you consider sacred can serve as a talisman to link you up with **yourself.**

Right about now you might be thinking I've lost it, but I do believe that the light of spirit is still shining here somewhere, and will in time clarify things, hopefully revealing a new perspective, not only for the reader, but myself, also.

Truth is understood differently by each of us, and since we have over five billion people on this planet and counting, there are exactly that many views available. A few years ago I was reading a book on "Zen." I recall an account about a monk who had meditated for years to find the answer to a certain "koan," and then one day while he was walking in the street, a prostitute approached him. Formerly he would have told her, "No way, woman: get lost!" but that day he went home with her.

Would you like to know what happened? Well, the moment this poor sex-starved monk penetrated the vagina of the prostitute with his sexual organ he experienced a great burst of illumination and voilá, the "koan" was solved! I've discovered that you can never know for sure just which direction the light of spirit may choose to sneak up on you when it decides to do so.

Knowing this I find it impossible to judge anyone's approach to God, nor even to criticize the kind of stuff they may be floundering around in while "doing" their lives. Probably they're only going through what they must until they learn how to do better. Which is what life is all about, anyway, whether this process is recognized as spiritual or not...

One night Sal and I attended a "wake" for an elderly woman who had been a friend of his family. Throughout the Mass I stored up all the impressions I experienced while observing the folks attending the "wake" as well as the bereaved husband, finding it difficult to say goodbye to the one he'd loved for so many years.

OLD MRS. DONNEGAN'S WAKE

Remember the night we went to old
    Mrs. Donnegan's wake?
From a block away we could hear
    the voice of the priest,
and I asked, "Whatever language is he
    praying in?
It sounds like he's saying Nail Mary!"

The rest was spun out in an unintelligible
    wail,
and when we entered the door of the church
    he was still saying it...
Afterwards we laughed rather furtively
when someone said that Father Reilly

from the "old country"
should learn to speak English better.

Then the conversation went around in a circle
like a lot of amateurs doing a reading,
until finally when we saw there wasn't
        any getting around it,
we followed the flower scent down to
        where she lay
in a pink net dress like a bridesmaid's
        with tiny pink satin slippers,
woodenly clutching a rosary and a
        prayer book...

Her husband was kneeling there
talking to her brokenly-natural like,
and looking down at the perfumed
incomprehension of her face.
After a while he got up and spoke to us:
"You see I was talkin' to her tonight
just like I done for the past forty years."
Then he knelt again and gave her three
resounding kisses on her waxen hands—
his lips puckered up like a small boy's
as though he found the noisy assertiveness
        of it somehow comforting...

While most of us, and that includes myself, look upon death as a
tremendous tragedy, perhaps those who've moved from here to life on
the other side are quite happy, grieving mostly when they see the
unhappiness of their friends and families who must remain here on
Earth. Although it's difficult to do, I'm now learning to look on death as

a kind of graduation into the next phase of existence. Usually we regard death as an end and fail to realize that every end always signals the beginning of something new.

On my visits to see Louis Untermeyer, after he'd finished reading what I brought him, he would often take a few minutes to discuss some of the deeper aspects of authors and writing. When he saw I was developing a philosophical, or perhaps even a mystical view right along with the sensuous imagery I loved to use, he introduced me to the writings of various Greek philosophers, as well as the work of Schopenhauer and Nietzsche. Oddly enough I was able to read these controversial philosophers with a certain detachment, not creating an argument with myself nor anyone else about them.

I've always felt that everyone has a right to their own view, psychologically as well as spiritually. Probably when Mr. Untermeyer saw this quality emerging he realized my future work might gravitate toward this outlook on life, and become highly individual in nature, although it wasn't until we moved to California that what he'd seen began to blossom. But that's all part of the work I would begin doing in Los Angeles after my marriage—when the time was right for it. Whatever knowledge we realize about our inner self, appears in much the same way a flower opens: in its own time and its own season.

In the meantime, Mr. Untermeyer accelerated the reading program I was doing. I became familiar with works that are considered classics, as well as some of the best writers of modern times. I was astounded at the writings of "Marcel Proust" who could extend one sentence to cover a whole page. Juxtaposed to that the books of "Hemingway" affected me with their amazing simplicity of line and structure, and yet revealing hidden depths on an inner level. I was so profoundly moved by his work, I even wrote several short stories or "vignettes" of my own adapted to his style. Mr. Untermeyer was duly impressed with my first attempts at prose, and after reading some of it, said with a touch of admiration, "This is damned fine writing. You don't deal with deeper issues, like most great writers of short stories have, but you do have a talent for writing prose as well as poetry."

In the final segment of this book entitled, "Forty Years Later" I'll include most of these stories so you can judge for yourself! After each story I'll write an "Epilogue" recording many of the changes which have taken place in my own life since then as well as in some of the characters portrayed.

In more ways than I can say, those first attempts at writing prose have opened the door for close to a hundred books of that "genre" written since that long ago time when I shyly presented my stories of Italy to Louis Untermeyer and almost held my breath until he'd commented on them.

I can't help wondering what he would say about all the books I've written since he left this world behind, or if he would simply smile and say that he always knew about that...

SECOND AUTUMN
IN NEW YORK...

As time went on and summer heat merged into the glory of autumn, I delved into "The Red Badge of Courage," and some of the books of "Steinbeck" whose humor and gift for story telling intrigued me immensely. After completing a small volume of my own short stories, I decided I was actually more interested in writing poetry, so I returned to it like a wayward wife goes home again to her husband, finding she loves him best after all!

I spent several years pulling this whole thing together in the work I've done in recent times, where I took the books of poetry I'd written over the years, many of them devoted to nature themes, and added a running commentary in prose. Here I created a rather unique blend of poetry and prose, which many friends have enjoyed reading. Unfortunately Mr. Untermeyer had left our earthly arena by the time I discovered this happy marriage of my talents, where the poet within myself was united with the writer of prose, hopefully giving birth to some interesting offspring that readers may enjoy in the future, when human sensitivity again enters an era of seeking for the higher Reality found in our own hearts...

At the end of my second summer in New York I'd become acutely aware of the passage of time, knowing that all too soon I'd be leaving behind all these wonderful sessions with my "mentor" to begin a new life with Sal in California. Mr. Untermeyer assured me that we'd still be in touch by mail and that I could send him my writings for his criticism. He cautioned me not to expect him to reply right away due to various commitments, but I was reassured of his continuing assistance and interest anyway. One day I put my feelings about all of this concern in a poem and called it appropriately enough, "Clocks."

CLOCKS

Only when we are apart
do I notice
the ticking of all the clocks
ticking, ticking—
endlessly ticking:
tick-tock, tick-tock…

Thieves of minutes,
hours, days and years—
benevolently bestowing
the gift of life
in the outstretched palm of Time
to reclaim it
minute by hour, by day
by year, by life!
And only when we are
together again
does all the ticking stop…

I've discovered that our lives here are bound to a pendulum of the opposites, buffeted by our own reactive responses from one extreme to the other, keeping us strapped to the back of Time! To live in a state of timelessness, or love itself, is the blessing that comes when life is set free from the domination of the opposites. You may wonder who sets us free of Time's bondage, and I must reply that of course **we** do when we enter that mysterious essence within ourselves called the "soul" where the pendulum comes to rest at last…

By the end of October that year, Sal and I were busy with plans for our upcoming departure in November. My final meeting with Mr. Untermeyer, which took place not long before Sal and I left was heart wrenching for me, although I was eagerly anticipating the return to California and my marriage to Sal, something we'd longed for since our engagement in Milano.

Although I expected to have children at some time in the future, nothing was sure about that either, since I'd probably have to undergo surgery before a pregnancy could even take place. For so many of us the future is at best an unknown quantum. Learning to live from day to day in the "NOW" of things is truly a saving grace few people ever discover, and that includes myself!

At last, in the latter part of November, Sal and I left in a new Buick he'd bought for the trip, loaded with our books, luggage and a few personal possessions of his along with my own. One of these was a pair of skis he wanted to take, hoping to go skiing somewhere in California, or perhaps Colorado. Those skis drew a few humorous comments from folks on the road, where strapped to the top of the car they pointed the way down endless stretches of highway between New York and Los Angeles. Although we made brief stops at several interesting places, we opted not to tarry, but to stick to our travel agenda, arriving in Los Angeles at least two weeks before our wedding on December l9th., as we'd planned to do for so long.

We did stop overnight at the "Grand Canyon" and made a firm resolve to return to that marvelous place as often as we could in the years ahead. While we stood looking out over this incredible Canyon, stretching for five hundred miles in length and over a mile and a half across, we saw the hand of time at work on this Earth and were simply awed by it. Even after all these years I still get goose bumps whenever we go there!

Actually we encountered very little snow during the whole trip, and only clear highways opened up before us all the way to L.A. where we arrived a little ahead of the two weeks we needed to get ready for the 19th. I discovered that Los Angeles hadn't really changed all that much since I left for Italy over three years earlier. I recall Sal being tremendously impressed by the palm trees lining Sunset Boulevard, and all the flowers still blooming in late November.

On the day we were married, at four o'clock, it was ninety degrees and the biggest worry I had was perspiring so much it would show on my wedding gown! Since I have no family of my own, our wedding was given by the same foster family who had sponsored my trip to Italy. Although I knew everyone would be disappointed with my decision to follow a new career in writing, I felt that in time my friends would accept this, and realize it was as right for me artistically, as Sal was the perfect man to be my husband...

Our Wedding Day

LOS ANGELES: "CITY OF THE ANGELS"

YOU CAN GO HOME AGAIN!

If I had to choose a place to live out of all those I've seen in the course of my life, my favorite would still be California, although if you're happily settled in Ohio or somewhere else, you may question that! For many years we had friends who spent every winter on the coast of Mexico, insisting it had California beat a mile, and even included maid service.

I'd say in retrospect that I love California, Los Angeles in particular, because I sense that the unfolding of my inner life, as well as the completion of this current physical expression will take place here. And it has, earthquakes and all! Or I might say, in spite of several large earthquakes, since sometimes thousands of people die in one of those things in countries throughout the world! The famous Northridge quake hit here around 4:30 A.M. and I couldn't believe the number of things I saw tumbling down throughout the house, although miraculously nothing was broken!

Not long after I moved to California, several years before I left for Italy, I'd spent a weekend on Balboa Island with friends. That night I was asked to sing at a cocktail party which several guests had been invited to attend. Among them was the character actress, "Beulah Bondi," who became a lifelong friend that evening until her death many years later. We never lost touch with one another even while I was living in Italy where I ultimately studied with a teacher who was a personal friend of Beulah's.

During the time I stayed in New York Beulah was in the city for a professional commitment and we invited her to spend the evening with us at the little "East Side" apartment where I lived. Sal fixed her a real Italian home-cooked meal which she thoroughly enjoyed, and from that time on she became a staunch supporter of our marriage plans, never losing interest in what we were doing.

After the birth of our sons, they became very dear to Beulah, also, and were remembered with gifts for birthdays and holidays. Often we shared family parties at her beautiful hillside home, although now and then she was invited to our more modest two story house in Hollywood for various celebrations. I've come to see the truth that only a few friendships in our lives are so harmonious they've obviously been forged over many lifetimes in which all the little personality snags have been worked out. As another friend expressed it, our auras no longer find reason to "bump!"

I've often thought about how Mr. Untermeyer and I must have shared a tremendously close relationship like this in the past somewhere, although I never remembered just where or when, nor even **what** that was! I finally concluded that only the life we're living now has any real significance anyway, since those in the past have merely served to bring us to the present and provide us with an opportunity to create a more meaningful "NOW"…

It wasn't until after our honeymoon was over and we got settled in the apartment where we lived until our home was purchased, that I got in touch with Louis Untermeyer, sending him a group of poems I'd written when my muse became active again. In my letter I enclosed copies of a few photographs taken on our honeymoon, and some from the "Grand Canyon" when we stopped there on the way to California. Mr. Untermeyer knew very little about my family in Los Angeles, having met my foster father on only one occasion in New York when he was invited to accompany us for lunch at the "Town and Country" restaurant. Below is his reply.

Letter #1

Dear Mildred,

Thank you for the charming letter as well as the equally charming pictures. I wish I had time to answer your good paragraphs (and the implications of the poems) in as much detail as they deserve, but I have just returned from Europe to a more-than-usually-cluttered desk. We spent two months abroad (France for sheer escape and England for rest mixed with research), and I am still resentful about resuming work and other responsibilities in New York.

*As to the choice of a future career, that, as I've told you often, is a choice that no one but you can make. There are probably more financial rewards—to say nothing of immediate audience responses—for a singer: the poet can scarcely expect to support himself on his product and he is lucky to find any audience at all! But poetry can be a compulsion as well as a pleasure, and when it **is** a compulsion, there is nothing one can do about it—except to write...Meanwhile, you have a career in which you are happy: the career of being a wife, a performance as well as a privilege which will take up most of your time.*

As to the poems themselves, I found them somewhat uneven. I feel that some of them ("Poets and Lovers," "Wedding Reflection," "A Caress Is All Things," (for example) are not only slight but trivial. On the other hand, such poems as "Lazy Afternoon," "Monkey on a String," "Valedictorian," "Night," etc. are full of the things which you do so well: the unusual image, the sharp observation, the distinctly personal tone. They make me wonder what you will be doing, say, a year from now... whether you will be doing more with your voice than with your verse.

But that is for the future. Meanwhile, you have much to do in your everyday life as well as your creative life, and I hope that all continues to go as happily as your letter and work indicate.

Sincerely, Louis Untermeyer

At this point following the letters I'll include copies of the poems in which Mr. Untermeyer found some merit. I'm not sure that I still have copies of those he called slight, or trivial! If he didn't like them, I no longer did either, although at the time I wrote them I thought they were rather clever, filled with cynical overtones I rarely employed and have since abandoned completely. I'm glad he indicated another direction more suited to my abilities, and I've been grateful to him for that ever since.

LAZY AFTERNOON

Just for us, my love,
one long, lazy afternoon—
dosing, somnolent,
easing its round, soft belly into sleep
as hot wet waves of air
swim up from the grass,
and one intrusive bee
bumbles and nuzzles the flower cups—
its wings too heavy for flight
like passion numbed by satiety,
and nodding in the lap of languor…
while the drowsy minutes topple
     out of the clock
and the silken hours spin their
     endless cocoon
through the whole long lazy afternoon…

Our honeymoon was scarcely over before family and friends started putting pressure on me to resume my singing career. I sang at parties, and in spite of having let my voice slide for so long, it had remained in remarkably good shape, which only added fuel to the argument in favor of my return to opera.

When people finally realized I didn't intend to do much more about it than I was already, that I simply wanted to enjoy my life of wedded bliss and a certain solitude in which to write, they either gave up in disgust or clicked their tongues showing their total disapproval of the choice I'd made. Probably the resentment I felt about all this pressure fueled the inspiration for the following poem! It seems that throughout life there are always people more than willing to push us into what **they** think we should be doing, with little or no regard for our own wishes...

MONKEY ON A STRING

God holds life it would appear,
like a monkey on a string,
and we, quite free to move to all
        its length,
barring any sudden reining in
can traverse at will its cunning
        little orbit.

We can dance and play the fool—
pretending to be oblivious of it,
indulge our minds in endless
discussions of poetry or philosophy,
like a cross-legged Buddha
expounding at the wake of civilization.
We can immerse ourselves in some
        religious escape,
remembering of course to shake our
        little cup
for tithes and dues to appease
        the keeper's wrath...

We can even play at love,
that old ubiquitous panacea:
no matter, it's all the same
and there's no escaping HIM!
HE burns us,
      HE drowns us,
           HE maims us,
and Oh yes—I forgot: HE loves us!
And when the poor dead thing hangs useless,
without a word HE cuts the string!

Yet didn't I hear just the other day
something about a state of bliss—
somewhere beyond all this?
But where it is I cannot say...

This poem pretty accurately expresses the state of mind I was in at that time, feeling I was neither fish nor fowl as the saying goes. Actually my whole life was in transition, after which I'd be moving from an Earth-based view into my ongoing investigation of the Truth behind this brief existence...

VALEDICTORIAN OF FIFTY-THREE

The world can wait—wait for me,
the valedictorian of fifty-three!
Atomic bombs and the communist scheme
to rule the world may seem
important to lesser mortals then I.
What care I if politicians vie
with each other—brother against brother,
for the topmost perch on the international
      roost,

when neither can keep it, nor boost
himself one century higher than he can fall!

There will be time—
time for me to hear the call
to fight their battles for them:
today I'm deaf!
The stirring of a leaf
is louder than a cannon,
and the burden of sixteen summers
is for me more weighty than a century
of global destinies!

This day in June brings greater triumph
than Earth's first rocket to the moon,
while I—frowning potentate in long
      black robe
speculate on the fate of nations,
searching a sea of upraised eyes
      for hers!
Their promise I well surmise,
and tonight the world waits
just for me,
the valedictorian of fifty-three!

The following poem, the last in the group mentioned in this first letter from Mr. Untermeyer, was written during one of those crazy moments that I periodically experience while waiting for my muse to come up with a more meaningful idea.

NIGHT WORLD

I love the way the furtive
      shadows creep
to rub their plump backsides
      together in the street—
brazenly, full in the face of Creator Moon,
like those two expatriates of Eden!

And I love as well the paradox of hush
beset by thunderous "twitter talk":
even the way the wind wrings mysteries
from the stuff of ordinary leaves!

But night's hypocrisies
are difficult to conciliate:
she slyly swings her cloak aside
to conceal a felony,
then smugly draws it in at once
to bed a pair of lovers!

In the following weeks I began writing in earnest again. The small
one bedroom apartment we lived in until we could find a home for ourselves was certainly no challenge to keep clean. One interesting note
which amuses me when I think of it, concerned Judy Garland's bed
from a beach house my foster father had bought in Malibu and still furnished with her stuff, which he moved to his garage in Hollywood for
storage. Since Sal and I fell heir to Judy's bed, maybe the next group of
poems reflects some of the volatile vibes she possessed, although I really
can't verify that!

I must have had some unidentified connection to the aura of this
great actress-singer, because a couple of years after our marriage when

my foster father died, he left us the option of a shared inheritance in Judy's former house in Malibu. Although we turned it down, I was again aware of this link.

Years later after our next door neighbors died, their house was purchased by Judy Garland's ex-husband, Mark Herron, and we shared a warm and neighborly friendship with him for many years until his death not long ago. I recall giving him a lamp that had belonged to his ex-wife, as a memento. I also remember the time Mark got a bit high while a party was in progress at his house and he dropped by our place to talk about his marriage to Judy.

"God, how I loved that girl!" he said. I was very touched that he still felt so strongly about his film legend wife, in spite of whatever difficulties they had. That **has** to be what love is…

When our sons were in their teens, Sal and I took them on a trip to visit the Italy we'd loved so long ago, and still do. While we were gone, Mark and the man who shared ownership of the house with him looked after our newly-planted vegetable garden, caring for it and our home as though it were their own.

Later Mark said laughing, "A lot of **our** tomato plants died, but yours are doing just great!"

Of course we shared some of our harvest with them since good neighbors are hard to find. Here's the next letter from L.U.

Letter #2

Dear Mildred

Those are excellent poems—practically every one has something to say, and says it in its (or your) individual way. You have, as I have said so often, an extraordinary gift for similes, strange comparisons, and startling figures of speech. I particularly like "Birth of a Poet," with "a garden of metaphor"; "White Wild Roses," with its "imminent Nirvana"; and the entire sequence of the seasons, especially "Autumn" with its half-pun about

Van Gogh gouging color and "Winter" with that fine line about "a white excitement...through a harem of trees." I return them herewith as I fear losing original manuscripts.

I hope that your hospital experience will be neither long nor painful, and that it will give you, after it is over, renewed vitality—although you do not seem to lack much in that department. If you expect to remain there long enough to read a rather lengthy book, you might have your husband get you my MAKERS OF THE MODERN WORLD which was published last week and which, I am happy to say, has already received some important and extremely gratifying reviews. You might also have a look at the September "Atlantic Monthly" which contains my two-page double-column poem, "Orpheus and his Lute," which is a kind of satire (with serious undercurrent) on certain phases of modern poetry—including parodies of Auden, Eliot, The New Critics, and others.

*Good luck to you before, during, and after the operation...and, as they say in Germany, **Gute Besserung**.*

Sincerely, Louis Untermeyer

The surgery Mr. Untermeyer referred to in his letter was considered necessary if I wanted to have children. And I did! Through giving birth to children we find a way to repay the universe for the life it has bestowed upon us. Having children also proved to be one of the most remarkable experiences of our marriage, inspiring several poems. The operation was, of course, a complete success, and I subsequently gave birth to two sons. Below is my poem on the birth of a **poet**, also a blessed event!

THE BIRTH OF A POET

Since I first discovered poetry
the world has never been the same:
say a haunting vision came
on wings as frail as butterflies

that floated past my "eye"
and left me such a longing
eagle's wings are not enough
to probe its depth of sky...

Now all things hold a mystery—
a core to peck from every heart:
thoughts that swim behind an eye
burn peacock bright with scandal!
A leaf before was a frail blowing thing
concealing its textbook in green,
and toads but purveyors of common warts
removed from their garden of metaphor.

I've plunged a bucket in the well
of a golden elixir supply
and raised it filled with subtleties:
the poet's Devotee am I!

When I was in school I had a very close friend, a poet who chose to live her life as a lesbian, although not with me, I hasten to add because I've been most definitely heterosexual in my own expression throughout my life. Although I've continued to love my friend all these years, my love is in spirit and always has been.

I've never found a truly valid reason to withhold my love from anyone, since the essence of love itself rises from the soul and doesn't belong to gender. If love is unconditional like that of the Christ, how could any sense of exclusiveness remain? When we separate ourselves from someone and sit in judgment on them, we've moved out of the soul essence and into the love-hate expression of this lower level founded on the opposites. We must again transcend it in order to dwell in the beauty of essence.

It's said that joy spills from a tiny hole in the heart that becomes an aperture for it. It has also been stated by certain eastern teachers that the whole world emerges from this tiny hole in the heart, although I can't verify that for you! It did become obvious in my own meditative work a long time ago that when we open our eyes each morning we recreate the world around us. Does it have a separate reality if we don't do this? You know something: that's a really good question!

WHITE WILD ROSES

You lay beside me in the sand,
remote and lonely as a sigh,
while all about us everywhere
      white wild roses grew,
oblivious at our feet—
their fragrance maddening and sweet
      as imminent Nirvana.

I plucked the virgin blossoms up,
crushed them hard against my face,
ravished them with greedy breath—
lying beside them where they grew,
felt their petals throb beneath
      my trembling penitent hand,
      groping in the sand,
and this at last I knew:

Beauty is too fleet a thing
for fingers ever to hold.
Whose vehicle is fire or wing,
to the grasp of force is cold...

One of the most enjoyable things I recall about the eastern part of the country is the change of seasons each year, spring and autumn standing out most in my mind.

Here in California it seems that an almost perpetual summer prevails, with now and then a lot of rain, particularly if we have "El Niño" paying us a visit. Occasionally there isn't enough rain and we have a drought.

Although many varieties of deciduous trees grow in California, including the Maples, the unique glory of an eastern autumn is absent, and certainly the winter's snow except in the high desert and surrounding mountainous areas...

SEASONS IN METAPHOR

AUTUMN

Autumn is the essence of frost,
     of flame, of farewell,
a wallflower summer become a
     nympholeptic belle!
A painter gone mad—
a Van Gogh truant from his cell,
gouging color on a canvas
     wide as a wood,
until dour-faced November—
his relentless chiaroscuro keeper—
comes to blow away
the insurgent madman's holiday!

WINTER

Winter's a dozing nonentity
locked in the hibernation of long
     frigid sleep,
yet there's pulsing within her

      quiescent stream
where life lies smiling in a dream
of springtime sin!
A white excitement spins through
a harem of trees with rumors of spring:
the triumphal homecoming of Sultan Sun!
A black indictment of eunuch Earth's
dark treacheries, the frozen one,
his forbidden beauties encircled
      within his icy embrace,
he forgets his impotence disgrace,
panting and longing surreptitiously
for the vernal rite of fertility!

SPRING

Spring is a time-release fireworks
display of exploding buds
in a landscape of sunlight,
puzzled clouds and wind-crazed day!
A potpourri of bloom
and demented buzzing things
in a world that seems to have gone—
not just to the dogs, but to wings!

If autumn's a flapper and summer a lady—
      winter an old one,
then spring must be a maid
three-quarters ready for love,
the rest of her a nun whose half-formed
velleity is scarcely a bold one,
and for a poet with autumn zest,
      mere prosody!

SUMMER

Summer's a floating adagio movement,
    a pensive mood,
a throb in the throat of the year—
    a time for summing up:
a balancing of debit spring against
    credit fall—
the prodigal tree scorns all reminders
    of husbandry!

A surfeit of sleep: onomatopoeia
    of ennui—
yet there's haunting diablerie
in her colloquies of wind and leaves:
they cannot keep their russet-red
and golden secret concealed
within those frosty sleight-of-hand
fingers of autumn's sorceries...

Of course now I'd find a way to write this poem with greater simplicity and economy of words, which must be what poetic maturity is all about! But since I was still learning to write and working to establish contact with my own soul, this must be taken into account. Perfection is seldom encountered on the first steps.

Mr. Untermeyer certainly knew how to push me into the discovery of those depths within myself better than anyone else I've known, with the exception of those few advanced spiritual teachers and sages I've been privileged to meet, and sometimes to work with at rare times throughout my long life here on this Earth. I've discovered that just as soon as we're ready a door opens to the next level of learning and all we have to do is walk through it...

A FURTHER EXPANSION

In between the time I received this letter and the next one, I'd made the acquaintance of a spiritual teacher who was to play an important role in my life for the next twelve years or so. While studying the "Teaching of Living Ethics" I became involved in a course of learning about things of an esoteric nature, finding right at the outset that my "Third Eye" was alive and mysteriously active! If you've experienced this, you'll understand why I say this "Blessed Event" brings great joy.

From then on my life was focussed in a different direction, and filled with a strange new significance which I'm sure Mr. Untermeyer sensed, although I never told him about it.

This next letter from him took quite a while arriving, making me wonder if he'd lost interest, even though I was pregnant with my first son at the time and pretty much involved in the many challenges that often come with this, morning sickness and all!

When Mr. Untermeyer's letter came at last, I understood why I hadn't heard from him and was quite overjoyed he hadn't forgotten about me.

Letter #3

Dear Mildred:

Your letter and the enclosures waited for me for weeks. I was away on a lecture trip with my wife who, though she had traveled in Europe with me, had never seen anything of America except the east coast. We covered most of America in a little less than two months, from New Orleans to the other extreme of color and climate, the state of Washington; from the desert of New Mexico to the sub-tropics of San Diego. By the odd booking of my agent, we were in and out of Los Angeles three different times, and by the oddest coincidence we were in your district: Hollywood 46 stopping with the John Weavers, (old friends of ours) who live on the heights of Hillside Avenue. Although we were continuously occupied (what with lectures and social obligations) I would at least have phoned you had I known your new address. Next time, I hope...

Meanwhile, I applaud the new poems. They have a tang, a tartness which reminds me of Emily Dickinson—they even have Emily's "off-balance" rhymes. You say what you want to say in your own way, however; the poems are you speaking, not a series of echoes from some other poet or some older tradition. Have you thought of trying "The New Yorker" or "Poetry; A Magazine of Verse," which has taken on a new lease of life with a new editor.

Congratulations on the house, which sounds enchanting, and the renovated Mildred, who seems to have emerged from the operation more zestful than ever. I can see you now, training those climbing roses—in spite of the name I recommend the climbing Herbert Hoover, who (which) was sprawling all over the Weavers' terrace.

To hell with Eleanor King. She sounds not only inefficient but impossible. Just keep on with your work, either in prose or verse, and let's hope and believe that the agents will come to you. Most important of all, keep well and happy...as I'm sure you are.

Cordially,
Louis Untermeyer

This was probably the only occasion when I might have seen Mr. Untermeyer again in person, or at least talk to him on the phone had he received my letter with our new address. As it turned out, our present location in Hollywood became our permanent residence throughout the balance of the twenty-four years I was in touch with Mr. Untermeyer, and has remained so ever since. Oddly enough I sometimes think the powers that be must have had a hand in keeping our relationship confined to inner levels of awareness, which for many people still remain unexplored.

Before I left New York Mr. Untermeyer had put me in touch with an agent who probably concluded that she didn't want to waste her time on a poet, so my door to "name and fame" closed before it could even swing open! Her rejection of my work is what he was referring to in the previous letter. I've discovered that when the right time comes, doors begin opening quite inexplicably, as they have for me so far throughout my life.

Next I'll transcribe a few of the poems Louis Untermeyer spoke of in his letter. Although I certainly wasn't imitating the work of "Emily Dickinson" here, she wasn't far from my mind! I also knew that Mr. Untermeyer admired her, not necessarily the form she chose for her poetry, but the mystical insights she revealed.

PAIRS OF MEANING

Truth is elusive as Siamese cats—
unapproachable and cold:
it prowls in pairs of meaning
from inscrutable to bold!

Slinks right past the wariest eye
then pops in unannounced
to claim a hearth more viable
and leave tradition trounced!

BY WHIM OF INFINITY

Reflection on life reveals to me
a dream tucked in 'twixt "Y" and "Z"—
snapped in and out of consciousness
by the whim of infinity!

On the breath of the insignificant
mortality relies,
the pertinacity of a sperm,
or the speed with which it dies!

The bleak alternative of an "if"—
a moment's reckoning:
what belated perspicacity
a tragedy can bring...

These two poems indicate the phase I was experiencing at that time. I've discovered that creativity, as well as one's inner awareness, progresses in cycles where there's never an end to anything, but only the beginning of something new. This as I've come to see, is how life reveals its scenario to us, also. Attempting to hang onto something that's flown by, or trying to grab hold of what we want before the time comes for it creates only a lot of personal frustration. I discovered, right along with the growth of my literary creativity, that my spiritual life was always taking a new and sometimes astounding direction toward a new level. Throughout the years ahead both of these would continue to reveal ever-deepening insights into the essence of myself.

This next letter from Mr. Untermeyer was written on "Easter Sunday"—a time when people seldom have time to complete everything related to that occasion, let alone answer mail! When he responded to my letters at such times, I was often bowled over by the peculiar feeling of intimacy it created, as though he were indicating I was part of his family. This letter also contained a rare summing up of what I'd accomplished so far in my work with him, obviously leaving the door open for a **lot** of improvement!

Letter #4   *Easter Sunday—full sun to show*
                                       that spring, too, has risen.

Dear Mildred:

You seem to be enjoying your Emily Dickinson binge—and there are no evidences of a hangover. I took the envelope of pages with me to Connecticut and read them in the quiet of the Connecticut hills and the purring of my Connecticut cats.

So far your work has reflected facets of many things: people, places, experiences, facts and fantasies. Although you have been subjected to many influences, there is always a quality which is distinctly your own. It emerges, disappears, discloses itself in another guise, and plays a kind of intellectual hide and seek. The style is equally fluctuating, almost kaleidoscopic, and—or but—neither your thought nor your style is quite fused. That is to say, the expression is uneven, the idea and the technique are not yet completely integrated, fluent and imaginative though the lines often are.

I think that this integration is the next step—and I think, moreover, that you are about to take it. At least I hope so.

As a reaction to Emily Dickinson's wayward whimsicalities, you might try the more rigorous discipline of such contemporary women as Louise Bogan, Léonie Adams, Elizabeth Bishop, Charlotte Mew and Sylvia Townsend Warner, all of whom are included in my MODERN AMERICAN AND BRITISH POETRY. The taste, I promise you, is different.

                              Happy Easter—lilies and all, Louis Untermeyer

Here I'll transcribe a few more of the poems that Mr. Untermeyer referred to. His letter had certainly served to shake me out of the confining E.D. phase I'd been stuck in and get me back to expressing my own "voice" in another direction.

I've discovered that one soon tires of imitation anyway, no matter what form it takes!

HORSES OF MY WILL

I drive the horses of my will
they know their master now!
and only on rare occasions do I
frivolity allow.

Though once in recent journeying
along accustomed ways
an apparition's baleful eye
assailed my docile bays,

who plunged beyond my proud control!
Since then "Lord Arrogance"
conceding fate's intractable
sits wary at the reins!

INEXPLICABLE AS WINGS

Beauty is the strangest thing:
it leaps around horizons,
curls up in a tiny pearl
and peers through the bars of prisms—
surrounds a modest cottage
or sweeps a castle wall!

Inexplicable as darting wings
that are far too swift for capture
by a greedy stalking mind,
eyes might well be made of agate,
and ears of buzzing cockle shell
if the heart were deaf and blind...

I feel quite sure now, while looking at things from the higher perspective bestowed through many years of meditation and writing, that Mr. Untermeyer didn't want to see me get hung up at any point along the way, not only in the development of my poetic abilities, but perhaps in my inner discoveries as well. His next letter reveals the truth of this, although I'd already begun moving into another phase of expression that would take a spiritual, as well as a philosophical direction, becoming permanent as far as my poetry was concerned, then later in all the prose work I did also. I suppose you might say this signaled the birth of my own creative "voice" which is always as unique as one's finger prints.

When it's truly yours it won't ever be exactly like that of anyone else, and any inclination to imitate totally disappears. In his next letter Mr. Untermeyer confirms my discovery.

Letter #5

Dear Mildred:

I'm glad to see that you are recovering from your Emily Dickinson binge. I notice a bit of hangover here and there; but mostly the poems are clear-headed, bright-eyed, and definitely your own. I particularly relished "Lawnmower," "Spirit," "Body of a Friend," and "The Eye," even though this last one has the E.D. twist of phrase. By God, you will sell one of these somehow, someday, somewhen!

As usual, I'm in the midst of things. I'm putting off the work on which I've spent considerable time—LIVES OF THE POETS—to do a volume for The Limited Editions Club. It's to be a selection of the best poems of Heinrich Heine (my own translations, based on a book I did some years ago) plus a new critical-biographical introduction. Later it will be issued as a book for the public, but the first edition will be deluxe and definitely limited.

After that, I will return to my labors with the poets of my own language, Please God.

I'm happy that you liked MAKERS. My own favorite chapters are those on F.D.R., Isadora Duncan, Charlie Chaplin, and Robert Frost, perhaps because I had so good a time writing them. I wonder what you thought of the pieces on Emily Dickinson and Dylan Thomas. The one on Mary Baker Eddy has been furiously assailed by Mother Church.

*No more for now. I'm in New York three days a week—sometimes no more than two—and I don't feel that I can cheat Decca out of **all** my (or, rather, it's) time.*

Best to you and the work—but, chiefly best to you.

Louis Untermeyer.

P.S. I love zucchini, (even though you Anglicize it to zukini" which looks Japanese), but I never had it in salad. How do you prepare it? Do you cook it first? And then chop it, or merely slice it like cucumbers? We've used oregano a lot—and mint, which grows all over our Connecticut meadow. But I don't know the taste of basil, unless that's what the Genoese put in their pesto sauce.

By the time I received this letter from Mr. Untermeyer I'd already planted an herb garden and made a little progress in learning to cook. In Italy Lucilla had done most of the cooking except for the soup and salad which I enjoyed making. In New York Sal did a lot of the cooking since he liked various Italian dishes which I hadn't as yet learned how to make, and he was actually teaching me to cook by example. Now he says my chicken cacciatore is better than his! My pizza's pretty good, too, for an Irish poet. Well, Irish and Scotch and French.

After we moved into our new-old brick house, my husband of course always mowed the lawn. Perhaps hearing the sound of the mower as he worked inspired the following poem…

THE LAWNMOWER

Convolutions of doom whir and
    descend
upon the lawn's green silences,
more cruel than winter's slow
    numbness,
or the cool blunt discipline
    of wind:
such elemental stringencies
have bred an ancient fortitude...

But
this—
this herbal
guillotine
holds carnival
in chlorophyll!
See how the head
of a dandelion
rolls with a
vengeful
    /

        plop
lying in golden
martyrdom atop
the common heap
that the ludicrous
loping barrow
bears to the compost
burial plot,

while from the huddled flower bed
rows and rows of coral bells
ring requiems for the fallen dead...

After writing this rather light-hearted fantasy about mowing the lawn and wreaking havoc on the grass, I entered a more serious mood for the next poems Mr. Untermeyer singled out. If he didn't like something at all, he wasted no time in letting me know about it, so I deduced that the poems he mentioned in his letters jumped out at him and aroused his interest immediately.

The following poem reveals that I was becoming frankly introspective about life and questing for the meaning it ultimately holds for anyone who decides to probe deeper. And I was certainly beginning to do that...

SEEDS OF SPIRIT

Oh could some spying deity
essay to analyze,
dissect and quarter—bare to eye
this core of loneliness:
obscure and unknown resting place
where the seeds of spirit lie,
enmeshed in mellow flesh,
secure and incorruptible—
their hard brown hidden spring
aloof and inviolate
as the verities they live by...

And we, so full of knowing
yet knowing so little!
Cognizant only of the growing
        and the dying,
and the vague impenetrable core
enduring somewhere at the heart
        of the thing...

Throughout my life on this Earth, or during anybody's life, someone's always dying, or lying mortally ill and waiting to do so. Like I always say, no one's going to get out of here alive! In this next poem I was again searching for that mysterious something which survives earthly life, or at least get a glimpse of it. Up to that point I'd had very little success...

THE BODY OF A FRIEND

Her corpse is an armful of unfinished
     living,
a hasty departure from a long-familiar
     house left in mute dishabille
on a one-way, round-the-sphere flight
bringing no postcard reassurances!

An unresolved chord of aching love,
resounding its single brainless note,
awaits the full-throated major
of a comforting resolution...

But zero plus zero plus zero,
     all added to zero—
make nothing, nothing, nothing
on this dark side of the wall
that surrounds the light
where understanding waits,
cloistered like a shy little nun
     who seldom speaks...

THE "EYE" THAT'S SINGLE

The eye is a strange phenomenon,
it sees and doesn't see—

lies and yet it doesn't lie,
quite paradoxically.

Looks on fame or anonymity
with flexible attention
and only through accustomed gaze
gains accurate dimension.

Or is it quite the opposite?
I'll seek the "eye" that's single:
a bloody cyclops then I'll be
and see just what I see!

In my meditation, as stated previously, I had very quickly experienced what is known as the opening of the "Third Eye" which occurred as easily and naturally as though it had always been present in my life. I never shared this with Mr. Untermeyer, since I wasn't sure he was interested in things of that nature. Years later I entered a period of intense experience on the inner planes, after which I began writing a volume of poems that may have clued him into the fact that something unusual was happening.

In the meantime, a lot of personal stuff was going on in my life, also. Earlier I'd become pregnant at around the same time my foster father learned he was ill with terminal cancer, which had already metasticized throughout his body. Going through bouts of morning sickness at the same time one is grieving for a loved one experiencing so much suffering was something I'll never forget!

Finally after the funeral was over and things had returned to some semblance of normal, I wrote Mr. Untermeyer about what had, and was still taking place. The following letter was his reply.

Letter #6

Dear Mildred:

Condolences and congratulations—life is, as the poet (or at least as a poet) said, full of entrances and exits. I well remember your father—I even recall the details of his talk and the charm of his presence at lunch—at Town and Country on Park Avenue. Death is always a horror to those who watch its coming on—but it is most horrible when it takes the form of cancer. I, too, have sat and watched a dear one literally fade away.

And now you are to be a mother. I spare you the conventional sentimentalities, but I know what this fulfillment will mean to you. Although I have never been a mother myself, the state of maternity is a popular (or should I say populous) one, and many of my best friends speak well of it. I expect you will, too—and volubly. Let me know more when you know more—including sex, name, color, career, etcetera.

About the poems: I like their spirit as well as their expression. I also like your experiments in the technique of assonance and rhyme—especially in "Death and the Lady," "On Butterflies" and "Viaticum". Caution: Watch out for too much of a mixture of metaphors—for example, "Grief." You are obviously getting a firmer control of your medium all the time. Further congratulations in your double role as creatrix.

As this letterhead may indicate, I do most of my work at home now. We moved from New York six months ago and come into the city only once or twice a week...Thanks for what you say about my books. I enclose a review of my latest, published a couple of months ago, and already doing well. Best to you and your creations.

Louis Untermeyer

P.S. I enjoyed the Edd-fi-cation pun, a new one to me.

As usual a letter from Mr. Untermeyer lifted my spirits and increased my enthusiasm for finding new material to write about. He seemed to sense exactly when I needed psychological support, and also when a subtle reminder was called for to let me know I was going off the path to my highest expression.

The poem "Death and the Lady" was subsequently retitled "School After School," since life here on Earth is certainly like attending school where we learn to move into increasingly higher levels of understanding. Following graduation, we may reside for a while in what we refer to as Heaven, but death could also mean a return to the drawing board of life where school continues until we find a way to "get it right" and matriculate to a higher level.

SCHOOL AFTER SCHOOL

I dreamed that life was like a school
let out for a long recess—
with pupils roaming all around
or lolling on the grass…

And there beyond its green compound
I saw a figure lurking,
handsome of form, and knowing of eye—
mysterious force exerting.

He drew me out into his arms—
a lover he was to me!
I quite forgot that school was called
and I was absentee…

At last he led me to a place
beside a lonely pool,
where the future rippled past my eye
with astounding clarity!

Neither birth nor death contains the key
to solve the riddle of life,
for all I saw looming up in space
was school after school—after school...

ON BUTTERFLIES...

Butterflies in cocoons are worms
        and butterflies are nerves
in abdominal cavities beneath a dancer's
        curves:
they're peculiar to actors, preachers,
and tenors: poets, politicians
and all sorts of folk who perform
        or speak after dinners.

They frequently turn social in nets of
        lace and tulle,
and at other times more serious
they also fly to school!
But to me a butterfly is more than
a charming symbol, or desiccated specimen:

It is threads of velvet spun on air
from luminous strands of light,
rich chords of silence resounding within
        the vibrant hum of space:
an ecstatic exile from this world
        of Earth-bound usefulness...

What collectors crucify between pages
of a book, we poets deify—
and the ways of God to man attempt
        to justify...

During one of our hanging-loose parties in the patio, our actress friend "Beulah Bondi" told us a joke about butterflies and I've never forgotten it… It seems that while having dinner together, four gentlemen engaged in conversation, looked up when a lovely butterfly came flitting across the table. The American pointed out the grace and beauty of a butterfly and how appropriate our English word is to describe its flight.

Another of the men came from an Italian background and on seeing the butterfly exclaimed, "Ah una farfalla! What a beautiful little creatura. Our Italian language is so perfect to express its movement: farfalla, farfalla"… He closed his eyes to enjoy the sheer beauty of the open vowel sound in the Italian language.

The third gentleman at the table was of French extraction. "I agree with you my friend, but I must say that the French language, spoken all over the world," he added proudly, "is a thing of great beauty, also. Papill-on," he said, repeating it several times and making graceful gestures with his hand in imitation of the butterfly's flight. "Can you imagine a word more appropriate for this lovely creature than 'papillon'?"

The fourth member of the group was of German lineage, and up until then had been quietly listening to the other three men. Suddenly without any prelude and perhaps a little defensively, he asked, "And vat's de matter mit Schmetterling?"

Of course everyone laughed, hopefully realizing that a butterfly is more than the name bestowed upon it by different races throughout the world. Like the nameless energy supporting its flight a butterfly lives everywhere bringing beauty to the Earth.

The idea of "viaticum" in the sense I use it for this next poem, means provisions for a journey, and not the usual connotation given it by the Catholic church. My poem "Viaticum" incorporates seriousness along with a growing sense of humor, something Mr. Untermeyer encouraged from the very beginning of our association. As I recall, he was well-known for some of the puns he came up with, coupled with an outrageous sense of humor.

My own feeling about all of this is that humor saves us from becoming sanctimonious about ourselves, being one of the greatest gifts we inherit from the father-mother-God of this universe. If we don't have humor, then we must work really hard to acquire it, since this is our "survival kit" for earthly existence! Most spiritual teachers recommend humor as an aid for transcending psychic blocks, also, where it may be applied like an antibiotic ointment to heal the sores of self-importance many are afflicted with, especially when we excel at doing something. Maybe writing!

On the other side of life, a poet, if he's lucky, will no longer be concerned with writing, having become the poem itself. The flickering glow of egotism never survives in the glory of the soul's luminosity, so we might as well find a way to jettison it while we're here! Otherwise we'll have to wait until some future lifetime for that to happen, in one way or another. It's said that to realize the highest truth we must be stripped of everything we hold dear, in a personal sense that is, since none of what we define as "personality" outlives us.

VIATICUM

What shall I have for viaticum
when that last unreasonable sleep descends,
what sort of provender, what dress
will serve immortal ends?

Shall I go fortified with jewelry,
the latest style gown, a divine new hat,
a fur or two to keep me—cold?
Oh no, I will leave all that!

What kind of state will Heaven be:
communist or democratic,
socialist, subject to royal dominion
or strictly autocratic?

I believe it's nothing quite so mundane
as these narrow divisions of the mind:
such petty ideas are happily mortal,
and these I will leave behind!

Might culture be a fetish there?
I'd love to take a book or two
to augment the introspective view:
but—my memories will do...

Will nature haunt those fields,
          will the sky
be the same stab of blue, the wind a thrill
of air on leaves as responsive as these?
Oh, I do so hope it will!

Does the sensual have its role to play
as part of Heaven's itinerary?
Or are souls a lot of cold-blooded wraiths
who'd reject an ecstasy?

Pleasure I know has its counterpoint
of pain that is played by a deft left hand,
but find a way to take joy I must,
and it's there I'll take my stand!

I'll have all the depths my soul has stored
of loving and losing—both too well,
and a plump little trunk I will take with me,
be it either to Heaven, or hell!

THE BIRTH OF A SON

On June 30th. three years after our marriage, our first son was born. Following that I sent Mr. Untermeyer a letter announcing his arrival. Somehow he got the idea that the Italian name "Nicola" was a girl's, since it sounds feminine. The post card he sent in response to my letter explains why I hadn't heard from him.

Letter #7

Dear Mildred:

Your letter-notice has remained unanswered until now because (1) I have had a severe, (but evidently not fatal) operation, (2) have been in Europe for two months recuperating, during which time I heard "Iphigenia" at La Scala and "Tosca" at Covent Garden, (3) have retired from Decca to spend all my time doing my own writing here in Newtown, and (4) trying to catch up with my unacknowledged correspondence, unpaid bills and unfulfilled commitments.

This, then, is nothing more than a hearty note of congratulations—to all of you. The best of everything to Nicola Anthony and her proud parents.

Sincerely, Louis Untermeyer

A few weeks after I received this I got another letter off to him, now that he was established in his Connecticut home. In this letter I enclosed a few poems I'd been working on in between my duties as a new mother. I discovered that while Nick was taking a nap was the best time for me to rest, also, and catch up on some writing. With a new baby in the house you sleep when he sleeps!

Earlier that year Sal and I had gone to visit our neighbors at their cabin near Crowly Lake in northern California, located at over seven thousand feet. I was simply awed by the mountain stream rushing down from the mountains outside the cabin. We even thought of buying property ourselves and building a cabin up there.

I must have had a rough night when I wrote the poem "On Motherhood!" The "Abandoned Apple Orchard" that Mr. Untermeyer mentions describes a place I was quite familiar with in Michigan, since we passed it each time we went to the river to picnic and swim. But first the post card from him.

Letter #8

Dear Mildred:

We're in something of a catastrophic phase. My wife just lost her darling Toy Yorkshire terrier, which she had brought from England, via France, and suddenly it succumbed to (of all things) meningitis! I've been limping around with a badly dislocated ankle. My oldest son (29) is going through a marital upset. And... But I won't weary you with our other troubles. I've just time enough to congratulate you on your growingly interesting poems, especially "On Motherhood" and "To A Mountain Stream" and "The Abandoned Orchard," as well as the growing Nicolino.

Best, as ever, Louis Untermeyer

Here are the poems that caught L.U.'s eye in the group I sent. "On Motherhood" was later retitled, "The Chain of Life." I often do this, putting down a tentative name at the start.

THE CHAIN OF LIFE

Is the goal of motherhood—
that maudlin departure from
the sanity of solitude,

to forge a chain of life
and clothe a consciousness
with flesh and a formula for grief?

Surely there must be
a wider purpose in it:
some veiled horizon past our sky

of diapers on a line!
If not, God stop this wheel,
this old unending serpentine

betrayal of the flesh:
it's been so long ago
since we revolted from the fish!

The poem, "To a Mountain Stream," was also renamed, becoming "Wench of the Woodland," a title I felt more accurately expressed what I wanted to say. We'll never be able to conquer nature, but only discover more about her ways, and then through adapting ourselves to nature's way, our own will be made clearer. Here we may also discover that we've become one with all things...

WENCH OF THE WOODLAND

Oh, wild, illusive mountain stream,
born of melting summit snows,
cavorting freely though the wood,
I've come, not just to acclaim your
        beauty
but to conquer you as well!
My strategy is already mapped,
and the plans have all been made
to defile your virgin whiteness...

Spanning your girth with a sturdy tree,
I'll drink of you, bathe in you—
gather your garlands of columbine,
reticent lilies and sweet brier roses.

Then to crown this rustic carnage,
your white-limbed Aspen court must fall,
stilling their green defiance!
Clearing your banks for a building site,
the rushing force of your heart
will be syphoned to make a scullery slave of you.

All this and more, much more I'll do
to tame the pristine spirit of you,
you virtuous wench of the woodland!
Yet knowing full well that in the end
it is you who will conquer me,
elude me and taunt me, flaunt your
                  dominion:
out-sing me, out-live me, plunge on
through the wood...

My brash intrusion no more to you
than the bustle of a leaf tossed high
                  on your foam,
a pebble's revolt to your current's caress,
or the feathery prick of a mocking
                  bird's wing
dipping low in your water's song...

Over the years I began feeling a deeper link with nature than any I'd
ever known before, although I've always had a profound regard and
respect for her many expressions since childhood.

From my girlhood in Michigan I recall seeing the "Abandoned Apple Orchard" dealt with next, and loved to walk past it, especially in the spring when the trees were blooming. Strangely enough half a lifetime later, and clear across the country in California, I have a deeper rapport with those invisible trees than I did with their living counterparts! Often I wonder what's real and what's unreal now, since the invisible world seems at times more real to me. This visible world is more familiar to most of us in this body and we'll always have a deeper connection to that.

ABANDONED APPLE ORCHARD

Solitary and self-sufficient as a
staunch old man,
the deserted orchard stands,
deep-rooted in the mystery
of wayward mingled grasses
curved into the palm of any wind
that passes...

Gone now the days of plough and share,
of morning milking sounds in the air,
the tug and pull of children's hands.
Only songs of birds and the nuzzle
of bees
echo through fields of serenity...

These sprawling forgotten trees
court the fading ardor of the seasons
with intermittent passion
in shadow-play of youth's green lust,
bearing in autumn their meager harvest

of stubborn tough-skinned russets—
distilling gnarled and ancient sweetness
mellowed like wine in autumn's peace...

Mr. Untermeyer's remarks in this next communication refer to a snapshot of the baby which I'd enclosed along with a poem written for him. I still have the poem somewhere in a notebook and if I find it I'll come back and insert it here later. I found it!

SIX MONTHS OLD AND ALREADY I SEE

Spirit of beauty peering at me:
Starlight, star bright,
first star had blue, blue eyes.

Spirit of truth's own naked glance:
Humpty-dumpty had a great fall—
now here's a fact to confound the wise!

Spirit of love's bright secret look:
Peter, Peter pumpkin eater—
the question here takes ancient guise...

Spirit of wonder spilling over:
Hey diddle, diddle, the cat and the fiddle—
a boy might do what a cow once tried!

Spirit of genius round his finger:
Little Boy Blue come blow your horn—
a dream I knew grew up and died...

Spirit of ego creeping up:
Little Jack Horner sat in a corner—
a god could well be slain by pride!

Spirit of greed in embryo:
Old Mother Hubbard went to the cupboard—
where treasure lies the heart must go…

Spirit of freedom with a frown:
Mary, Mary quite contrary—
Mothers are nice, but a fellow must grow!

Spirit of God in mortal guise:
Mary had a little lamb—
a rhyme and a fact eternally so..

Letter #9

Dear Mildred:

The picture and the poem resemble each other to a remarkable degree. Both radiate health, happiness and—what else begins with an "h"? ah, yes—humor. The young one and his mother look wonderful and it is evident that they enjoy each other. The poem was also enjoyable—I especially like the way you threaded the nursery rhymes throughout… I've just finished a new "guided" anthology: it's to be called THE GOLDEN BOOK OF POEMS FOR YOUNG PEOPLE and should be out late this year or early next.

Best to all the household,

Louis Untermeyer

The pace of Mr. Untermeyer's own career seemed to be picking up remarkable speed at that time. Not that his life was ever uneventful, but a lot of new things were happening that kept him occupied and apparently on the road. There seems to be a time in our lives when a certain festival of spirit takes place, bringing a joyous culmination and sense of completion to all our efforts.

Letter #10

Dear Mildred:

That was a most attractive Christmas card. The boy looks lovely, lively, and full of California vitamins—and so do you. I did not have time to answer much of my holiday correspondence. I still haven't. I quit Decca two years ago this May, and my wife resigned from SEVENTEEN exactly a year ago. Both of us planned to retire and do a minimum of work. Instead we find ourselves forming a collaborative team and contracting to produce so many different types of books that our two studies seem parts of a literary factory.

The pressure now is a little greater than usual, for we are leaving for Italy in less than a month. Our schedule does not permit more than five weeks altogether, but it will be an exciting break in our routine. We'll have to miss La Scala, we won't get further north than Florence, where we will spend a week. The rest of the time will go between Naples, Rome, and the hill towns. By the way, what is the rest of Lucille's name?

It's good to know that Sal is doing so well and that you have not abandoned poetry. Best to all of you. The next you hear from me will be a postcard en route.

Cordially, Louis Untermeyer

What I'd never told Mr. Untermeyer about was my own spiritual life, which was picking up new momentum, or that for some time I hadn't written anything. When I finally began again, it would follow a new devotional direction which has embodied the mood and subject of all my work since then, whether it took the form of poetry, or the prose volumes I would write later.

What I haven't mentioned before was that now and then I'd started making phone calls to Mr. Untermeyer, not only to hear his voice again, but to receive his critical suggestions. For these conversations, usually on Sunday, I of course have no record, and can only tell you what I've retained in my memory all these years. Since he was so busy with his own career at that time, phone calls worked out well for both of us. A couple of years after Nick's birth I'd become pregnant again with our second son, Anthony, and when he was born I was busier than ever, with little time left to devote to writing or anything else except caring for our sons.

Earlier that year before Anthony's birth, Sal and I had flown to New York to see his family and of course to show off our adorable son, Nick. I'd hoped to get in touch with Louis Untermeyer and perhaps see him again in New York, but that, too, was not to take place. The following card from him explains why.

Letter #11

Dear Mildred:

Good about the poems; it's good that you are writing again. But not so good about your trip East—at least as far as I am concerned. My new book, LIVES OF THE POETS, is being published at the very end of this month, and I'll be busy all over the place, traveling, interviewing and lecturing hither and yon. I wish I could meet you in New York, but that is not possible, alas.

Your letter sounds happy and out-giving, and I hope that is the way it is with you and yours,

Sincerely, Louis Untermeyer

In August our second son was born and a month or so later I sent some pictures to Mr. Untermeyer to show him off. He was duly impressed with our two beautiful sons, but still caught up in so much work it was mind-boggling to me, following my daily routine with the children, and sometimes getting bogged down even in that! His next letter explained what was going on in his life.

151 / Mildred Marshall Maiorino

Letter #12

Dear Mildred:

My correspondence in general and in particular has been most irregular. I've been finishing one huge work—the just published BRITANNICA LIBRARY OF GREAT AMERICAN WRITING—and am midway through another. What makes it the more grueling is that the creative efforts have to be done between lectures, trips to Europe (part pleasure and part research), reviews, and other chores.

This is not to complain but to explain. If you don't hear from me for long stretches it doesn't mean that you've been forgotten.

Thanks for the pictures. The children look lovely, and maternity (to judge from the snapshot) becomes you better than moonlight. Nickie seems so intent at the wheel that you can almost hear the engine roar. And the baby seems ready to appear on any magazine cover.

Best to you and all the family.

Cordially, Louis Untermeyer

A little later, I received another letter from Mr. Untermeyer which was tremendously interesting. I was happy he'd found time to fill me in on a lot of the things that were happening for him, particularly concerning a book he was doing on the letters of Robert Frost, in which he added his own biographical commentary.

Letter #13

Dear Mildred:

The poems sound as if you were in a creative upswing. So does your home life. Who could, as the song has it, ask for anything more?

*You are fortunate in the children of your brain and of your flesh—
although your husband can claim some credit for the latter. More power
(and perhaps) more brain-and-flesh children to both of you.*

I'm in the grandchildren stage—there are ten of them,

*and they are with me from time to time. At the moment I'm enjoying a
two-week visit from Mardi and Sheila Moore—their grandmother is the
poet Virginia Moore, my second wife, whom I married some thirty years
ago.*

*As for my brain-children, they too continue to increase. At present I
have just delivered the manuscript of a volume of letters from Robert Frost,
with a running biographical commentary, and my wife and I have completed a series—18 volumes!—a Golden Library of Literature for Young
People. I am now faced with a new assignment for the Britannica... So
back to the grindstone and the drawing pad.*

Sincerely, Louis Untermeyer

Between this letter and the next communication I had from him, I
decided to devote my efforts entirely to the new expression I'd discovered. At first the poems were openly devotional in nature, and would
only later become more objective in the views they expressed. Actually,
this is somewhat like the development we go through while learning
about almost anything. At first we look to something, or someone outside ourselves, only to discover at last that the true source lies within.

I could see right away that Mr. Untermeyer liked the new direction
my work was taking. He lost no time in telling me so, both in his letters
and during our occasional phone conversations concerning the poems I
mailed to him.

Letter #14

Dear Mildred:

I like your devotional poems—they strike a note which is new as well as distinctly personal. Perhaps you should pursue this recent method and manner; poems like "Weighed in the Balance" are rare these days.

Not many poets are writing in this vein today, But, since you ask what others may be doing in a religious attitude, I might call your attention to WAGE WAR ON SILENCE by Vassar Miller, recently published by the Wesleyan University Press, a beautiful book.

Sincerely, Louis Untermeyer

I was delighted that Mr. Untermeyer liked my devotional poems, since this particular approach became an ongoing reality for me, and has never ceased throughout all the years that followed. Although intrigued and perhaps somewhat curious he never asked the source of my interest.

WEIGHED IN THE BALANCE

Alone in the night I wait, my Love,
with an onerous bundle of gifts
for you:
here is my anger that for half the day
flung bright red veils around my mind
to prostitute all thinking…

And here is a potpourri of petty
      thoughts
that grew like weeds in the garden
      of my mind,
tangling among the roses
I'd intended to gather for you!

Hardly had the day begun
when I lost the thread of joy!
Now, see how the cloak I was weaving
     for you
is all torn and filled with holes!

Oh! how can my love—lying
     huddled in my heart
the whole day long with eyes
     tight closed—
balance the scale and call you near?

I will not be surprised
if you do not come tonight
but Oh, my Love—my Love!
I cannot promise you
that I will not weep and long for you
the whole night through...

The next brief communication of Mr. Untermeyer's was mailed from Washington, where it seems his busy life had just gotten busier than ever!

Letter #15

Dear Mildred:
   A card from Washington where I'm now installed as Consultant in Poetry at the Library of Congress. I'll be here most of the year except for some journeys abroad and intervals back to Connecticut. Your new poems strike a new and deep note.

                          Best, Louis Untermeyer

Since Mr. Untermeyer didn't mention here which of these poems he'd read I can only presume they were excerpts from the latest collection of devotional poems I was writing, entitled "Songs of Yearning." This was a rather lengthy volume, preparing me in many ways for the later collection of "Love Play" poems which became sort of a landmark, or turning point in my spiritual life, also.

My mentor always seemed to sense what was going on in my inner life, and responded with just what was needed. I've had very few friends who could fit into that category!

Letter #16

Dear Mildred:

I'm acknowledging the poems and letter from Sanibel Island, the shell hunter's paradise in the Gulf of Mexico where we are spending a sun-and-surf drenched week. The poems continue to achieve a blend of personal emotion, and impersonal devout spiritualism.

Good luck, Louis Untermeyer

Perhaps it was during one of these apparently rare retreats at his home in Connecticut that Louis Untermeyer found time to write the following letter. Probably he also wished to be near his old friend, Robert Frost, during his final illness...

Letter #17

Dear Mildred:

*These are revealing poems, a passionate mixture of sensual and spiritual ecstasy. Body and spirit are so inextricably fused that they seem inseparable in these lines. I wonder which magazine will have the taste and temerity to publish them? You might start with **Poetry**, the Chicago monthly.*

This has not been a happy season for us. Apart from the worst winter we've had in years, many of my best friends are seriously ill. I spent yesterday at the bedside of Robert Frost in Boston and, though there are good signs of his ultimate recovery, he is pitifully frail. The same is true of one of my other most intimate friends, Van Wyck Brooks, who lives nearby, while two other poet-friends, William Carlos Williams and Alfred Kreymborg, are fighting hard against the ills of old age.

My wife and I are about to leave on a lecture trip which will take me through the country for about a month. My itinerary hasn't yet been "finalized," and it's possible that I'll have time in Los Angeles for more than a lecture. But all is still uncertain. If time permits, I hope I can get a glimpse of you, even if it is en passant.

Best always, Louis Untermeyer

As fate would have it again, whatever plans Mr. Untermeyer had for seeing me in Los Angeles never materialized. I'm not surprised, because as I said earlier, I really don't think we were destined to meet in the physical again in this life.

Just when I began hoping L.U. would be having more free time to relax at his home in Connecticut, a new and seemingly more active phase was about to start, indicated by the following card!

Letter #18

Dear Mildred:

The poems continue to sound like you. I wish I could go into more detail, but I've just come back from Washington. Moreover, as soon as I can get my desk and mind clear, my wife and I are taking off for Japan where the State Department is sending me for a month's lecturing at various universities.

Best to you always, Louis Untermeyer

Here I'll quote a couple of poems from the "Songs of Yearning" volume that Louis Untermeyer was referring to, and although he didn't mention the titles, I knew which ones he meant.

THE SOURCE

At last—you spoke!
You came and caressed me:
where is the vessel
that can contain the ocean
        of my joy?
You: all grace, all love,
        all beauty—
all are combined in YOU!
What need have I of another source:
is there another source?

FIELDS OF RIPENING GRAIN

At your touch, my Love,
a shudder of delight
takes possession of my being
like waves of wind caressing
fields of ripening grain.
All else is forgotten—
utterly forgotten
in the sweeping wonder
        of our love...

All my life I've adored the wind as it moves over fields of grass, or grain, or flowers, and especially through leaves: it really doesn't matter which because it's all wonderful! To me it's as though the air, like the soul within ourselves, is kissing its Beloved. And that brings up another interesting point to consider: everything and everyone is the **wind's** Beloved!

I recall one occasion when my husband and I had to change planes on the way home from somewhere. I sat looking out the window at a nearby field of grass blown by the wind, and almost forgot to get off the plane. Since we had to catch another plane, my husband was quite unsympathetic, reminding me that this was definitely not the time to be carried away by the wind blowing!

Here's another poem I sent to L.U.

OH THOU DIVINE SHOWMAN!

I know you: at last I have
     found you out,
Oh Thou Divine Showman,
Oh Thou Master Magician!
You dazzle the whole world
     with your tricks—
tossing useless baubles to the crowd,
but only the undeceived—
your nearest and dearest,
do you admit to your inner
apartments
and invite to dine at your
     table!

Letter #19   *October l, which happens*
to be my birthday.

Dear Mildred:
   This will have to be the curtest sort of reply to your letter of more than a month ago. I have been, and still am, up to my hair follicles in work. Some of it is in connection with a new project which is keeping me from practi-

cally everything else; the rest is cleaning up odds and ends of things in manuscript or revising old editions.

Lately I have had to interrupt the progress by going in and out of New York for radio and TV shows as well as interviews, mainly concerning the book of Robert Frost's letters (see the enclosed) which is having a most gratifying reception and has had spectacular reviews. Today's New York Times has a half-page advertisement featuring some of the handsomest quotes.

As to your poetry I have said before that it is time you should try what Frost called "the test of market." I say it again. It isn't an easy test, and you will get rebuffs before you begin to get acceptance. But it is a test you should face, and soon, if not now. Best to you.

Sincerely, Louis Untermeyer

Again Mr. Untermeyer urged me to get busy sending my work out, although it wasn't until many years after his death that I became acquainted with another poet who'd just seen the same film I had at Universal, and the seed was planted. We were comparing notes on writing while fixing our makeup, when she expressed an interest in my poetry and I offered to send her one of the books my husband had published for a Mother's Day gift, a lovely book entitled, "A Tale of Leaves" with drawings done by a friend, also a poet.

This book is fairly typical of dozens of nature volumes I've written since Mr. Untermeyer's death.

After I'd sent my new friend the book I didn't hear from her. Many years later I discovered she was acquainted with another close friend who had also lived in Santa Fe, New Mexico. The thank you note she sent for the book had been lost in the mail, providing just another example of how things seem to happen at the right time in my life and not before!

And now I'll tell you how I got to teach Mr. Untermeyer something! Every year at Christmas time we sent him a gift which was delivered by mail: fruit or candy or something like that, and in return he sent us one of his books, personally autographed, either from the past, or some recent success. Below is a thank-you note he wrote one Christmas.

Letter #20

Dear Mildred:

What a rich and toothsome surprise! It's foolish to protest that you shouldn't have done it, for it would be ungracious to say so after such a generous fait accompli. You have excellent taste, these are unquestionably the best pears I've ever tasted. Thanks from my wife and myself and whatever guests we permit to share the fruit.

*I am sending you a book not so much as a return for the pears as for your poems. It is a book of my own selected poems (**Long Feud**) and I hope you don't have it. If you have, please return it. I have purposely not inscribed it for fear you may have a copy, in which case I'll send something else. **Lives of the Poets**, perhaps if you don't own it.*

Most of the last two years has been spent away from here, either for the Library of Congress in Washington, or abroad for the State Department. Now I'm back "in residence"—literally snowed in at the moment—here at home. Stimulating and often exciting though the travel has been, I'm happy to be doing my own work in my own place.

You and all the other Maiorinos are, I hope, flourishing. Holiday greetings go along with this letter which also carries the best wishes for the coming year.

Sincerely, Louis Untermeyer

It seems he'd already sent a copy of "Long Feud," a wonderful book of his own poems, so he mailed the book of sonnets that he mentions in his next letter. In the meantime I'd been talking to the "friend of a friend" who wanted to bring out some of my poetry, but the whole thing fell flat. Obviously he wasn't really qualified as an agent of poetry, so again it wasn't time!

Letter #21

Dear Mildred:

I'm sorry about that second copy. Soon, however, I hope to send you a small but, I think, interesting little collection of sonnets illustrated by—of all people—Ben Shawn.

I thought I had previously indicated that your poems had deepened in insight, in expression as well as feeling. I also thought I told you it was time for you to send some out for what Robert Frost called the test of the market. I should imagine several of the religious magazines—and your library should be able to give you a list of them—would be interested.

I, of course, will be interested to learn what happens.

Sincerely, Louis Untermeyer

In his next letter Mr. Untermeyer again mentions his friend, Robert Frost, as an example of the patience I should develop.

Letter #22

Dear Mildred:

As before the new poems should please you. And Sal is quite right. Your poems are certainly better than those of the good French father. I'm glad that you are finally sending some of them out. Don't, I warn you, expect too much or too speedy an acceptance. And don't be disappointed if the response is not immediately encouraging. Remember that Frost had to wait more than twenty years before he was recognized.

Meanwhile, my best hopes. I'm leaving here for another trip, this time through the Midwest, but I should be here and hereabouts most of the summer.

Cordially, Louis Untermeyer

After a while I think Mr. Untermeyer gave up trying to push me into the arms of potential publishers when he saw I really had no interest in doing anything about my work, not at that time anyway. In fact, I'd taken up oil painting, along with a return to singing, even surprising myself in that regard, especially when I discovered my voice came back rather easily with a few scales.

My affair with oil painting lasted for about two years after which I discovered I was allergic to the oils I used, so I lost interest and returned to writing, or I should say, I simply renewed my interest in doing so, since never at any time have I really stopped for long. Mr. Untermeyer's next letter again discloses more of his own current activities...

Letter #23

Dear Mildred:

What a (literally) sweet thing to do and send—especially to (and for) one who has a mouthful of sweet teeth. I appreciate the gift as well as the pun: Partyfours!

*Although they are just a bit young for it, I am sending Nickie and Anthony my latest volume: **The World's Great Stories: 55 Legends that Live Forever**. Nickie will certainly enjoy some of them now, if you will read them to him, and both boys should relish the others a little later.*

My wife and I have been to Europe and back. This time we spent all our time in southern France and Northern Italy. We were in Milan twice and, although we stayed at the Marino alla Scala, so close to the opera house that we could open our hotel window and almost scrape the sides of the building, we neither saw nor heard a single note. The entire troupe were playing Verdi and Puccini in Moscow!

May 1964 be a good year for you and yours. The picture of you and the boys certainly displays robust happiness, showing a healthy present and promising a splendid future.

Cordially, Louis Untermeyer

In his next letter Mr. Untermeyer got upset with me: the one and only time I can ever recall that happening!

The reason? It was concerned with the gift we sent him each Christmas. Without knowing Sal had already put Mr. Untermeyer's name on his list for one gift, I sent another, fortunately choosing a different one.

I never found the courage to confess that the two gifts we sent him had resulted from a communication mixup here in California. The following letter expresses how he felt about it.

Letter #24

Dear Mildred:

Thank you again. But you embarrass me—and that's not just a polite phrase. You really do. I appreciate your friendship, but I don't want it expressed in gifts. Much though I value your generosity, I honestly ask you not to send any more presents. Instead, let me take the thought for the deed. It would really be better that way. The thought is the most important. All the best to all of you for the coming year and all the other years.

Sincerely, Louis Untermeyer

Of course, I felt tremendously rebuffed by his letter! After I received it, I found out about the mixup on our Christmas list. I didn't mention this in my next letter to him, however, but pointed out that although he certainly knew how to give, and I could testify to that, I didn't think he'd yet learned how to **receive** and that this was something equally important to work on.

After receiving my somewhat indignant letter, he wrote again, but this time it was a letter of apology.

Letter #25

Dear Mildred:

I'm afraid I sounded like an ungracious recipient of lovely gifts. I'm sorry if I did—the more since the de luxe pears are as delicious as the "partyfours." Both are being relished gratefully. I might almost say religiously.

Speaking of religion, I like your new series. At first reading those that struck me most were "I Won't be quiet" and "I am Tired of Play," and of the others, "Oh Great is my Good Fortune," and "Would You Say the Heart can Think?" I hope it won't be too long before some of the poems appear in public.

By this time the book should have arrived. If it hasn't come, drop me a line and I'll either trace it or send another copy. Best to you all,

Cordially, Louis Untermeyer.

Again I had to go on a search for the poems Mr. Untermeyer mentioned and so far I've only found one of them which I'll quote, having discovered it under a new title. Instead of "Would You Say the Heart Can Think?" it became

THE RAIN OF BLISSFUL WISDOM

Would you say the heart can think?
It can, but wordlessly.
While you might call it feeling or emotion,
what I refer to is more than that:
more than sentiment,
and beyond what's called intuition—
although this is closer to what I mean.

This kind of thinking doesn't go anywhere
in the sense of a step-by-step conclusion,
since it's already here,

more like the essence of what thought is
than the tedious performance of it,
like lightning instead of a slow-burning bonfire.
Why dig in the earth of our minds for water
when the rain of blissful wisdom
descends in torrents to our hearts?

For some time after this communication, I didn't send any more poems, nor even write any. I'd become tremendously busy with my oil painting, which I really enjoyed. While I never took lessons, I somehow seemed to have an innate knowledge about mixing colors and getting them onto the canvas, although I wasn't very good at sketching. Oddly enough I think I must have done some form of painting in a past life, because I no longer felt any challenge to continue it after two years had gone by. At that time I'd completed some fifty canvases, many of which have been given to friends, one being sent to Louis Untermeyer for his birthday.

The next short letter came early in the month of December. Apparently his mail order Christmas gift had arrived ahead of time.

Letter #26

Dear Mildred:

*You shouldn't pamper me. You really shouldn't, said he, with a mouthful of chocolate truffles. My calorie counter warns me to limit your gift to one a day, but my natural gluttony will probably overcome my caution. Thank you for the thought **and** for the excellent choices in pampering.*

Not as a return, but as a token of something which we poets share, I am sending you my latest publication. I hope it gets to you before New Year's. The best of holidays to you all.

Sincerely, Louis Untermeyer

Sometime after this I mailed some color photographs of a couple of my paintings to Mr. Untermeyer to show him what I'd been up to instead of writing. Of course, like most of my friends who saw the work I was doing, he was quite surprised by it, as can be seen in his letter of thanks that came in time for the holidays. I must point out again how pleased I was that he would take the time to write to me on these special occasions when most people are doing all kinds of things, other than writing letters!

Letter #27

Christmas Eve, 1965
Dear Mildred:
  This is an added note of thanks and surprise. I didn't know you had so much talent as a painter—I might have known that you could express yourself in pigments as well as in words, but I didn't expect anything as expert as your two canvases. I don't know which is the more skillfully executed, the floral still life or the mountain landscape. Both are colorful and, what's more, convincing. My heartiest congratulations—and I hope that your painting will be more than a mere interlude. Renewed holiday happiness to all the family.

Sincerely, Louis Untermeyer

After learning how much Mr. Untermeyer liked my paintings I decided to send him one for his birthday on Oct. lst., so I put the finishing touches on a floral that I'd done expressly for him and got it off in the mail, hoping it would arrive in time. Although it arrived a bit late, his next letter confirms that he'd not only received the painting, but was delighted with it.

Letter #28

Dear Mildred:

What a colorful surprise! What gay flowers and what a lovely thought!

The painting came just after my birthday and it renewed the liveliness of that day.

New England is at its autumn best—hillside and roadside flaunt their colors with a flamboyance that seems to grow more brilliant every year. Soon, alas, the reds and golds will turn to brown, fall to earth, and leave bare branches. That is the time I will appreciate your painting particularly. It will bring more warmth and light, as well as delight.

Incidentally, let me congratulate you on your third expression in the arts. Musician, poet, and now artist! You are among the fortunate. May your good fortune continue for many tears.

Faithfully, Louis Untermeyer

While I wasn't writing much at that time, a great deal was going on in my spiritual life, perhaps revealing the next step I'd take where I entered a new phase of development that would have a profound effect on my inner life, as well as present a new expression for my poetic abilities.

I won't jump the gun on that now, however, but simply transcribe the next letter.

Letter #29

Dear Mildred:

If we had partridge, we could make a most elaborate pear tree for it to roost in. If we did this, however, the pears would not hang for long. They are so tempting that I probably will forego all other sweets until the last one is spooned into my greedy mouth.

*The gift was appreciated all the more because it seems a kind of appropriate equation: pears * poetry * painting.*

On its way to you is an advance copy of the new (9th) printing of THE ROAD NOT TAKEN, a book about (and by) Robert Frost which I did some years ago. I hope—I know—you will like it.

The best of everything to you and your family in the coming year.

Cordially, Louis Untermeyer

Of course what can't be recorded here are all the phone conversations I had with Louis Untermeyer. I think he regarded these as a continuation of my visits to him while I lived in New York, and just as he did then, he didn't hesitate to set me straight when he sensed I was getting off course, or to say something to change my direction. The truth is, a very big change was brewing which he would learn about later.

Letter #30

Dear Mildred:

I am happy that you like "Songs of Joy." It is also good to know that you are being president of your mothers club—it was an inevitable choice. As for the poems, they keep on getting simpler and more devotional. You should make a selection of them for publication. I'm fairly sure that a publisher who specializes in religious works would consider them. I don't know the names of any of these publishers off-hand but you might go to the library and look them up. Your librarian can probably help there.

Best to you as always,

Louis Untermeyer

L.U. never quite gave up prodding me to start sending my work out to publishers, but I simply didn't feel sufficiently moved to do so. Whatever contact I had with him, in addition to the exciting phase that was developing in my spiritual life was so engrossing that nothing else had much importance. I do recall that he often mentioned the three "P"s, and how important it was for a new author to practice using "patience, persistence and postage stamps." Anyway, I thought that was an amusing way of expressing it…

I soon decided to send him a few of the new poems I was writing at this time just to get some kind of feedback from him, but it wasn't until about a month later that I mailed him the first booklet of poems from a collection I called "Love Play." I later added a subtitle "Between the Soul and God."

This next letter is his response to the first sampling of my future spiritual direction…

Letter #31

Dear Mildred:

It is good to learn that you have had a return to poetry. I am sure that the new outburst has given you renewed pleasure.

I particularly like the way you mingle reverence and irreverence. You save religiosity from becoming sanctimonious by your whimsical and sometimes amusing images.

Some day I am sure that you will make a selection of the best of your efforts and submit them for publication.

Meanwhile a particularly good 1968 to you and yours.

Sincerely, Louis Untermeyer

A month or so after his last letter Mr. Untermeyer returned home, and found "Love Play" waiting for him. He never quite got over the impact this had on him, and quite frankly I never have either!

"LOVE PLAY"

Letter #32

Dear Mildred:

I have just returned from almost three weeks of seminars and other sessions, mostly on the Berkeley campus—my wife was with me and we had an exciting series of conferences with the students. Friends from L.A. joined us, for we couldn't find time to go further south in California.

"Love Play" was waiting for me here. The only thing about it which puzzles me is the sub-title. It seems more of a monologue than (as you call it) a dialogue. I hear your voice—or the voice of your spirit, soul, or whatever you choose to call it—but not God's. It is a highly personal and passionate voice, a voice that is not afraid—even exults in declaring its sensuality. It is, I would imagine, the bold mixture of the sensual and spiritual which give the poems their directness.

Do I detect a hint in your letter that the poems may soon be published? If and when they are, I would be interested in the reactions. The more rigidly religious readers will probably be shocked by the forthright physical teasing, the "love play," with all its sexual symbols, the "wild, sweet union," the self-acknowledged lustful delights. I wonder.

Sincerely and curiously, Louis Untermeyer

Just so you'll have some idea of the kind of poems I was engrossed in writing for this "Love Play" volume I'll quote a few of them here.

HEART TALK

Vain, all vain is this attempt
to express the inexpressible
in words!

I am like the bee
still seeking the blossom
with a loud disturbance of buzzing...
Drinking the nectar it falls silent:
truly heart talk is all talk!

OCEAN OF DELIGHT

Long have I sought you, my Love,
in countless spheres of striving,
and now at last you have come—
rising like a wave
from the ocean of delight!
How then to express my joy
in this tiny stream of words?

SO SWEET IS THE RAIN

So long I have waited for you!
Despair followed hope like two
        fleet runners
in an endless race of love...
And now, what can I say?
Only this:
that after the long dry season of waiting,
sweet, so sweet is the rain!

WILD SWEET UNION

How could it ever happen
that you have given me this:
this feeling of wild sweet union
that only lovers know in their hearts?
What good have I ever done
that you should bring my heart

to this state
and **keep** it there?

"HOT LINE"

How strange, my Love,
that since a certain brief encounter
with you,
there seems to be this "hot line" open—
wide open, between your heart and mine...

THE SWING

Children play on swings as everyone knows,
and grown people, too, sometimes!
I know I do...
But for me, my Love,
your arms are the swing
and our love the push.
Higher and higher we go
and in your arms could
I ever know fear—
however high we go?

MORE AND MORE THIRSTY

Can there possibly be something
about me
that you don't already know?
You and I know
that like a baby wants milk
I want love!
And so you have shown me the Truth:
each time I come to you
I must bring you a bigger cup,
since all the while I keep getting
more and more thirsty!

These poems have all been collected in a book entitled "Love Play" between the soul and God. I later wove them together with a prose commentary running throughout. For this next and final poem, I'll repeat the commentary that precedes it.

...A long time ago when I was studying opera, I appeared on a television show done **live** in those days, and not the pre-taped procedure usually observed these days. This was a performance of "The Marriage of Figaro" in which I sang the role of "Suzanna." For those who are familiar with Mozart's opera you know that this leading character spends a lot of time on stage, or as in this case, before the cameras. As I recall there were two cameras in use and a monitor, indicating which camera was being selected to telecast the scene as it was filmed.

I can say just one thing about this live show thing: you really had to stay on your toes, not only watching your entrances and exits, but also paying attention to which one of those cameras had its "eye" on you! I remember one horrifying moment when I was off stage and discovered the camera was picking me up anyway. I sure did a lot of fancy improvising then to cover the cameraman's mistake! I don't think he was very familiar with Mozart...

I'm relating all of this to you only to indicate the difference between a "live" show and one on film. Big difference! The spontaneity, the unexpectedness taking place in the live show of spirit remains a constant source of amazement to me, also, and I don't think I'll ever get used to it. Did you know that getting used to something kills it, whether it's a marriage here on Earth, or the "love play" taking place in the spiritual heart?

However, you don't need to worry much about the one in the heart. The "Beloved" is a Master with a thousand tricks to keep things stirred up and prevent you from becoming complacent, keeping you constantly on your toes. Live show...**big** difference!

A "LIVE SHOW"

While it's true that I used
to dream about you, now that you're here
there's no further need for that!
It's the difference I suppose
between a live show and one on film,
and as you know, my Love,
anything can happen in a live show!

Again nothing came of the effort to contact a publisher in England, made by a friend while on a visit to London. Actually these "Love Play" poems have little or no connection to organized religious beliefs. Even for the time they were written, which was still rubbing shoulders with the burst of freedom released in the sixties by the Hippies and the popularity eastern teachings had assumed in the west, my writings would have been considered controversial at best!

The only source I could find to relate it to were the writings of poet and mystic, Kabir, who lived back in seventeenth century India, although I don't imagine many people have read his work, and if so, have absorbed much from his explicit revelations concerning the soul's relationship to God. Clearly, the words always come from the devotee's heart, and not from any form of God, whoever it might be. God's part here is the revelation of himself to the soul, and there are no words to express these touches, no matter how hard the poet, or the devotee tries to do so. Much of the time he sounds like a loony-tune to many of those reading his work!

The next portion of "Love Play" was sent to Mr. Untermeyer a couple of months later. By then he was spending more time at his home in Connecticut, so his response arrived faster then usual.

Letter #33

Dear Mildred:

Your second series of love poems—(lyrics? epigrams? spiritual-sensual jottings?)—is in tune and tone with the first. Truly, you seem to find endless variations on the theme of a love affair with God. Sensual they are, in spite of your occasional disclaimers, but sensual in an unearthly way. Sometimes they strike me as a curious combination of the mystical moments of Kahlil Gibran and the unashamed eroticism of Walter Benton's "This is my Beloved."

(Parenthetically, did you ever see my Uninhibited Treasury of Erotic Poetry" published by Dial-Delacorte a few years ago? Benton is in it with a couple of pages.) But your lines derive from no one. Their mixture of sophistication and naivete, of religious intensity and physical excitement from love-play to orgasm, of traditional poeticisms and current slang, is your own.

I wonder what publisher would venture presenting it. What, if any, progress toward that possibility has been made by your friend? It amuses me to think what the editor of the average publisher would (or will) make of your easy alternations of reverence and impudence—chiding God for staying away one night, defying him to love anyone else, telling him if he has "others," to do it with them on his own time, calling him a scoundrel, a rascal, insatiable and shameless, making you more and more hungry for the ultimate ecstatic union. As I say, I wonder. In any case, I hope that some day someone will have courage enough to publish a selection from the two series.

Cordially, Louis Untermeyer

One Sunday after this I called Mr. Untermeyer and we had an unusually interesting conversation during which we got to talking about the Hippies and their investigation of eastern religions. Then I brought up the subject of "Kahlil Gibran" and the remark Mr. Untermeyer had made in a previous letter where he'd compared my work to that of Gibran.

Mr. Untermeyer replied, "While your poems remind me of the metaphysical expression in Gibran's writing, I like your work better. It's deeper than Gibran's."

I was shocked to hear him say this because you can still go into almost any book store and buy Gibran's books. "Do you really think that's true?" I asked, somewhat doubtful of what he was telling me. "Maybe you're just saying that to make me feel good."

He replied somewhat indignantly, "I never do that. If I see the potential for something I say so. I believe your work will not only be published one day, but that it will be as widely read and loved as that of Kahlil Gibran."

That stunned me into silence for a moment, and then he added, almost apologetically, "Would you excuse me, my dear? I left our dinner guests at the table while I talked to you and I really should get back to them." I suddenly realized that we'd been talking for close to thirty minutes.

I said, "You should have told me you had guests and I would have called another time."

He replied, "But I really wanted to have this conversation about your work." Shortly after that we said "Good-bye"…

I'll never forget retreating to sit on the stairway with the phone so I could talk to him, since the family was unusually noisy in the dining room that day with a game they were playing.It's strange how something like this can stay in one's mind, almost like it was photographed and placed there for future reference. Whether or not his prophecy regarding my work ever takes place, I was happy to hear how he felt about it anyway!

Our relationship had truly become "An Affair of the Heart," something clearly evident to me at certain times. Does this mean he said things he thought I wanted to hear just to please me?

I honestly don't think so, since he was too committed to his own integrity as a professional to do anything like that for anyone. He called it like he saw it and most of the time he was "right on" in his intuitive knowledge regarding the potential of those he worked with. Were there many of those?

I once brought up this subject and he very quickly set me straight about it. "I don't have time to work with all the people who send me their manuscripts to read, so mostly they're returned unopened."

In New York I'd shown him some poems written by someone close to me and would have been delighted if he'd accepted it. I was rather surprised when he told me in no uncertain terms that he simply didn't have time for it, and that I was his only student, at that time anyway...

As the years went by I felt more and more fortunate that Louis Untermeyer had shown such interest in my own work, and even more importantly, that he'd become my **friend**. That was the best part of all.

Letter #34   *December 31st. 1968*

Dear Mildred:

I thought New Year's Eve was an appropriate time to read your latest communion with the God of all years. So, putting aside the eggnog, I devoted myself to your devotions.

As before, the poems are a curious and sometimes almost incredible combination of uplifted thoughts and very earthy locutions, unions of soul and body—even bawdy—intercourse. You mix the spiritual and the vulgar without hesitation or shame, and your forthrightness will evoke shocked as well as pleasurable, and always surprised—responses.

Perhaps I've said—or at least indicated—all this before. At any rate, the beginning of a new year is a good time to say it again.

The best of 1969 to all of you.

Cordially, Louis Untermeyer

Mr. Untermeyer had indicated several times when I spoke to him that the poems I wrote for the "Love Play" volumes had at last attained the mysterious quality of "integration" that he'd been looking for, where thought, feeling and form enter a mergence.

I can only hope that this mergence has continued to blossom throughout the volumes I've written following Mr. Untermeyer's death when he left this Earth to continue his work in those invisible dimensions on the "other side." I truly feel this is only the other side of life. It seems that today, as we near the end of the twentieth century and enter the year two thousand, more and more people are becoming interested in things of a spiritual nature. The fact that many young people have chosen to do this through the use of drugs, doesn't mean that's the best way to do it, since this proves mostly to be a sidetrack on the way home.

I must have done drugs in a previous life, or perhaps several of them because throughout this re-embodiment I've been aware that drug use is a **trap**. From the beginning of my own investigation into meditative techniques and related practices I've seen the fallacy of turning my spiritual "power," even my health, over to drugs. I've also seen the truth that if someone thinks he has to drink cactus juice, beetle juice or whatever, to give himself a push in the direction of "home," I have no right to sit in judgement on what he does. My personal feeling is that drugs in addition to creating dependence on their continued use, leave finger prints in the inner layers of the aura to be dealt with later on...

As our sons grew older and more active in school, Sal and I also became more involved in various activities there. For a while I worked with a friend training children to perform in little plays put on for the public. This proved to be so much fun I mentioned it to Mr. Untermeyer in my letter, and included a copy of a message on "Love" which I'd done for the little paper published by the parents' club.

This was where I began to re-discover whatever talent I had for writing prose...

Letter #35

Dear Mildred:

So now you're a teacher, an editor, and a message-bringer as well as a poet. Also a hula dancer. Is there no limit to your roles? Congratulations.

Louis Untermeyer

After I'd gotten around to writing some more "Love Play" poems in the seemingly never-ending saga by that name, I sent them to Mr. Untermeyer, hoping my letter would arrive in time for his birthday on Oct. lst., and it did.

Letter #36   *October 2, 1969*

Dear Mildred:

Thank you for the good wishes—they came on a day that was gratifying in every sense.

As for the poems, you seem indefatigable, your energy is unflagging and your images proliferate amazingly. I continue to marvel at the combination of devotional ideas and casual speech—you unite spirit and sense, and, what's more, suffuse the blend with humor.

I look forward to the time when some publisher will take a chance on what you've done and are still doing.

Cordially, Louis Untermeyer

This next poem was in the last group I sent Mr. Untermeyer. These poems used various imaginary scenarios to express my mood...

A SHEIK OF LOVE

Like a Sheik of Love you came riding
across the desert of life,
bearing my heart away with you

into the burning night.
My feeble protestations
were as naught to you, my Love!
Oh ravisher of my heart—
who there within your gold pavilion
laid siege to all my senses:
assaulting me with wings of bliss
and caresses never-ending...

Later that year I sent L.U. some more of the new work I'd done, which as it turned out would also be the last of the "Love Play" poems, because I became involved in singing a role for a semi-professional production of "The King and I." Although this wasn't as challenging as the "Marriage of Figaro," it was perhaps more fun. But first Mr. Untermeyer's note.

Letter #37

Dear Mildred:

We've just returned from two glorious weeks in Grenada. Your new collection of "Love Play" was waiting for our return. I'm acknowledging it now before turning to the pleasure of reading it, which must wait until I get rid of the clutter accumulated during our absence. I continue to hope that the poems will eventually get published.

Your comments on her book pleased my wife very much, and both of us enjoyed the photo with Number Two clowning son.

Cordially, Louis Untermeyer

Mrs. Untermeyer had written an interesting autobiography about their life together in Connecticut, "Memoir for Mrs. Sullavan." I truly enjoyed the copy they sent me for Christmas, in which I discovered how much they both liked cats, just as I did. Oddly enough, cats also play leading roles in several books of fact and fantasy I've completed in recent months.

Later in the year Mr. Untermeyer sent another brief note informing us of his latest work. Everything he did was always so important, compared to my own achievements, which appeared trivial to me at that time. Now I'd say that nothing we do is trivial, although our attitude towards it may be!

Letter #38

Dear Mildred:

Your continued activity (and that of those around you,) make for good cheer at any time of year. Some of it made the cross-country trip intact and radiates from your letter…I have made and revised a new anthology that Random House will bring out next year, and Travel and Leisure will soon be publishing a jeu d'esprit of an article I wrote on reading. So you can tell we're not doing too badly on the east coast.

Best wishes to all the Maiorinos.

Louis Untermeyer

Later that year we finally got the show on the road for our production of "The King and I" and when it turned out to be a great success, people again began asking me why I was wasting my life writing **poetry** when all the while I could have been singing!

Letter #39

Dear Mildred:

So you are back on the stage: congratulations. I'm sure you will present a resonant and colorful—and convincing—Lady Thiang… And your gift for poetry seems to have been inherited. Congratulations again. Nicky's lines are expressive, and your "Editorial" is sweeping in its simplicity.

A more than usually happy and productive year for all the Maiorinos.

Cordially, Louis Untermeyer

After this last letter I became involved in so many activities, including two more performances of "The King and I," along with increased participation in my work with a spiritual group I belonged to, that I actually ceased writing for a while. Although I still kept in touch with Mr. Untermeyer, it was mostly through cards and an occasional call during the holidays.

I was also probing deeper into my own artistic storehouse, seeking a new direction for my writing skills, while Mr. Untermeyer seemed quite content to devote his life to the reduced activities most of us must observe when the years start catching up with us. After all, he was nearing ninety, and although he was still mentally clear and alert, I'm sure his body was beginning to feel the effects of his advancing years.

About a year before he died I sent him a letter hoping to amuse and distract him with some of the stuff that had been going on in our neighborhood. The following letter was his response.

Letter #40   *Dec. 24, 1976*

Dear Mildred:

Your letter is both amusing and, in some ways, amazing. I had no idea that a boy's haircut might come to $50. And I had even less idea that a decent district in L.A. could be ruined by 16 massage parlors. The fact that there are, or were, three of them on your corner was bad enough, although I admit that they must have entertained their customers with such titles as "The Church of Spiritual Sexuality," "The Institute of Oral Love," and "The Club for Sexual Gourmets." What a neighborhood! Emphasized by pornographic movies around the block!

I wish I could agree with you that something good must come out of all this. I do agree (as you put it) that "mankind must grow weary of interminably inspecting the contents of its interracial garbage can." Perhaps channeling our thoughts and energies in a new direction may bring about something of a change if not a transmutation. But I am less hopeful than you.

In any case, I am glad to see the new spirit in your tone. There is a vigor and freshness which augurs well not only for your attitude but how you may express it.

Meanwhile, I found your sister's Christmas rhymes clever and comprehensive. Good luck to her novel. And, of course, to you.

Cheers, Louis Untermeyer

This was sadly the last letter I had from Mr. Untermeyer which embodied his old spirit and in this case a somewhat guarded sense of humor. I think that physically he must have been suffering from the ravages of poor health, signaling his departure from this Earth. As usual he'd gotten a premonition of the poetic inspiration brewing within myself, even before I knew just what direction it would take.

Not long before Mr. Untermeyer's death, he sent a response to my letter, in which I'd attempted to communicate a flow of psychic energy his way. This was the final, and most poignant note I ever received from him, penned on a postcard that was a reprint of one of Van Gogh's paintings: "Field with Peach Trees in Blossom."

On it was the following commentary which also contained L.U.'s own heart tugging message, expressed in the photograph of Van Gogh's painting and in the accompanying printed description.

"This luminous field where peach trees blossom, immersed in the vibrant Provence light, is one of Van Gogh's most lyrical works. The artist seems to have achieved a moment of perfect communion with the nature he sees and creates with stupendous harmony of color, contrasting brush strokes that highlight the profiles of the hills, and colors that burn brightly in the peach blossoms and in the sky.

"He had come to Arles from Paris in search of light and in order to create a more intense, truer painting style. And his masterpieces of the first months spent in the French Midi (southern France) reflect his hope for serenity."

A short hand-written note followed the preceding printed message, acknowledging receipt of a letter from me for the last time. The hand-writing was still firm, but labored, and I knew Mr. Untermeyer was already envisioning the glorious vistas of life's continuation in spirit's invisible worlds beyond this.

Letter #41

"I appreciated your explicit and interesting letter. You have certainly succeeded in changing and enriching your ways of life."
Louis Untermeyer

As you can imagine, this brief note tugged at my heart like no other communication from him ever had! Death always has that strange power to reach down into our very depths and shake us in a way nothing else can...

The day Mr. Untermeyer died our family had gone to Disneyland, a birthday celebration for one of our sons. Throughout the whole time we were there thoughts of my treasured friend filled my mind, like a haunting fragrance that can be sensed flowing everywhere, and yet nowhere.

I thought of him constantly throughout the whole day and of what our wonderful relationship had meant in my life. "Oh Great Was My Good Fortune," as one of my poems states. When we returned home that evening, newscasters gave reports of the death that day of well-known poet and critic, Louis Untermeyer... While death on this Earth is always an ending that catapults the soul into a new beginning in another dimension of awareness, for those of us who must remain behind, death is truly final, signifying an irrevocable end to our lives together here on this familiar earthly plane of existence...

The void left by Mr. Untermeyer's departure has never been truly filled by anyone else. Although there have been many people since then who've been helpful in my long career, none of these have entered that dimension where "An Affair of the Heart" unfolds its magic, changing one's life forever. Only in recent times have I begun to realize that spiritually Louis Untermeyer hasn't gone anywhere, but is still present as part of my own awareness. The truth is, I've felt it very strongly all the while I've been writing this book.

Perhaps someone might say, "That's only because you've been going over these old letters and sifting through the ashes of memory. Wouldn't it make more sense just to admit he's gone?"

I've come to see, as my spiritual life opens up new vistas for understanding, that actually no one ever comes or goes anywhere. They're always present in the hologram of existence. Our task, it appears, is to remove any stubborn sense of separation we may still feel within ourselves that's preventing communion in spirit.

This I believe is the challenge everyone must face during the coming "New Millennium" here on this planet…

JOURNEY
INTO THE DESERT...

Several years after Mr. Untermeyer's death, my husband took a job that required occasional business trips to Phoenix, which as you probably know is located in the middle of the Arizona desert. Here in California you don't have to drive very far before entering some astoundingly vast desert regions. Los Angeles itself is simply reclaimed desert and without water would become so once more, reverting to rolling stretches of sand and cactus...

By that time I'd modified my poetic style greatly, and the desert poems that follow here were in a way only "teasers" for the books I'd begin writing subsequently. These were dozens of nature volumes to which I later decided to add a running commentary in prose. Would you believe this inner change, not only in the kind of poetry I was writing, but in myself, also, began unfolding while we were traveling through the desert?

Various friends have reported having all kinds of strange experiences in the desert, not the least of which is seeing a UFO. So you might say the desert's a spooky place, this being the effect it has on many people, both in the past as well as the present, often initiating an inner metamorphosis.

On one of our trips we narrowly missed a "Flash Flood," but we did go through a "Dust Storm" and experience the "Noon High" in my poems. At least I did. While many spiritual realizations have come to me in the desert, burning bushes, and alien visitors haven't been among them! On one trip I observed the meditating tree described next, and felt an inexplicable rapport with her…

TWILIGHT TREE

One lone tree at dusk
sinks absorbed in her twilight trance,
feathery clumps of invincibility
drawn into a cloak of evening mauve
around her smoke-green shoulders.

Oblivious to cicada static
surging rhythmically on heated sound waves,
or the velvet swirl of shadows on the sand,
she surrenders to rich opiates of silence
pulsing through the desert night…

FLASH FLOOD

Without warning
this serpent of terror
sweeps through the desert
sucking everything it touches
into a hissing maw of rushing sand
and water.

No time to turn back,
and no time to finish the journey
before it strikes,
bringing each year wide devastation
and sudden death…

We missed that "Flash Flood" because the driver of our car recognized ominous signs of trouble brewing in the area and drove more than eighty miles an hour to get us out of there. The next day we went back over the same road and were amazed to see the wide swath that had been covered by the flood in which two people had lost their lives when their car was swept away...

In the desert one may exteriorize from the body rather easily, scarcely realizing it has occurred. One evening as we were driving back to our motel after dinner, I was completely absorbed in the golden sunset which inspired this next poem.

A GOLD PATINA

A sunset raw and clean,
its sun enlarged to outsize proportions
       in the clear air,
covers the desert floor
with a gold patina...

Burnishing slowly to evening lilac
       and indigo,
it gives birth to stars
and long Saguaro shadows writing mysteries
in dry tree-swept arroyo beds...

As I stated previously, when you're driving through the desert things often take on an unreal appearance, resembling a kind of mirage where quivering images shimmer on the horizon, creating their own reality in a world already unreal for sages advanced in meditation. At these times one begins to wonder if burning bushes and talking serpents might actually appear and call one to view invisible worlds more real than this earthly dimension!

This peculiar new feeling of detachment I felt toward things of the Earth continued its hold on my heart until long after our return to the city. The following poem captures that strange mood I frequently feel in the desert.

NOON "HIGH"

Watery heat lies in pools on
    the road ahead,
dissolving the highways's hardness
until it shimmers and disappears
in a flowing hypnotic haze
that covers the desert terrain...

In the distance heat waves
    initiate mirages
where groves of beneficent palms
growing from emerald green depths
    of coolness
entice nomadic hearts to remain forever,
merged in the purple silence
of far-away mountain ranges...

I started realizing in the years following Mr. Untermeyer's death that not only my spiritual life, but my literary creativity, also, had begun to enter what might be called the "high country" of my own understanding, which now and then comes after the trial in the desert of our own "aloneness" has been undergone. I started seeing the truth that Louis Untermeyer hadn't devoted so much time to assisting me for twenty-four years just to have it all fall apart after his death. Hardly without my knowing what was taking place there had been the insemination of a higher form of creativity into my awareness, which would be given birth many years later and result in the writing of nearly a hundred and fifty books of poetry and prose, a couple of them still not finished.

Often these books utilized both poetry and prose where the poems were strung together like a strand of beads interwoven by paragraphs of prose commentary to make a necklace of thought. Often in an introductory chapter I would tell how the inspiration for a particular volume was given. Sometimes the birth might take place right away, but now and then years would pass before I started writing it. This seemed to be all tied in with the fabric of unfolding events in my life, the whole thing becoming imbued with touches of inspiration drawn from a higher understanding.

What is that like, you may wonder, and perhaps I can explain it as I see it now anyway. One night we were flying into Los Angeles on a return trip from the east. For a long time the lights of the city beckoned and shone below us, twinkling with magical significance. Viewed from the ground, each segment displays its own facet of reality, but from high in the air everything appears to be moving in a huge network of light, revealing how it all fits together to form this "city of lights" that we call Los Angeles.

When we become so caught up in any facet of existence that we lose our capacity to zoom up for an overview, we may succumb to the negative pull of this Earth and keep ourselves grounded. From somewhere I can hear a voice saying, "Don't we spend most of our time on the **ground** anyway and not looking from an aerial view? Is it possible to live here and still have that higher perspective you're talking about now?"

Finding out the answer to that question is the goal of all spiritual search! There isn't anyone I know who can look from the heights all the time, since the function of "schoolhouse" Earth is to ground the light and keep it here until the job we returned to do has been completed. Our work is certainly cut out for us if we want to project our awareness upward for that higher view.

You may wonder what that is. When we're locked into envy or jealousy, and any desire to harm another, even ourselves, we lose the higher perspective and the beauty it bestows to our whole existence. If someone doesn't want to let go of these negative qualities, then they're free to continue living with them. God, or energy, whatever name we give to it, lets us go on doing life until we get it right.

I do believe that "getting it right" means living here on Earth and maintaining as much as possible this higher view.

I'm sure many folks may wonder if I learned all these things while working with Louis Untermeyer. The truth is that I've learned it, not only while working with him, but from all the illumined souls who've appeared in my life, both before and after Louis Untermeyer's death. I've found that spiritual discovery as well as artistic development is a continuum from this to that, and not a jumping off place anywhere. There's simply nowhere you can say, "Ah-ha! I've arrived," and cease moving forward to discover a new level of understanding.

Life itself won't permit us to do so!

A NEW DAWN
ON THE HORIZON

In the years that followed Louis Untermeyer's death, I floundered around for a while, seeking a new direction in my work. Then, through a chain of seemingly strange circumstances, I met a woman who'd been associated with the poet, Don Blanding. She was also, at one time, on the staff of a small poetry magazine here in Los Angeles which Mr. Untermeyer had mentioned to me not long after my marriage, suggesting I submit a few poems. Of course I didn't!

The magazine was defunct by the time I met this woman, a poet, known as "Dr. Grace" to many of her friends. She admired Louis Untermeyer and the contribution he's made to poetry, not only through his own fine poems, but in his brilliant anthologies which have been immensely helpful, especially to students of poetry.

Following our meeting "Dr. Grace" proceeded to introduce me to various poetry groups here in the city as well as several clubs that support musical and literary activities, like the "National League of American Pen Women." One day I invited my new friend to have lunch with me. Afterwards I showed her some of the poems I'd done while working with Louis Untermeyer. As she read them, she now and then glanced through the glass door that leads to a "porte cochère" built over our driveway.

"I just saw a man passing by the door out there," she said.

"Oh," I replied, running to look outside. "I didn't see anyone there, Grace! You must be seeing things!"

"That's about right," she replied cryptically.

She read some more of my poems and then a few minutes later explained. "The man I saw a while ago wasn't from this world. I've seen people like this several times before. One evening during a party at my home a man joined us that no one else knew."

"But you did?" I asked.

"Oh yes," she replied. "He's been dead for many years. I guess he just stopped by to say hello."

In a way I understood what she was saying, having known others who've experienced spooky things like this, including myself.

"What did the man you saw a while ago look like, Grace?"

"He was an older man, not too tall, and with grey hair."

"Well your description fits several elderly men I've known in my life! Can you be more specific?" I asked, laughing.

"This was someone who loves you very much. He seemed quite interested in what we were discussing, as though he'd come by for that reason."

"And that was my poetry, Grace, which you've just been reading!" Now I was more puzzled than ever.

After this we discussed some other things and then she asked, "Have you ever thought of writing some poems using Japanese forms, such as the 'haiku,' 'tanka' and 'sedoka'? These are based on a strict syllabic count instead of rhyme and meter."

I admitted I'd never been interested in these forms, then "Dr. Grace" suggested I try them. "Why don't you take something from nature and write about that? Japanese forms are ideally suited to working with nature."

"You may be right, Grace. I'll try it."

Subsequently I found the five line "tanka" more adapted to my needs than any of the others she'd suggested, so I began creating whole segments around a chosen subject, using the "tanka sequence" where although each verse is complete in itself, it's connected to the whole…

When I attended our next poetry meeting I had a big surprise for "Dr. Grace," having done a whole book which I entitled "A Tale of Leaves." I'd completed the layout and most of the poems in a single day, and that of course included part of the night.

Grace was quite impressed with what I'd accomplished, and everyone seemed to enjoy my new poems with their thought-provoking stanzas. So on that note of encouragement I began traveling in a new direction, which held me and my literary talents spellbound for many years as I discovered that nature's rich storehouse of ideas is inexhaustible.

Ultimately this led to the addition of prose commentaries to these books of poetry, creating a tapestry woven of poetry and prose. Although now and then I employed other forms like the six line "sedoka" or the more comprehensive "choka," I always returned to my "tanka" as being the most appropriate. I continued writing these thought provoking "nature" books until like the old woman in the shoe I had so many of them I didn't know what to do!

Each volume deals with some particular aspect of nature, chosen previously, and covering every aspect of the subject I could envision. I suppose you might say this is like studying each facet of a gem in order to reveal the entirety of it. Here I'll transcribe one of these poems, along with the introductory prose commentary that precedes it, taken from a volume entitled "What the Moon Sees." If anyone should ask me which poem I consider truly representative of my later work, at least in this genre of nature studies, I'd say it's this one entitled "Moon Drinkers."

So with no further "computer" talk, here are a few paragraphs from the book, followed by the poem...

...Imagination, or the act of "imaging" plays a big role in the creation of any form of art, although reflection or remembering, is also important for a poet since usually one picks up one's pen after the fact, or following a memorable experience. At the time something significant is happening, it becomes so all-absorbing nothing else can, nor even needs to be added to it: it is complete in itself!

So to write a poem like "Moon Drinkers" I began by recalling something which occurred one night where we'd set up camp in Yosemite National Park. A full moon was beaming down, reflected on the water, and for quite a while I watched a deer drinking up its light spilling into one of those exquisite meadows. Then the title, along with the idea for "Moon Drinkers" was imaged in my mind, pulled from the depths of my own perception, and rising as a joint phenomenon from the storehouse of memory.

I call this process spiritual, and it often inspires work that might be considered "new" by those reading and experiencing it through the vision of its creator. Here I must clarify again that when I use the term "spiritual" in my writing I don't attach any religious connotation to it. I've discovered that a spiritual realization may take place completely removed from, or outside the fold of any organized religious belief. However, I certainly don't wish to imply that spiritual experiences don't take place for those belonging to various religious groups, but only to state that I never limit my own creative expression to any specific path or approach to truth, but to finding out the truth itself.

In India children are told: "Uncle Moon is every child's moon." To see the moon you only need to look up, whether it's in Yosemite, or your own back yard! When we look from the depths of ourselves, it becomes "seeing," and often opens the door to meditation, or contemplation, which is a more dynamic process.

"MOON DRINKERS"

The moon sees his clear
reflection on the surface
of the lake, knowing
it is the same image cast
on myriad moonlit lakes.

The **real** moon, he
knows, floats serenely in space
untouched by all these
images, but does the deer
nosing the cool water know?

Startled, yet she drinks
the bright liquid, ingesting
a whole moon before
she is replenished: never
once looking up at the sky!

Like her, we too are
"moon drinkers" of our own hearts
reflected within
the lake of life: rarely do
we see the reflection's source...

You might wonder after reading the preceding poem, what I think is so important about "Moon Drinkers" and I'd say it's because in this poem I see the reflection of "every man" in the light of the Infinite. This act of unconscious drinking continues until we look up and seek the source of the moon's light within ourselves, realizing we're only a reflection of that here on Earth.

"But won't we still be drinking our own reflection in the lake of life?" a close friend once asked when we were discussing "Moon Drinkers."

"Same moon. Only now we've become aware that we're drinking a reflection, and that the source of ourselves lies in spirit."

"Do you think Louis Untermeyer would have liked your book, 'What the Moon Sees'?"

"I really don't know that for sure, and since he's no longer here I can't wait for his response in a letter! I do feel in some very deep place within myself that he'd like it. Of course, the fact that **he** liked it doesn't mean others will. Everyone has his own literary taste! I suppose that's what Robert Frost's advice, conveyed to me by Mr. Untermeyer to try the "test of market" implies. Finding that out, I mean."

"And what if people don't like what you've written?"

"Then they don't like it! But haven't you noticed that tastes are always changing? Even in the world of fashion, something that's popular and admired for a few years soon begins looking ridiculous when another trend takes its place."

"But aren't there books that remain classics no matter how many others are published?"

"I'd say there are."

"Do you think you've written anything that will become a classic?"

"I'm not sure I have, but I really don't think that matters."

"Then what is it that matters to you?" my friend asked.

"The joy I find in writing. If the joy weren't there I truly feel I'd be wasting my time, which would be better spent doing something else!"

"Like singing opera in your next life?"

"Maybe!"

That was a clever question my friend asked, and I really don't know the answer to it! Like the poem Robert Frost once wrote about two roads that diverged in a yellow wood, I took the one not many people wanted me to travel by. Who knows, next time I may choose the other one, like my friend, Lucilla, did in Italy, and know the thrill of touching thousands of hearts from a stage.

This, too, can be a life of "moon drinking," depending on whether it's done consciously or unconsciously. I've known singers whose lives ended in bitterness when the vocal instrument declined, and nothing more significant had been explored.

That something "significant" is all that ultimately matters. If we're lucky we discover that the source of the music lies within ourselves, and has been all along. Then if we look up at the glorious light of the soul, we may drink of the ineffable joy pouring from those invisible dimensions **consciously**, while still dwelling here in this earthly one…

My friend, "Dr. Grace," left this world a week or so after the Northridge earthquake hit our area several years ago. I have a feeling that she encountered Louis Untermeyer on the "other side" and found out for sure if he were the one she'd seen that day walking past the door outside our living room.

I recall another occasion when Grace told me about an experience she had many years ago when she lived in Sacramento. One evening at twilight she was returning home when she suddenly looked up and saw a huge space ship hovering in the sky, emanating a strange purple light all around itself.

"Come on, Grace," I said, "I know from various discussions we've had that you don't believe in space ships and all of that weird stuff. You told me yourself that you think all these people who do are 'kooks.'"

"Well I guess I didn't believe it until I saw a UFO myself. I haven't seen another since then, but I never forgot that one."

"Maybe that's why you saw it, Grace, so you wouldn't forget."

"Forget what?" she asked, a little puzzled.

"Who you are," I said.

I knew that Grace liked my poem, "Moon Drinkers" so I said, "Unlike the deer in my poem, Grace, you looked up into the sky of yourself and let that look change your life."

"I'm a Unitarian," she said, with a certain familiar tilt to her head. "I don't believe that God takes the form of any man.

"Like Jesus, or Buddha, or Krishna you mean?" I asked.

"That's right," she said. "They were just men."

"You didn't believe in space ships until you saw one," I said. "Maybe the same thing's true about everything. That old adage about 'seeing is believing' may reveal a certain truth for us to think about here."

"But those so-called Divine beings are all dead now."

"Are they?" I asked. "Maybe like Mr. Untermeyer they've only become invisible to our physical eyes, but not to the 'EYE' within ourselves that looks up at the 'moon' and drinks of Reality."

After Grace left this world a few friends suggested that perhaps Louis Untermeyer is channeling all the books I've been writing for so long since his death, or at least someone is.

My reply would take the form of a question: "Who is the channeled, and who's doing the channeling? Aren't they the same?"

Throughout the years of his life on Earth, Louis Untermeyer poured the light of his vast literary understanding into my aura, imbuing it and inspiring me to reach into my own potential. This is after all the greatest form of teaching there is and the highest endowment we can make to others. In the house of our spiritual ancestors, while the door to their life on Earth has closed, the "windows" of their spirits remain open, allowing us to move freely in and out, still communing with those who have become invisible, although the world may call them "dead."

You may wonder how this is done and the answer's simple. Whenever we tap into the same vibration we're in touch with them.

I've been asked if this is some kind of psychic contact, and I must say that I really don't think so, since it goes much deeper than that, into the very essence of ourselves where all separation disappears. This will ultimately reveal the whole secret of our existence here in the "schoolhouse" during the coming "Millennium," affording humanity a quantum leap into the arms of Truth.

Someone asked me recently, "Why don't you write a book about your own spiritual life and the discoveries you've made?"

That's a good idea, and maybe it will be the next one I'll write, although I do believe that all the books I've done so far have been dealing with this very subject! Just as our bodies reflect what we eat, our spirits mirror the totality of what we **are** in essence. Any separation has been created by the mind coming from a lower level, filled with information but rarely with the light of wisdom…

CIRCLE OF LOVE

Perhaps this next little story I'll use to conclude this third segment will serve as a prelude for the next one!

As the years go by I've found that life is a lot like the five-line "tanka" which I lifted from one of my own books entitled "A Matter of Perception." The name for this book was given to me at least a year or more before I thought of writing it, while the family was vacationing at "Bryce Canyon." Each time we were there, my husband and sons had gone hiking down in the Canyon, but I never went with them, preferring to look at all those translucent rocks while comfortably seated on a bench near the rim.

Later that night in a **dream**, which unfolded in full living color, I was walking along a trail at the base of the Canyon with a group of people when suddenly I stopped to look at one of those incredible rock formations. On it was carved, "A Matter of Perception," and below that, as though for clarification a subtitle had been added: "Seeing the Unusual in the Usual"...

Many months later I was shown the truth of these words, and soon afterwards began writing a book about it. Only as we begin "seeing the unusual in the usual" do we affirm for ourselves that we've started living what is loosely termed a spiritual life. Before that we're simply "moon drinkers" of the lake of life, doing this unconsciously and seldom if ever looking up at the moon...

Here is the tanka from that book which I'll use to introduce this next story.

ARROWS OF LIGHT

Each day discloses
new wonders concealed among
sunrise leaves: shot straight
from the eyes of love, they pierce
your heart with arrows of light...

—Tanka from "A Matter of Perception"

In recent years so many extraordinary experiences have appeared in my spiritual life that I'm sometimes almost overwhelmed by everything that has been and still is happening! More and more I find that people are drawn to this inner light, not to me, but to the light of the "Holy Spirit" shining through me. I often wonder if this isn't what returning home truly means, then wherever you are subsequent to that realization, will be your home.

Perhaps only in this way can Heaven be here on Earth right now in our hearts and become our own portable paradise! A further discovery might be that every soul is part of God's universal awareness, and the substance of what sages call the SELF. The following encounter, which took place a few years ago when a group of friends and I paid a visit to a local "Rose Garden" and Museum, gave me at least a glimpse of that all-encompassing light.

On the day this outing was scheduled, I'd seen in my early morning meditation a circle of exquisite flowers, half of which were royal blue, and the other half dazzling white, arranged in a yin-yang design. This was followed by a view of several young girls with angelic faces, each one connected to a rose-colored segment of phone cord leading straight to the area I think of as my spiritual heart.

To tell the truth, I had no idea what these symbols meant until later that day, when at the park we "Poets Four," as we called our small group, attended a movie, then decided to go for a walk through the "Rose Garden" before having lunch. As we were leaving, one of my friends spoken of in the previous chapter, "Dr. Grace," who had been quite ill, expressed a desire to rest, seating herself on one of the large benches outside the garden. The other two ladies decided to keep her company.

"I think I'll walk on down to the corner," I said, "and talk to my Deodar." This is a large Pine tree growing beside the "Rose Garden" protectively shading a white stone bench beneath it. Since my friends knew how much I love Deodars, they understood.

I walked on as though some part of myself were being magnetically drawn to that tree. On approaching it I saw that a group of young girls, eight of them as I recall, had arrived before me and were occupying, or standing around the bench I was contemplating for myself.

As I drew closer, the oldest girl in the group, in her mid-teens perhaps, approached me and asked, "Mam, can you tell us what a circle means to you?"

"Sure! For me the circle is a symbol of the Infinite."

She and the younger girls with her, all looked at one another, and then at me like little beings out of "Star Trek."

"The Infinite: what's that?" they asked in puzzled voices.

"Oh, the Infinite: you know, God!"

"Oh-ooo," they chorused almost in unison, then pleaded, "Oh, please could you tell us some more about the circle?"

Intrigued by this whole thing I did as they asked, proceeding to point out, "If you could hold a circle in your hands, pulling it out from the top and from the bottom, it would become a stretched circle, or a spiral, symbolizing Infinity. This is also life without beginning and without end."

Again the "Trekie" extra-terrestrial whispers rose among them, after which they surrounded me, requesting my autograph.

Each one asked, "Would you please put your phone number on it, too?" This was followed by a lot of frantic searching through pockets and purses for bits of paper, some of the girls sharing what they had with one another by tearing it in half.

As I wrote, I said, "It's strange you should ask me about a circle because I recently finished a book of poetry about that." This evoked a tremendous outburst of awe and interest.

They looked at one another and repeated in hushed voices, "She's even written a **book** on circles!"

"That's true, but I've also written over fifty others."

This was really beyond their comprehension. I said to the older girl, "I'll tell you what I can do. If you give me your name and address, I'll send you a copy of 'A TALE OF LEAVES' one of my poetry books that was published a while back, and you can all read it." That seemed to make them tremendously happy. "Tell me, why are all of you so interested in the circle?"

The older girl replied, "It's a project we're doing at summer camp, and three of the girls here all had the **same dream** this week." She then pointed the three "dreamers" out to me.

"In the dream they were told to go and wait beneath the tree from India, across from the Museum, and someone would come by who could tell us about the circle."

Obviously all the girls were as stunned and delighted by this whole thing as I was.

I explained, "The tree from India is called 'Deodar' and its name means 'Gift of God' since it's filled with energy. If at any time you feel ill, or low in energy, you should look around for a Deodar and touch its branches."

Suddenly one small girl noticed my earrings, which were metallic circles within circles, gleaming with rainbow colors in the sunlight. I'd put them on that morning almost as an afterthought. This was followed by more "Trekie" whispering, then the little girl who had pointed out my earrings dived into her small purse and brought out two tiny foil replicas attached to a piece of paper which she'd tucked inside it.

Tugging on my sleeve, she said delightedly, "Look, these are the same as the earrings you're wearing now!" All the girls looked at her earrings, then at mine, then at one another, forming a circle of wonder and love around me. Everyone was laughing and hugging one another, totally delighted with what was happening. Each of them eagerly took turns to hug and embrace me, also, some of them almost forgetting to let go.

After what seemed quite a while, I said, "I really must leave now and go to lunch with my friends, but in a few days you'll receive a copy of my book." With great reluctance we all said good-bye. As I walked away I saw only light-filled eyes following me, their innocent sweet gaze of love fixed upon me for as long as they could see me.

It's so easy to be adored when you're adoring back! It has been said that if we take one step towards God, HE practically trips over himself in his haste to come running to meet us. The truth is, I don't merely believe this to be true any more, since now I **know** that it is!

I've often wondered who could have set up all the details for this close encounter in the soul but that wondrous light of the "Holy Spirit" mirrored so perfectly in the form of Jesus two thousand years ago, when HE lived and walked upon this Earth, breathing the same air we breathe today, and touching the hearts of everyone he met along the way... Same air, the same love!

DECCA RECORDS, INC.

50 WEST 57th STREET, NEW YORK 19, N. Y. · COlumbus 5-2300

June 21, 1955

Dear Mildred:

Thank you for the charming letter as well as the equally
charming pictures. I wish I had time to answer your
good paragraphs (and the implications of the poems) in
as much detail as they deserve, but I have just returned
from Europe to a more-than-usually-cluttered desk. We
spent two months abroad (France for sheer escape and England
for rest mixed with research) and I am still resentful about
resuming work and other responsibilities in New York.

As to the choice of a future career, that, as I've told you
often, is a choice that no one but you can make. There
are probably more financial rewards -- to say nothing of
immediate audience responses-- for a singer; the poet
can scarcely expect to support himself on his product
and he is lucky to find any audience at all! But poetry
can be a compulsion as well as a pleasure, and when it
is a compulsion, there is nothing one can do about it--
except to write.... Meanwhile, you have a career in which
you are happy: the career of being a wife, a performance
as well as a privilege which will take up most of your time.

As to the poems themselves, I found them somewhat uneven.
I feel that some of them ("Poets and Lovers," "Wedding
Reflection," "A Caress is All Things," for example) are
not only slight but trivial. On the other hand, such
poems as "Lazy Afternoon," "Monkey on a String," "Night,"
"Valedictorian," etc. are full of the things which you
do so well: the unusual image, the sharp observation,
the distinctly personal tone. They make me wonder what you
will be doing, say, a year from now... whether you will
be doing more with your voice than with your verse.

But that is for the future. Meanwhile, you have much to do
in your everyday life as well as your creative life, and
I hope that all continues to go as happily as your
letter and work indicate.

Sincerely,

Louis M. Fremeeye

P. S. I'm returning the poems, since I hate to keep
other people's manuscripts. I've lost too many things
moving about.

DECCA BUILDING
NEW YORK

Letter #1

CABLE-DECCORD NEWYORK

DECCA RECORDS, INC.

50 WEST 57TH STREET, NEW YORK 19, N.Y. · COLUMBUS 5-2300

September 1st, 1955

Dear Mildred:

Those are excellent poems -- practically every one has
something to say, and says it in its (or your) individual
way. You have, as I have said so often, an extraordinary
gift for similes, strange comparisons, and startling
figures of speech. I particularly like "Birth of a Poet,"
with "a garden of metaphor"; "White Wild Roses," with its
"imminent Nirvana"; and the entire sequence of the seasons,
especially Autumn," with its half-pun about Van Gogh
gouging color, and "Winter" with that fine line about
"a white excitement...through a harem of trees." I
return them herewith, as I fear losing original manuscripts.

I hope that your hospital experience will be neither long
nor painful, and that it will give you, after it is
over, renewed vitality -- although you do not seem to
lack much in that department. If you expect to remain
there long enough to read a rather lengthy book, you
might have your husband get you my MAKERS OF THE MODERN
WORLD which was published last week and which, I am
happy to say, has already received some important and
extremely gratifying reviews. You might also have a look
at the September "Atlantic Monthly" which contains my
two-page double-column poem, "Orpheus and his Lute," which
is a kind of satire (with a serious undercurrent) on certain
phases of modern poetry -- including parodies of Auden, Eliot,
The New Critics, and others.

Good luck to you before, during, and after the operation...
and, as they say in Germany, Gute Besserung.

Sincerely,

Louis Untermeyer.

Letter #2

CABLE-DECCORD NEWYORK

DECCA RECORDS, INC.

50 WEST 57th STREET, NEW YORK 19, N. Y. · COlumbus 5-2300

February 21st, 1956

Dear Mildred:

Your letter and the enclosures waited for me for weeks. I
was away on a lecture trip with my wife who, though she had
traveled in Europe with me, had never seen anything of America
except the east coast. We covered most of America in a little
less than two months, from New Orleans to the other extreme
of color and climate, the state of Washington; from the desert
of New Mexico to the subtropics of San Diego. By the odd
booking of my agent, we were in and out of Los Angeles three different
times -- and, by the oddest coincidence, we were in your
district: Hollywood 46, stopping with the John Weavers (old
friends of ours) who live on the heights of Hillside Avenue.
Although we were continuously occupied (what with lectures
and social obligations) I would at least have phoned you
had I known your new address. Next time, I hope....

Meanwhile, I applaud the new poems. They have a tang, a
tartness which reminds me of Emily Dickinson -- they even
have Emily's "off-balance" rhymes. You say what you want to
say in your own way, however; the poems are you speaking, not
a series of echoes from some other poet or some older tradition.
Have you thought of trying "The New Yorker"? Or "Poetry: A
Magazine of Verse," which has taken on a new lease of life
with a new editor.

Congratulations on the house, which sounds enchanting, and
the renovated Mildred, who seems to have emerged from the
operation more zestful than ever. I can see you now, training
those climbing roses -- in spite of the name, I recommend
the climbing Herbert Hoover, who (which) was sprawling all
over the Weavers' terraces.

To hell with Eleanor King. She sounds not only inefficient
but impossible. Just keep on with your work, either in prose
or verse, and let's hope and believe that the agents will
come to you. Most important of all, keep well and happy...
as I'm sure you are.

Cordially,

Louis Untermeyer.

Letter #3

Easter Sunday -- full sun to show
that Spring too has risen
LOUIS UNTERMEYER
TAUNTON DISTRICT
NEWTOWN, CONNECTICUT

Dear Mildred: You seem to be enjoying your
Emily Dickinson binge -- and there are no evidences
of a hangover. I took the envelope of poems
with me to Connecticut and read them in the
quiet of Connecticut hills and the purring of my
Connecticut cats.

So far your work has reflected facets of many things:
people, places, experiences, facts and fancies .
Although you have been subjected to many influences,
there is always a quality which is distinctly
your own. It emerges, disappears, disclosed itself
in another guise, and plays a kind of intellectual
hide and seek. The style is equally fluctuating,
almost kaleidoscopic. And -- or but -- neither
your thought nor your style is quite fused.
That is to say, the expression is uneven, the
idea and the technique are not yet completely
integrated, fluent and imaginative though
the lines often are.

I think that this integration is the next step --
and I think, moreover, you are about to take it.
At least I hope so.

As a reaction from Emily Dickinson's wayward
whimsicalities, you might try the more rigorous
discipline of such contemporary women as Louise
Bogan, Léonie Adams, Elizabeth Bishop, Charlotte
Mew and Sylvia Townsend Warner, all of whom are
included in my MODERN AMERICAN AND BRITISH POETRY.
The taste, I promise you, is different.

Happy Easter -- lilies and all.

Letter #4

DECCA RECORDS, INC.

50 WEST 57th STREET, NEW YORK 19, N. Y. · COlumbus 5-2300

July 10th, 1956

Dear Mildred:

I'm glad to see that you are recovering from your Emily
Dickinson binge. I notice a bit of hangover here and there;
but mostly the poems are clear-headed, bright-eyed, and
definitely your own. I particularly relished "Lawnmower,"
"Spirit," "Body of a Friend," and "The Eye," even though
this one has the E. D. twist of phrase. By God, you
will sell one of these somehow, someday, somewhen!

As usual, I'm in the midst of things. I'm putting off
the work on which I've spent considerable time -- LIVES
OF THE POETS -- to do a volume for The Limited Editions
Club. It's to be a selection of the best poems of
Heinrich Heine (my own translations, based on a book I
did some years ago) plus a new critical-biographical
introduction. Later, it will be issued as a book for
the public, but the first edition will be de luxe and
definitely limited. After that, I will return to my
labors with the poets of my own language. Please God.

I'M happy that you liked MAKERS. My own favorite
chapters are those on F. D. R., Isadora Duncan,
Charlie Chaplin, and Robert Frost -- perhaps because I
had so good a time writing about them. I wonder what
you thought of the pieces on Emily Dickinson and Dylan
Thomas. The one on Mary Baker Eddy has been furiously
assailed by Mother Church.

No more for now. I'm in New York three days a week --
sometimes no more than two -- and I don't feel that I
can cheat Decca out of all my (or, rather, it's) time.

Best to you and the work -- but, chiefly, best to you.

Louis U

P. S. I love zuchini (even though you Anglicize it to
"zukini," which looks Japanese), but I never had it in
salad. How do you prepare it? Do you cook it first?
And then chop it, or merely slice it like cucumbers?
We've used oregano a lot -- and mint, which grows all
over our Connecticut meadow. But I don't know the
taste of basil, unless that's what the Genoese put
in their pesto sauce.

DECCA BUILDING
NEW YORK

Letter #5

January 31, 1957
LOUIS UNTERMEYER
Great Hill Road • Newtown • Connecticut

Dear Mildred:

Condolences and congratulations -- life is, as the
poet (or at least as a poet) said, full of Entrances
and Exits. I well remember your father -- I even
recall the details of his talk and the charm of
his presence at lunch -- at Town and Country on
Park Avenue. Death is always a horror to those
who watch its coming on -- but it is most horrible
when it takes the form of cancer. I, too, have
sat and watched a dear one literally fade away.

And now you are to be a mother. I spare you the
conventional sentimentalities, but I know what
this fulfilment will mean to you. Although I
have never been a mother myself, the state of
maternity is a popular (or should I say populous)
one, and many of my best friends speak well of it.
I expect you will, too -- and volubly. Let me know
more when you know more -- including sex, names,
color, career, etcetera.

About the poems: I like their spirit as well as
their expression. I also like your experiments in
the technique of assonance and rhyme -- especially
in "Death and the Lady," "On Butterflies," and
"Viaticum." Caution: Watch out for too much of
a mixture of metaphors -- for example, "Grief."
You are obviously getting a firmer control of
your medium all the time. Further congratulations
in your double role as creatrix.

As this letterhead may indicate, I do most of my
work at home now. We moved from New York six months
ago and come in to the city only once or twice a
week... Thanks for what you say about my books --
I enclose a review of my latest, published a couple
of months ago, and already doing well.

Best to you -- and your creations.

Louis

P. S. I enjoyed the Edd-fi-cation pun, a new one
to me.

Letter #6

LOUIS UNTERMEYER · GREAT HILL ROAD · NEWTOWN, CONNECTICUT

January 26, 1959

Dear Mildred,

That was a most attractive Christmas card. The
boy looks lovely, lively, and full of California
vitamins -- and so do you. I did not have time
to answer much of my holiday correspondence. I
still haven't. I quit Decca two years ago this
May, and my wife resigned from SEVENTEEN exactly
a year ago. Both of us planned to retire and do
a minimum of work. Instead we find ourselves
forming a collaborative team and contracting to
produce so many different types of books that
our two studios seem parts of a literary factory.

The pressure *now* is a little greater than usual,
for we are leaving for Italy in less than a
month. Our schedule does not permit more than
five weeks altogether, but it will be an exciting break in our routine. We'll have to
miss La Scala -- we won't get further north
than Florence, where we will spend a week. The
rest of the time will go between Naples, Rome
and the hill towns. By the way, what is the
rest of Lucille's name?

It's good to know that Sal is doing so well and
that you have not abandoned poetry. Best to
all of you. The next you hear from me will be
a postcard en route.

Cordially,

Louis Untermeyer.

Letter #10

LOUIS UNTERMEYER · GREAT HILL ROAD · NEWTOWN · CONNECTICUT

August 25, 1959

Dear Mildred,

      Good about the poems; it's good that you are writing again. But not so good about your trip East -- at least as far as I am concerned. My new book, LIVES OF THE POETS, is being published at the very end of this month, and I'll be busy all over the place, traveling, interviewing, and lecturing hither and yon. I wish I could meet you in New York, but that is not possible, alas.

      Your letter sounds happy and out-giving, and I hope that is the way it is with you and yours,

          Sincerely,

Louis Untermeyer

Letter #11

Dear Mildred:

My correspondence in general and in particular has been most irregular. I've been finishing one huge work -- the just published BRITANNICA LIBRARY OF GREAT AMERICAN WRITING -- and am midway through another. What makes it the more gruelling is that the creative efforts have to be done between lectures, trips to Europe (part pleasure and part research), reviews, and other chores.

This is not to complain but to explain. If you don't hear from me for long stretches it doesn't mean that you've been forgotten.

Thanks for the pictures, The children look lovely, and maternity (to judge from the snapshot) becomes you better than moonlight. Nickie seems so intent at the wheel that you can almost hear the engine roar. And the baby seems ready to appear on any magazine cover.

Best to you and all the family.

Cordially,

Louis Untermeyer.

Letter #12

LOUIS UNTERMEYER · GREAT HILL ROAD · NEWTOWN, CONNECTICUT

July 13, 1961

Dear Mildred:

The poems sound as though you were
in a creative upswing. So does your
home life. Who could, as the song has it,
ask for anything more?

You are fortunate in the children of your
brain and of your flesh -- although
your husband can claim some credit
for the latter. More power (and perhaps)
more brain-and-flesh children to both
of you.

I'm in the grandchildren stage -- there
are ten of them -- and they are with me
from time to time. At the moment I'm
enjoying a two-week visit from Mardi and
Sheila Moore -- their grandmother is
the poet Virginia Moore, my second wife,
whom I married some thirty years ago.

As for my brain-children, they too continue
to increase. At present I have just delivered
the manuscript of a volume of letters from
Robert Frost, with a running biographical
commentary, and my wife and I have
completed a series -- 18 volumes! --
a Golden Library of Literature for
Young People. I am now faced with a new
assignment for the Britannica... So
back to the grindstone and the drawing
pad.

Sincerely,

[signature]

Letter #13

LOUIS UNTERMEYER · GREAT HILL ROAD · NEWTOWN, CONNECTICUT

January 22, 1962

Dear Mildred:

Those are revealing poems, a passionate
mixture of sensual and spiritual ecstasy.
Body and spirit are so ~~inextricably~~ fused
that they seem inseparable in these
lines. I wonder which magazine will
have the taste and temerity to publish
them. You might start with <u>Poetry</u>, the
Chicago monthly.

This has not been a happy season for us.
Apart from the worst winter we've had
in years, many of my best friends are
seriously ill. I spent yesterday at
the bedside of Robert Frost in Boston
and, though there are good signs of his
ultimate recovery, he is pitifully frail.
The same is true of one of my other
most intimate friends, Van Wyck Brooks,
who lives nearby, while two other poet-
friends, William Carlos Williams and
Alfred Kreymborg, are fighting hard against
the ills of old age.

My wife and I are about to leave on a lecture
trip which will take me through the country
for about a month. My itinerary hasn't yet
been "finalized," and it's possible that
I'll have time in Los Angeles for more
than a lecture. But all is still uncertain.
If time permits, I hope I can get a glimpse
of you, even if it is en passant.

Best always.

Louis Untermeyer

Letter #17

LOUIS UNTERMEYER • 50 WEST 72ND STREET • NEW YORK 23, N.Y.

October 1, which happesn to
be my birthday, 1963

Dear Mildred;

This will have to be the curfest sort of
reply to your letter of more than a month
ago. I have been -- and still am -- up
to my hair follicles in work. Some of it
is in connection with a new project which
is keeping me from practically everything
else; the rest is cleaning up odds and
ends of things in manuscript or revising
old editions.

Lately I have had to interrupt the progress
by going in and out of New York for radio and
TV shows as well as interviews, mainly
concerning the book of Robert Frost's
letters (see the enclosed) which is having
a most gratifying reception and has had
spectacular reviews. Today's New York Times
has a half-page advertisement featuring some
of the handsomest quotes.

As to your poetry, I have said before that
it is time you should try what Frost called
"the test of market." I say it again. It
isn't an easy test, and you will get rebuffs
before you begin to get acceptance. But
it is a test you should face. And soon, if
not now.

Best to you.

Sincerely,

Louis Untermeyer

Letter #19

LOUIS UNTERMEYER · GREAT HILL ROAD · NEWTOWN, CONNECTICUT

December 26, 1963

Dear Mildred:

What a rich and toothsome surprise! It's foolish to protest that you shouldn't have done it, for it would be ungracious to say so after such a generous fait accompli. You have excellent taste; those are unquestionably the best pears I've ever tasted. Thanks from my wife and myself and whatever guests we permit to share the fruit.

I am sending you a book not so much as a return for the pears as for your poems. It is a book of my own selected poems (Long Feud) and I hope you don't have it. If you have, please return it -- I have purposely not inscribed it for fear you may have a copy, in which case I'll send something else: Lives of the Poets, perhaps, if you don't own it.

Most of the last two years has been spent away from here, either for the Library of Congress in Washington, or abroad for the State Department. Now I'm back "in residence" -- literally snowed in at the moment -- here at home. Stimulating and often exciting though the travel has been, I'm happy to be doing my own work in my own place.

You and all the other Maiorinos are, I hope, flourishing. Holiday greetings go along with this letter which also carries the best wishes for the coming year.

Sincerely,

Louis Untermeyer

Letter #20

LOUIS UNTERMEYER · GREAT HILL ROAD · NEWTOWN, CONNECTICUT

April 13, 1964

Dear Mildred:

As before, the new poems should please you.
And Sal is quite right. Your poems are
certainly better than those of the good
French father.

I'm glad that you are finally sending
some of them out. Don't, I warn you,
expect too much or too speedy an
acceptance. And don't be disappointed
if the response is not immediately
encouraging. Remember that Frost had
to wait more than twenty years before he
was recognized.

Meanwhile, my best hopes. I'm leaving
here for another lecture trip, this
time through the midwest, but I should
be here and hereabouts most of the summer.

Cordially,

Louis Untermeyer.

Letter #22

UNTERMEYER · GREAT HILL ROAD · NEWTOWN, CONNECTICUT

December 23, 1964

Dear Mildred:

What a (literally) sweet thing to do and send -- especially to (and for) one who has a mouthful of sweet teeth. I appreciate the gift as well as the pun: Partyfours!

Although they are just a bit young for it, I am sending Nickie and Anthony my latest volume: The World's Great Stories: 55 Legends that Live Forever. Nickie will certainly enjoy some of them now, if you will read them to him, and both boys should relish the others a little later.

My wife and I have been to Europe and back. This time we spent all our time in southern France and Northern Italy. We were in Milan twice and, although we stayed at the Marino alla Scala, so close to the opera house that we could open our hotel window and almost scrape the sides of the building, we neither saw nor heard a single note. The entire troupe were playing Verdi and Puccini in Moscow!

May 1964 be a good year for you and yours. The picture of you and the boys certainly displays robust happiness, showing a healthy present and promising a splendid future.

Cordially,

Louis Untermeyer

Letter #23

LOUIS UNTERMEYER · GREAT HILL ROAD · NEWTOWN, CONNECTICUT

February 26, 1968

Dear Mildred:

I have just returned from almost three
weeks of seminars and other sessions,
mostly on the Berkeley campus -- my wife
was with me and we had an exciting
series of conferences with the students.
Friends from L. A. joined us, for we
couldn't find time to go further south
in California.

"Love Play" was waiting for me here. The
only thing about it which puzzles me is the
subtitle. It seems much more of a monologue
that (as you call it) a dialogue. I hear
your voice -- or the voice of your
spirit, soul, or whatever you choose to call
it -- but not God's. It is a highly
personal and passionate voice, a voice that
is not afraid -- even exults in --
declaring its sensuality. It is, I would
imagine, the bold mixture of the sensual
and spititual which gives the poems their
directness.

Do I detect a hint in your letter that the
poems may soon be published? If and when
they are, I would be interested in the
reactions. The more rigidly religious
readers will probably be shocked by the
forthright physical teasing, the "love
play," with all its sexual symbols, the
"wild, sweet union," the self-acknowledged
lustful delights, etc. I wonder.

Sincerely and curiously,

Louis Untermeyer.

Letter #32

LOUIS UNTERMEYER · GREAT HILL ROAD · NEWTOWN, CONNECTICUT

July 18th, 1968

Dear Mildred:

Your second series of love poems -- (lyrics?
epigrams? spiritual-sensual jottings?) --
is in tune and tone with the first.
Truly, you seem to find endless variations
on the theme of A Love-Affair with God.
Sensual they are, in spite of your
occasional disclaimers, but sensual in
an unearthly way. Sometimes they strike
me as a curious combination of the
mystical moments of Kahlil Gibran and
the unashamed eroticism of Walter Benton's
"This is My Beloved." (Parenthetically,
did you ever see my "Uninhibited Treasury
of Erotic Poetry" published by Dial-Delacorte
a few years ago? Benton is in it with a
couple of pages.) But your lines derive
from no one. Their mixture of sophistication
and naiveté, of religious intensity and
physical excitement from love-play to
orgasm, of traditional poeticisms and
current slang, is your own.

I wonder what publisher would venture presenting it. What, if any, progress toward
that possibility has been made by your
friend? It amuses me to think what
the editor of the average publisher would
(or will) make of your easy alternations
of reverence and impudence — chiding God for
staying away one night, defying him to
love anyone else, telling him if he has
"others," to do it with them on his own
time. calling him a ~~lusting~~ scoundrel, a
~~shameless~~ rascal, insatiable and shameless,
making you more and more hungry for the
ultimate ecstatic union. As I say, I
wonder.

In any case, I hope that some day some
one will have courage enough to publish
a selection from the two series.
                    Cordially, *Louis Untermeyer.*

Letter #33

FORTY YEARS
LATER…

"MOONLIGHTING"

Last week I was cleaning out some shelves where I keep original copies of my writings stored, and suddenly came across several short stories, or "vignettes," written over forty years ago in New York! Rather than throw this work out, or forget about it again, I decided to find a place for it in this current volume which among other things, relates the story of my meeting with Louis Untermeyer, followed by twenty-four years of study with him.

While typing these "vignettes" on the computer I was amazed at the insight they sometimes revealed which even now after all this time, seems to have been far beyond my perceptive capabilities when they were written. I considered myself a poet then, "moonlighting" to discover whatever hidden talent I might have for writing prose. Forty years later, I could perhaps answer that question, because prose is what I've been doing now for the past fifteen years or more. So calling the final segment of my book "Forty Years Later" opens a door for this early work. Hopefully you will enjoy it as much as I did writing it.

At the time I wrote these stories Louis Untermeyer was very patient with my side trip into prose for a few weeks. I do think he was happy, though, when I returned to poetry, leaving the prose to others more talented in that field. He did comment, after reading some of these stories that it was "damned fine writing."

As you can imagine, that pleased me a whole lot! No doubt it still would, especially if it were said about my current endeavors...

This first short story, or "vignette," as Louis Untermeyer called it, was written not long after I'd read some of Ernest Hemingway's work, at Mr. Untermeyer's suggestion, and like many other readers had become fascinated with this great writer's style. I discovered that he could reach into some very deep part of myself and awaken a certain feeling of pathos, which didn't let go until long after I'd put the book down.

In this story I chose to create a more intimate connection to our artist friend and his painting, called "Bird In a Wicker Cage," by becoming a male participant, something I do now and then in my poems, also. Gender doesn't matter all that much anyway since the soul is neither masculine nor feminine, although it may be both when we learn to tune into the "androgynous" side of ourselves.

The location I chose for this meeting of two old friends was one I was familiar with, having visited it during the Italian "feast" with my future husband while living in New York. Sal had also been there with Peter on several occasions in the past, since they were boyhood friends and had grown up together.

But enough about that. Perhaps my first short story here about Peter's painting which we'd seen while visiting him in Paris, will reveal greater insight into the friendship we had with him and its inner significance, than any further discussion can at the moment...

Mildred & Sal—40 Years Later

BIRD IN A WICKER CAGE

We pushed our way through the crowd until we came to a booth where they sold fried "salsiccia." The big fat Italian sausage smoked and sputtered pungently on the grill and I said, "Hey, Pete, how about a hunk of that?"

"O.K." he agreed. "Looks good."

The girl, a preoccupied blonde, thrust the sausage between big pieces of bread and we ate hungrily as we walked on up toward the intersection. The "feast" was in full swing and noisy as hell. Rows of lights had been strung across Mulberry Street for blocks, down which the crowd moved in a serried mass like the current of a stream, broken into little eddies by the vociferous obstruction of concessions lining the curb.

"Two years ago in Italy," I shouted, "I went to one of these feasts at Casamicciola. Not much different from this one except that here there's more of everything."

"Yeah," Pete agreed, "In America we got everything and too much of it!"

"Let's get out of here and go some place where we can talk. There's a café up on the corner where they serve pretty good espressos."

"O.K." Pete said, without much enthusiasm.

It was one of those hot sticky nights in New York and tables were set up outside. We got there just as a couple were leaving and sat down. The waiters were all inside. "You'd never know there were so many Italians living here until you go to one of these feasts," I said, looking back at the crazy mob surging by, without seeming to have any sense of where they were going.

"Remember how we used to sit around at the 'Deux Magots' in Paris?" Pete asked.

"Yeah, those were great times. Heard anything from Klara?"

"No."

"Think you'll go back to Paris, Pete?"

"Maybe. Not for a while though. But Christ, I miss it. Home two weeks and I'm homesick for Paris!"

"I know, only for me it was Rome. But you get over it." The waiter finally came and we ordered two espressos and some pastry. While we ate I remembered the night I'd met Pete at "Deux Magots" last year. Klara had been with him then. Damned clever girl Klara. Refugee from Germany or something like that, attractive and smart as hell.

Pete said, "Klara's been a big help to me. She can look at a painting once and pin-point a weakness I wouldn't even admit to myself until I'd worked around it for days!"

Klara was a regular little polyglot, too. Her French made mine sound like doggerel, and she spoke English almost without an accent. It wasn't until I went up to their apartment, or I should say attic "room," the next week that I realized they were living together.

"But why not, this is Paris!" I thought. Their room was on the top floor of an old ramshackle building on the Left Bank, furnished with an odd assortment of junk: an alcohol stove, a three-quarter bed that was only a mattress on the floor, an easel, dozens of canvases, and an ingenious collection of packing boxes. One of them doubled as a cupboard and another as a bookcase, while the largest one covered with oilcloth served as a table.

We sat around on cushions and had a great meal of ham and eggs, coffee, jelly and a three-foot long loaf of bread that I wondered how you brought home from the bakery! There was a big basket of fruit and a bowl of bright red peppers, too, big ones curled up into all sorts of queer shapes.

Klara said, "Eat the fruit, but leave the peppers. Pete wants to paint them."

Pete said, "Yeah, I'm doing vegetables now, nothing but vegetables! You know it's taken me three years in Paris to learn that vegetables have a soul?"

"Hey, Pete, I wouldn't like to think of that while I'm eating them!"

"Oh, go to hell!" Pete said with a laugh. "Here, look at this," he called, carefully selecting a canvas from a dozen or so leaning against the wall. It was a big artichoke that had flowered into a blossom like blue flames.

"There!" Pete said, standing back and pointing triumphantly towards the painting. "You can see it can't you? That artichoke lives, it's complete: it has a soul!"

"Yep," I agreed, "it does have a soul. At least you've given this artichoke a soul, and that's the important thing!" Encouraged Pete brought out other canvases of big red onions, a basket of leeks, some oddly-shaped peppers and squash, bunches of carrots, and finally a study of some eggs.

"They're good, Pete," I said, "but I don't think any of them has a soul like the artichoke does!"

A couple of weeks after that I invited Klara and Peter to have dinner with me at a little restaurant near the Folie Bergere where we had plates of escargot and the best barbecued capon I've ever eaten. Later we went to a café for coffee and Pete asked if I'd like to go back to their place so he could show me his latest work.

"I'm not doing vegetables any more," he said with a laugh.

I thought the canvas he showed me was the best thing of his I'd ever seen. Although the work he'd done before going to Paris was technically good, and had some innovative touches in style, this was different.

"You see now," he said jubilantly, "why all that work on vegetables was so good for me? Of course I haven't found what I'm looking for yet, but some day I will!"

The painting Pete showed me really had something unique I thought. Maybe it was its simplicity: what you saw, or rather didn't see stirred the imagination and made you wonder about the story behind it. A young man with sort of a mask-like expression sat beside an open window, and in front of him on the table was a wicker bird cage with the door open. That was all and yet it created an emotional response that was quite inexplicable. Even after you'd studied it for a long time you couldn't be sure of the precise feeling behind the man's enigmatic expression.

"You've created a peculiar kind of impact here, Pete."

"You see it, too!" he said. "You know, I tried for weeks to put a bird in the picture but I couldn't get it right, then one day Klara said, "Why don't you just take the bird out?"

"I did like she said and I had it!"

"I think so, too, Pete. I like your painting a whole lot!"

Pete sighed and turned the canvas to the wall. "Some day I'll get it," he said without much elation…

…We ordered two more espressos. "Well, Pete," I asked, "have you gotten it yet, I mean did you find what you were looking for in your painting?"

"Do you ever find it?" he asked with a laugh. "Maybe it's like that damned bird I took out of the painting you saw! It always escapes you one way or the other in the end."

"Why did you come home, Pete?"

"Well for one thing my passport had expired." Just then, two men drunkenly boisterous seated themselves at the opposite table.

"Then you'll go back to Paris?" I asked, raising my voice.

"No, not yet. Not for a while anyway. I'd reached a sort of impasse. It's kind of difficult to explain, but a man has to get back to his own country now and then. Sharpens your perspective."

"I see. So that's why you're here."

One of the drunks called loudly, "Hey waiter, where's that food we ordered?"

"You know, Pete," I went on, "some day you'll be a painter. I think you'll be a very great painter!"

The fellow who had called for the waiter leaned over confidentially from his chair. "Did you say painter? Hey pal, are you a painter?"

"Yep," Pete said, obviously disgusted with the guy.

"Well I need somebody to paint my house. How 'bout it?"

"I'm not that kind of painter!" Pete said dryly.

"Don't make no difference!" The drunk belched benignly. "What kind of painting you do?"

"I'm an artist: I paint pictures." Pete said tensely, like he was starting to get sore at the drunk.

"Oh for Christ's sake," I said, getting up to leave. "This sounds like a comic strip. Let's go, Pete!"

"Don't make no difference!" the drunk muttered to himself. "Painter's a painter: don't make no Gad damned difference!"

Pete threw a tip on the table. "Let's get out of here," he said.

"Forget it, Pete!"

The next week he left for Paris.

EPILOGUE:
FORTY YEARS LATER...

As stated in the beginning here, the foregoing "vignette" was written more than forty years ago while I was living in New York and studying with Louis Untermeyer. What I didn't say, though, was that I was also trying to decide whether to continue preparing for an operatic career, or devote all my creativity to writing. After reading the work of various modern authors like "Steinbeck" and "Hemingway" I tried my hand at prose, and this along with several other "vignettes" were the result of my efforts.

At first I was influenced strongly by "Ernest Hemingway" during the writing of some of these true-to-life accounts, or character sketches about many friends and acquaintances I'd met in Italy and elsewhere. When this story about him was written Peter had already returned to Paris where he continued to study oil painting for the rest of his life. I later mailed him a copy of "Bird in a Wicker Cage" and he loved it, sending me a poem he'd composed to express his gratitude. It's actually quite a deep poem!

Pete rarely returned to America, remaining abroad where he became a well-known artist. Many of his paintings have been displayed in museums in Europe, and perhaps still are. He died some years ago, and although I never saw him again following the year and a half I lived in New York before moving to California to be married, I truly hope Pete found what he was seeking! Few people ever do. Artists paint scores of pictures, and authors write millions of words throughout their lives, a small number being accorded worldly fame and recognition, but in the end there may be only one "artichoke" with a soul!

If we're lucky we solve the mystery behind the "Bird in a Wicker Cage" from which the bird of spirit has flown. I've personally found that to do so, we must learn to follow the bird in its flight, soaring into those invisible dimensions where the answer we seek may be found. In my own long quest to escape this cage of flesh and explore the "other side," I've also discovered that like a teacher of modern times once said: "Through art thou hast the light."

After all this time, and nearly a hundred and fifty books of poetry and prose written since then, I'd say that art, along with the many spiritual teachers who appear on this Earth to lend their assistance, can only give us a push into the light. What we do with that "push" is entirely up to us.

Perhaps this is the reason not many artists have moved beyond the open door of the body's cage to follow the bird of the soul in its flight! There have been a few, and some have gone mad, not understanding the force they'd tapped into. The renowned artist "Van Gogh" was one of these. His paintings indicate this, to me anyway, since I've encountered some of those dimensions in my own inner quest.

It was said that the famed ballerino, Nijinsky, took the art of ballet to such great heights literally that he discovered the psychic power of levitation, but being unable to control it, or call upon it at will, he became unbalanced. These "powers" which many have encountered, are never a plaything, but merely stepping stones to greater awareness. Although I still believe that working with any form of "art" opens the door, I also know that further study is required before you can fly away on the wings of your soul and find the way home again!

You may wonder if it's necessary to work with a spiritual teacher in order to do this, and I must affirm from my own experience that I do think it is. Peter, studied art with many teachers, although his own natural gifts helped him soar into realms no teacher can bestow, where "self help" enters the scene.

I've also worked with several spiritual teachers on my way to finding that "Supreme Teacher" within myself who knows how to open the cage of this body and set the bird of the soul free at last. I've discovered that I must then do my own flying, and like a homing pigeon set a course straight for home! Since the teacher always dwells in our own heart, even when we're looking at him in a form outside, we're never at any time without the teacher! He is the perfect artist, the poet, the Beloved, and the "Teacher of TEACHERS" who resides forever within ourselves. Through all of this HE now and then permits our personal "devil" to have his day, attempting to throw us off the path and prevent the bird of the soul from returning home.

I've met people who question what I'm saying now, doubting that the devil has the power to do this. From my own experience I'd say he does, but I've also found that it's only for a little while. Learning is a continuum, and not a jumping off place!

This next poem was the one Peter wrote for me and sent in a letter of thanks for the story I'd done about him.

T'IS ONLY ME!

If by chance in wooded dells
the pine trees' wind-blown murmurs linger
in the air, like muted bells
struck by some invisible finger,
reaching for your very soul,
and seems not fancy but reality,
for you feel the toll has found its goal:
t'is only me, t'is only me…

If you along some coast alone
the storm's relentless fury brave,

watch break against unyielding stone
the huge and countless host of waves,
and mark the flight of the driven gull,
or a great ship smashed by a maddened sea
that casts ashore the shattered hull:
t'is only me, t'is only me…

If when at night the gentle rain
courses down upon this thirsty land
and softly taps your window-pane,
dream on! This is no stranger's hand
that seeks to break your quiet rest,
intrude upon your reverie,
or banish peace within your breast:
t'is only me, t'is only me…

If at dawn you wake and find
you've lost the haunting melody,
search deep around within your mind
for what was found will always be.
In solitude, or when at play
it's always there for you to see.
Awake, or asleep, don't turn away:
t'is only me, t'is only me…

> For Mildred, By Peter A. Marcasiano

I've never forgotten my friend, Pete, even though I never saw him again. In spirit there's no separation as his poem states, so we're still together. I've discovered that this is the only true "oneness" we ever find on this Earth. In everything else the mind creates division in one form or another. While the soul may employ thought for its own purposes, the mind is merely a reflector for it. Doesn't it seem a strange paradox that in all of our seeking thought always perceives itself as the only reality?

In much the same way we look in the mirror of life at an image we believe to be ourselves, seeing reflected there only a body the soul is using. Even more puzzling is our projection of another form into the external world where we fall in love with it, identify with it, and then perhaps blame it for all of our unhappiness! It seems superfluous to add that this constitutes the very nature of illusion. Strangely enough, only now, after more than forty years of spiritual seeking I've come to see at last the deep truth in what was just expressed.

This next story is written about the third and final voice teacher I worked with in Milano before returning to New York where I encountered my new destiny as a poet. When I first arrived in Milano I'd studied with "Madame Carmen Melis" and later with my friend Lucilla's teacher, "Maestro Montesanto." Not long before I left for America I decided to work with Marsha, a personal friend who lived there and had at one time been a professional singer herself. Oddly enough she'd offered to help me explore a new direction for my voice which she felt would be significant to my future as a singer. One of her suggestions was to learn lighter roles in the lyric coloratura repertoire, such as she'd sung.

At the final session I had with Marsha she assured me that if I could remain in Milano and study with her for another year I might very well become one of the most sought after sopranos in all of Italy. At that time we were working on "The Barber of Seville," an opera she'd once sung and which I'd never studied. Since the lessons were entirely "gratis," I could only conclude that Marsha meant what she said! So often we seek only ego gratification no matter what the cost, yet as my story about her reveals, we must learn to follow the call of destiny stored in the depths of our heart, no matter what sacrifice it calls for. If we fail to do so, the outcome could be tragic, as it clearly was for Marsha.

THE PHOTOGRAPHS
I ASKED FOR

The photographs I asked for came in the mail this morning. They aren't bad of her, but then again they aren't particularly good either! If they were in color instead of black and white, then at least you could see the beauty of her coppery red hair and green eyes like heroines have in stories.

There's one thing sure: not all women of forty-five still look that good! But then Marsha wasn't like anyone else I'd ever seen, even in the movies. On the back of the pictures it says they were taken at "Taormina," but I'd know that anyhow because I was there myself two years ago.

If I close my eyes it's easy to picture every detail of that bus ride up from "Messina," the way the crazy driver swung around the curves and sat on the horn while we passed through the little villages. An Italo-American I'd met on the ship was teaching me to say, "L'autista guida come un pazzo! The driver drives like a crazy man!" Very true in English or Italian.

In one little village the bus came to a stop while an old man muttering imprecations maneuvered his cart into an alley. The street was narrow and fetid, with people and animals oozing out of open doorways and onto the little balconies. In front of one house an old woman sat lymphatically munching a roll filled with some kind of stringy green leaves hanging from it, probably ciccoria, or chicory as it's called here.

A teenage boy on a bicycle, singing "Anema e Core," meaning "heart and soul," had a surprisingly good voice. Boys mature early in Latin countries. A good-looking young man standing in front of a "marcelleria" ogled a young girl carrying a market basket. She didn't look like she was wearing a bra because the nipples of her breasts showed through the cotton stuff of her dress. An almost naked baby playing on the curb with a dispirited dog, took time out to urinate, grasping his tiny phallic appendage and sending a cherubic dribble of water into the gutter...

After that the street was clear and we plunged onward to what seemed vertiginous heights, where "Mount Etna" loomed in a blue haze on the shoreline. Everything suddenly turned to blue, blue, blue: blue flame, blue light, blue ache in my throat from so much beauty! When I just couldn't take any more of that feeling, I stared through the windows on the other side of the bus at all kinds of little villas set back among fig and orange trees, with flowers burgeoning and spiraling exultantly everywhere.

Mostly I remember the bougainvilleas writhing redly on rooftops and walls. Their color was so bright it hurt my eyes if I looked too long, like staring into flames, and I could still see it moving kaleidoscopically across the retina of my eyes even after I looked away. "Seeing" then became an outer as well as an inner experience, and remained like that all the way up to the ruins of the Greek Theatre at Taormina. I do think my "Third Eye" was born in Italy although I only realized what that is later in America...

During the following winter, while living in Milano, I had many occasions to remember all that color and beauty because Milano was drab and dull like most big cities. It had a horrible climate, too, with fog that clung to everything throughout the winter months. The Milanese called the fog "la nebbia," and I once heard some silly woman say she thought it was "simpatica," like a person!

Marsha, or "Signora Luigi Antonelli," which was her married name, hated the climate in Milano, too. I recall her saying so the first time I went to see her. That was in late October and already so cold we had to keep our coats on in the apartment while we drank cup after cup of scalding hot tea to keep warm. This, of course, was in post-war Italy.

Marsha said, "Every year I get more and more annoyed with the way these people do things!"

"But since it's so cold, Marsha, why doesn't the landlord just turn the heat on and make the tenants comfortable?"

Marsha laughed. She was quite beautiful when she laughed. Something went on inside her like an electric light and you could tell right away that she'd been a real personality on the stage.

"The contract says we get heat from November first until April first and that's all we get! So every year for the past twenty years I've frozen and cursed the landlord through April and October, but it doesn't do any good."

I mumbled something sympathetic while she sighed, then asked, "And how is dear Beulah?"

Beulah was my accompanist in Los Angeles. At one time she'd been Marsha's accompanist, too, and it was she who gave me a letter of introduction to Marsha. "Beulah is very busy and happy," I said. "I had lunch with her just before I left in August."

Marsha's eyes took on a certain glow of remembrance. "Isn't she the most marvelous accompanist? How many times I've wished I had her here in Italy!"

I went on, hoping she'd tell me more about herself. "Beulah has often talked about the wonderful career you had before your marriage."

"Yes I guess it was rather fabulous," Marsha agreed, "making my debut at La Scala and all that!"

"Tell me about it, Marsha. How did all of that take place?"

Until then Marsha had seemed more like a correct and beautiful society matron than the flamboyant artist I was prepared to meet, after talking to several mutual friends in America who had given such glowing accounts of her career. Suddenly a mysterious energy animated Marsha's whole being and she came to life right before my eyes! She was someone who knew how to soar, and I could see that she must have been a marvelous performer.

"I'd been in Italy about a year. My God, but how I worked! Eight hours a day of piano, acting, languages, voice lessons, everything! Then one night I went with my teacher, Maestro Mateo, to a 'prova' at La Scala. That's a dress rehearsal you know, and afterwards he introduced me to the conductor."

"'Feruccio,' he said, 'here's a voice I want you to hear some time!' Then the conductor, Feruccio Brancaccio, said 'Why not now?' So right then and there I sang for him and they were so excited about my voice I signed a contract that very night to make my debut the following season at La Scala!"

"What a thrilling moment for you!" I said.

"Yes, it was," Marsha agreed, "but I'm afraid that would be a rash procedure for most young singers to follow." Her green eyes slanted into thoughtfulness. "I truly think it's safer to come up the slow hard way, and make a habit of success instead of wearing it like a first ball dress!"

She hesitated for a moment. "I'm not at all sure that moving more slowly wouldn't have been better for me, too!"

"And how did it go, your debut at La Scala?" I prompted, since Marsha seemed lost in her memories.

"Oh, it was a marvelous success! Wait a minute and I'll show you the notices." Marsha got up with a grace that was still natural to her as she walked down the marble-floored hallway. A moment later she returned with a scrap book, while her dog, a spoiled black French poodle pattered importantly behind her.

"The critics were very kind," she said as she opened the large portfolio. Of course the notices were all in Italian, and since my knowledge of the language was still undeveloped at that time, she translated them for me. I thought the critics were not only kind, they were rhapsodic!

Marsha turned a page. "Here are some pictures from my first season in South America."

"What exquisite costumes!" I exclaimed, "especially this one from the 'Barber of Seville'!"

"Oh yes, I loved that role. I got the lace for the mantilla from Spain. That was the year I was introduced to Luigi."

"Oh I do hope to meet him soon, and your children, too!" I glanced again at some beautiful photographs of her son and daughter on the desk.

"My husband usually gets home late, but Maria should be coming in from school any time now."

"Does Maria sing?" I asked.

"Well at fourteen you can't tell much about it, but it seems a pleasant, sweet little voice. She seems more interested in American popular music at the moment than operatic training!"

I turned again to the scrap book. The notices had dwindled to a few scattered reviews of concerts. "As you see," Marsha explained, "after I married Luigi, my career dropped off to almost nothing."

"Why?" I asked curiously.

"Well, for one thing, Luigi's family were all opposed to my singing, my husband especially. You can't imagine how possessive Italian men are of their women! Then I discovered that I was pregnant, and after our son was born my health was poor for a long time. So you see, my dear, if you want a career, don't get married!"

I laughed. "No danger of that at the moment! Tell me, do you miss America?"

Marsha's face crept into a mask of poorly disguised bitterness. "I get so homesick for it sometimes I could die! Of course we've returned a few times to visit, but that only makes the longing worse when we get back to Italy!"

I was afraid to ask if she missed her music, but Marsha read my thought. "Sometimes I feel like I'm only half a person without my singing, as if there's some part of myself that doesn't exist any longer. If it weren't for Luigi and the children I don't think I could bear it"...

During the following months I went often to visit Marsha and became well acquainted with her husband and daughter, since her son was at school most of the time. Maria was a lovely young girl who spoke English surprisingly well. Actually they were a wonderful family. I could see that Marsha loved all of them dearly and they adored her, almost to the point of idolatry.

But there was something about Marsha that made me think of a wild thing in captivity. While it may be true that women were intended by nature to be wives and mothers, I'm convinced that for certain artists this role must become no more than an accompaniment to the larger song of the creative expression crying for release within themselves. If as in Marsha's life the song is completely silenced, then it becomes like a wound, or a cry of pain, and remaining suppressed, appoints itself an executioner...

After I returned to America, Marsha and I exchanged letters faithfully, then a few weeks ago she wrote that the whole family was going to Taormina for a long vacation together. I recalled the day I'd told her about my own visit to Taormina, and couldn't believe she'd lived in Italy for twenty years without seeing it!

How I envied them that trip as I read the letter, because like I said at the beginning of this story, I'd been there myself two years ago. Now while I'm looking at the pictures her family sent to me, I can almost see Taormina again, and feel the enchantment of that bus ride all the way up from Messina.

And there she is, Marsha I mean, standing on top of a cliff overlooking the sea, smiling out at me like a goddess from the glorious ruins of the Greek Theatre. But what I simply can't believe yet, no matter how hard I try, is that she's dead.

Some forms of cancer like Marsha had work very fast, and destroy the body swiftly...

EPILOGUE: FORTY YEARS LATER

The shock of hearing about Marsha's death came not long after I'd returned to America and was living in New York, waiting to make the trip out west where Sal and I planned to be married. Although I, too, would be leaving my own aspiration for singing opera behind, the chief difference between myself and Marsha, was that I would not be giving up a spectacular career such as hers had been. Fortunately, during my stay in Italy I'd been introduced to an even more gratifying expression in the field of the arts, and have continued working at it for over forty years.

I do think that after all this time, though, I've discovered something even more important than doing creative work one enjoys, and that's finding what we loosely call a "spiritual" life and devoting oneself to that. Once this happens everything else becomes secondary, although outwardly few people would detect much difference in the way you live, compared to someone else doing the same kind of work. When you're deeply involved in this inner life, you eventually find that it has become the most vital thing for you, clearly revealing that you've chosen the "better part!"

As you discover a way to fit all of this together like a giant mosaic, or tapestry, your life will be complete no matter what career you follow, whether it's that of an ordinary clerk, or a great operatic star like my friend Marsha was. There will be joy in doing it, and while not doing it as well!

I do think this is the true test of our success in life and not some kind of personal attainment, no matter how great…

The setting for this next story is on the "Island of Ischia," one of my favorite places in all of Italy. Just why that is I really can't say. Perhaps this feeling was aroused by the fact that my fiancé and I spent a lot of time together there. I've found that something incredible taking place inwardly will often evoke the same response from my surroundings, like a marriage of inner and outer worlds where the invisible joins hands with the visible to create the deathless dance of the soul.

And that, too, may endure for only a little while in this kaleidoscopic world of continual change, where joy comes and goes like the sun appearing from behind the clouds to play its game of hide-and-seek with our hearts through endless cycles of learning and growth...

In these stories of Italy, I've changed the names of the leading characters, since at times I took certain liberties with the story line. Probably most of my readers will see right away that when I write about "Laura" I was really talking about my life long friend, "Lucilla," and some of our life changing adventures together in Italy, never to be forgotten.

A SCENE FROM TOSCA

At seven, Norina, the maid at the villa, woke us as we'd asked her to the night before while having "cena" on the terrace.

"Signorine, signorine, svegliatevi, wake up!" she called standing uneasily at the foot of Laura's bed.

"Grazie, Norina, thank you," I said. "We'll have our coffee on the terrace. In about fifteen minutes!" I called after her.

Of course I always spoke to Norina in Italian, since she understood little or no English. She opened the shuttered doors of our room and went outside, moving ponderously, her wooden-soled "zocoletti" clattering behind her as she walked.

"Come on sleepy head, dormirone!" I said to Laura as I slipped into my paisley print sun dress. "Time to rise and get started."

Laura yawned and rolled over. Being a "night" person at heart she hated getting up in the morning, so I decided to try a little psychology on her. "I think today I'll use that roll of film I got from home and take some pictures of the Island. Be nice to have a couple of shots of you in that red peasant outfit your sister sent!"

Laura sat up immediately. She loved having her picture taken. "Oh darn, I don't think my red dress has been ironed yet!"

"Never mind. Norina can do it while we're having breakfast." Laura got up and started rummaging around in the wardrobe looking for her crumpled red dress. Since I was already dressed, I went out on the terrace and immediately the big police dog, Arno, came running up to nose my hand.

"Buon giorno, Arno!" I said, stroking him gently. "Come stai, eh?" I always spoke Italian to Arno because it worried him when I lapsed into English!

After a few minutes I stood up and looked down the steep slope of the Island to where the Mediterranean moved and sparkled in the oblique spotlight of the sun, with the shoreline of Naples curving far away in the distance, like a theatrical backdrop. On any clear morning we could look at Naples from the terrace like that while having our "colazione"—breakfast with a terrific view.

All down the sharply descending hillside, little white villas sat complacently, like cats in the sun, a light breeze lipping through the fig leaves and the grape vines covering the arbor. In the garden a sort of pungent fragrance drifted up from the tangerine trees, and the air was filled with that pristine freshness it always had in early morning on the Island. I remembered to breathe deeply, exercising my lungs and my diaphragm also, since singers can't ever forget about that!

I strolled over to the arbor where grapes hung thickly in clumps of small green nuggets. "Be another couple of weeks before they're ripe," I mused to myself, giving them a tentative pinch or two. Over on the wall a crimson bougainvillea clung wantonly.

Already the crickets were beginning their rhythmic chirping, and I thought about how this was a sign it would be another hot day. Or so I'd heard. After a moment I walked over to where Norina had the table all set up on the terrace, spread with a big red and white checked tablecloth. In the center sat a cut-glass bowl filled with apricots and plums nestled glaucously in the cool water. Norina came out just then with a tray of rolls, butter and plum marmalade, accompanied by pitchers of hot coffee and milk.

"Ecco, signorina. La colazione e pronta."

Just then Laura came out with her red dress looking like she'd slept in it, and asked Norina to press it for her. Norina took it, grunting a dispirited, "Si, signorina," as we sat down to eat.

"God, but it's another perfect day, Laura! Have you ever seen so many heavenly days in a row in your whole life?"

"Never!" she agreed. "The Maestro sure did himself and us, too, a big favor when he decided to come here for the summer. The heat must be murderous in Milano!"

"It was already awful when we left," I said, breaking a plump, seeded roll in half. "I think Ischia is ever so much nicer than Capri anyway. I'll bet so many tourists are there now it's like an anthill with a housing shortage!"

Laura chuckled. I always found her response to my corny humor gratifying. I glanced at my watch. "We better hurry. It's past eight o'clock, and we have to walk down to the piazza and get a carriage. That's a long hike, too, you know!"

Laura took a big gulp of café-latte. "I know. Hope we can find Antonio!" He was our favorite driver.

An hour later, we were in the piazza looking for him, but he wasn't there so Laura began haggling with another fellow. When he saw that we knew what the rates should be, she got him down to two hundred lire for taking us to the beach at San Montana, and another five hundred to pick us up there and drive us back to the Villa Martinelli. It sounded like a bargain, especially when we split the cost as we usually did with everything. That would get us to the Villa in time for lunch, which is dinner in Italy, and served on the terrace unless the weather was unpleasant.

As soon as we were settled in the "carozza" the lively little horse took off at a brisk trot down the road, following the curve of the sea all the way to San Montana. Later, about mid-morning after a long leisurely swim, we lay stretched out on the sand, cool, sleepy and at the same time exhilarated. Beneath the big towel the sand felt hot when I burrowed into it with my knees.

"That water," I said wonderingly, "I've just never felt anything like it. It's so soft it makes you feel like going swimming in the nude, like that cute baby down there!"

Laura giggled. "Doesn't it? It's as though the water's alive and caressing you: almost makes you feel indecent!"

"Not me!" I said. "I love it. Would you look at how brown we're getting?"

Laura inspected her white arms and sighed enviously. "You've got a much better color than I have. Olive skin like yours always tans better."

"I don't think so. It's just that this white suit makes me look darker." My two piece suit, laced up the side, exposed a lot of "skin", and was at that time somewhat daring.

Laura sat up suddenly and asked like a little girl, "As soon as our suits are dry, honey, could we take the pictures?"

"Sure. First I'll get a shot of you in that turquoise bathing suit, then one in your red dress, and if we see someone with a camera who looks like he knows how to take pictures with it, I'll get him to shoot one of us together!"

Laura lay down again on her tummy utterly relaxed, then after a moment I saw her muscles tighten. She'd been all tensed up like this for the past week, which puzzled me.

"What's the matter?" I asked.

Laura was kicking the sand with little jabs of her foot. "Oh sometimes I get so mad at the Maestro. Honestly I just dread thinking about my lesson this afternoon because I know I don't have the right feeling for that scene with Scarpia, and he'll be cross with me again!" She sighed. "I just can't seem to get it like he wants."

"I thought it sounded better the last time I heard you."

"But I still can't get the feeling of wanting to kill someone, at least not the way the Maestro expects me to!"

"I think you worry too much about it and that makes you tense. You'll see," I reassured her, "after this nice relaxing swim it will go better this afternoon."

"Well, I don't know"... Laura said, her voice trailing off.

"I do!" I told her. "Now shut up for a few minutes while I go over the words of 'Caro Nome' and make sure I know them. If I don't get this darned aria memorized, Maestro will be mad at me, too! Boy he can sure get mad faster than anyone I've ever met here, or in America, either!"

That afternoon at four o'clock when Laura had her lesson, I could hear right away that she wasn't doing the scene any better than she had before. I was sitting on the terrace just outside the door studying my score so I heard every word the Maestro said.

"No, no, NO!" he bellowed. "There's no fire! You're singing it just like an American!" as though that were the worst insult he could think of. "Now, let's do it again, and put some life into it. Vita!" he roared, banging the old upright piano with his fist.

I knew that Laura was furious with the Maestro for making that crack about Americans. I could hear it in her voice as soon as she started singing. There was fire all right, but it sure was phony!

Right in the middle of it the Maestro stopped her. "No, no, cara, that isn't what I want! It's better," he added more kindly, "but it isn't right. We'll let it go for today. Get some rest, read the score and think about the dramatic content. Tomorrow we'll try it again."

When Laura came out she was almost in tears, so I told her to take a nap until time to eat. "Go to sleep and don't worry. You'll get wrinkles!" I said. "I'll call you at six."

At seven we were both dressed in fresh cotton dresses and lounging in the curved canvas chairs on the terrace, chatting and waiting for "cena" which was usually pasta or soup, salad and some fruit. Laura began talking about that scene from "Tosca" again. She just couldn't seem to get it out of her mind. Closing her eyes she leaned back in her chair. "If there were only some way I could get the right feeling for it. I mean, killing someone!"

"Well, there isn't much here in this deliciously monotonous way of life on the Island to give you a feeling for murder!" I said laughing, hoping to keep her from getting all worked up again. "Unless maybe you can think about how you'd like to kill the Maestro when he cuts loose on you!"

"Silly!"

"Wait a minute, I suddenly remembered something. A long time ago I read a book on acting by some Russian drama teacher, Balaslavsky I think it was, and he told this young girl student, when she asked him about getting the right emotion to do the part of a murderess, that she should just think of killing a mosquito."

"A mosquito!" Laura laughed.

"Sure. He said that the feeling of violence and hate you have just before you 'smack' it should create all the motivation you need for working with the emotion of murder!"

I stared at some angry red blotches on my arm. "If these darn mosquitoes here on the Island were bigger you might get in a little practice, but they're so small and sneaky you never know they've been around until the next morning when you get up and start counting the bites."

"And they itch so, too, don't they?" Frowning, Laura pushed up the sleeves of her embroidered white peasant blouse. "Just look at these new ones on my arm that I got last night!"

"Yes sir," I said, knowing I'd soon have Laura laughing. "Just give me a big healthy American mosquito any time! You can hear him coming, feel him light, and then get in a good swing at him before he can sink his stinger in!" By then Laura was giggling and completely relaxed.

We just sat there not saying anything more while the last rays of the sun fingered through the petals of the white daisies in the flower bed. It was so peaceful and still with just the dinner sounds and a sort of muted chatter coming from the kitchen.

Now and then a lemon fell in a distant grove with a warm, languorous thud. Out in front of the villa we heard two girls come down to get water from the well by the gate, then the slow diminuendo of their voices as they walked back up the hill...

Suddenly from out of nowhere a tiny black thing that looked like a winged mouse came darting down the walk in front of us, with little frightened squeaks. "What on earth is that?" I asked.

"Oh my God, it's a bat!" Laura screamed. "Look at its wings!" She was almost as frightened as the bat was. "Oh I can't stand those things!" she wailed, pulling her feet up under her in the chair with a shudder.

"But it's just a baby, Laura! Probably trying to find its mother! Look, I think it's been hurt!"

"Oh no, get it away!" Laura shrieked, staring at the little creature darting everywhere but obviously finding nowhere it felt safe to stay. I hoped it would make its way into the deep shrubbery at the back of the garden and hide there, but by then the padrona heard all the racket we were making and had come out to see what the trouble was. When she saw Laura huddled in her chair looking scared to death, she grabbed a broom leaning against the wall of the villa and started trying to hit the little bat with it, but it wasn't solid enough to execute a death blow.

"This is so silly!" I said. "It's harmless. Besides I read somewhere that bats eat insects and bugs in the garden."

But nobody paid any attention to what I said, and the padrona continued scuttling around after the bat, flailing the walk with the broom. Once in a while she managed to bring the broom down with a sickening whack on top of the little bat, but it always contrived to wriggle free again, its darting and squeaking getting more frantic all the time.

Just when it looked like the conflict would never end, the maid, Norina, came out of the kitchen, gingerly carrying the big cut-glass bowl filled with fruit. With one glance she took in the situation, set the bowl on the table, and waddled over in her wooden-soled zocoletti. Then with amazing agility she sprang toward the terrified little creature before it had time to scud away and began stomping on it methodically with her feet.

After the first blow or two and a short, agonized crescendo of squeaks, the little bat was dead, but Norina kept stomping venomously on it until it was nothing but a bloody black and red mess on the cobblestones terrace. All the while Laura and I had been watching Norina's face, which was a study in cold, concentrated hate, utterly ruthless and determined.

Finally I started breathing again and mumbled to Laura, "Oh, how awful. What a horrible thing to do!"

Hearing that the padrona called sharply, "Norina, basta!"

After that she went over with the broom and swept the lifeless blob off the walk into the shrubbery where Arno came and sniffed at it in short tentative lunges. Norina, still breathing hard from all the exertion, said at last, "Oddio quelle bestie: I hate those beasts!"

"Bring some water and clean off the walk!" the padrona ordered sternly, and Norina lumbered obediently off toward the kitchen with the padrona following behind her.

"Well, Laura," I said, staring at the red stain on the walk, "that should give you all the feeling you need for the murder of Scarpia!"

Laura just sat there with her feet still drawn up, an expression of wonder on her face. "Did you see Norina's eyes when she was killing that thing?"

"I sure did! And I've just lost my appetite!"

"Oh honey," Laura said softly, still in some kind of trance-like state, "Tomorrow I think I can do that scene right, the way the Maestro wants it. I know I can do it now!" she added with a certain exultance in her voice.

"Ugh," I said, watching as Norina came out carrying a pail of water and started scrubbing the dark red stain off the walk with a dirty rag. "If you don't mind, I think I'll just stick to good old Balaslavsky and mosquitoes!"

EPILOGUE: FORTY YEARS LATER

After more than forty years of perspective here, along with the flow of events that followed, I can state without any doubt that Laura-Lucilla learned to do the scene from "Tosca" right that long ago evening on Ischia, since in subsequent years she's sung many successful performances of it throughout the world.

Although I never saw her personally sing this particular role on stage, we did have the privilege of attending her performance of the fiery Principessa in "Turandôt," presented here in Los Angeles by the San Francisco Opera Company many years ago. Whatever methods the Maestro employed for training singers, he was amazingly successful with Lucilla!

Just how much our experience of the "bat" episode did for her I can't be sure, except that after her lesson the following day she came out with the biggest smile on her face. I noted however, that each time she passed the reddish brown stain on the walk where the little bat had died, she'd shrug and walk on, appearing to feel a certain sense of remorse about it. In retrospect, I suppose there was some way we could have taken charge and rescued the baby bat, but I'm not sure now, over forty years later, just how that might have been done.

Anyway I refused to feel guilty about it at the time, nor even to be overly disturbed by all the distress and poverty we witnessed in post-war Italy, although the situation was pretty desperate then. In Naples when you saw a mother with a baby in her arms begging, it wasn't some kind of "scam" to make money like you see in the streets here sometimes. This was real, and not a scene from an opera, either.

I've found that guilt is a very strange thing. Like the glue holding pictures in an album, guilt retains the feeling of injustice, or anything else in our subconscious mind, flashing it back over and over until the "Savior" helps us let go of it, or the psychiatrist, or our spiritual teacher who knows about all of that.

Although the event itself may be long gone, we keep mulling over whatever that image was: good, bad, indifferent or just plain horrible and our awareness gets stuck there. As I said in one of my poems, written after I returned to America, "Our freedom comes in letting go!" After all, the image doesn't attach itself to you, since you're pulling it to yourself through memory...

Maybe you think that seeking some form of "amnesia" through drugs, or even psychoanalysis would free your mind of the whole thing, but I've yet to see much success resulting from that. Escape of this nature doesn't bring a lasting solution, since the image still remains buried in the subconscious. The process of "letting go" comes through spiritual understanding of what has happened, and not by running away from it. I've found that ignorance is to continue seeking some form of escape, while wisdom is seeing that pleasure can never free us from the hurt.

After all these years I also see that freedom, or clarity, doesn't come through any form of "art." Although the light within ourselves expands, only by merging with the one who creates the art, then coming to know the "ONE" standing behind both do we experience a successful clearing on all levels, which includes the subconscious. This is usually done with the help of a spiritual teacher, I might add.

Below is the poem I mentioned previously, taken from a collection written during the years when I was studying with Louis Untermeyer. I believe I was referring to that same "stickum" of attachment in our lives, and not whether we've decided to call those images good, or "bad." An image is neither one nor the other, except when labeled as such through the conditioning of the mind. What appears "good" may have been in reality not so at all, while something which we believed was "bad" might have been only the "hand of God" pulling us closer to himself.

Certainly the essence of every experience is stored in the light itself, becoming an immortal part of ourselves. If there's any purpose and meaning to this long earthly journey, surely it's that! What I call soul essence exists beyond form, and doesn't fall into any category thought assigns to it, being only pure, unconditioned energy and awareness...

LET THEM GO...

As the years go by I cross them off:
images of this face and that...
This one provoked a revolution
on battle grounds of consciousness,
ending in stalemate: no resolution...
Put malice aside, just let it go.
Our freedom they say comes in letting go!

That mind, filled with sterile,
invidious thoughts
like a flat of damp-off seeds
that never grew a bloody thing
but useless invasions of weeds!
She with the vain perennial eye
that winked away the years
until that day when one came by
quite unannounced, to stay.
Release them all, just let them go:
our freedom they say comes in letting go!

Even those faces loved
and preserved like carvings of ivory
In curio cabinets of the mind:

let these go, too, crossed off
with firm but gentle strokes
on pages well-thumbed and dear,
that have been turned and turned
for years,
time in and out of mind:
let all of them go...
Our freedom they say comes in letting go!

My life-long friend, Lucilla, who discovered the potential gift I had for writing in Italy has now gone to dwell on the "other side" where as her sister said, she's teaching the angels to sing.

I can only agree with that since Lucilla's voice and the light of her soul were very great...

My next story concerns a particular incident in the life Lucilla and I led together in Milano. Of course it also reflects how I perceived what happened then, since we all see things differently, and perhaps Lucilla remembered it in another light...

Lucilla in Turandôt

"GIANNI": THE DELIVERY BOY

Laura and I really liked our apartment in Milano. In fact, we'd come to like Italy, also, and even after living there for three months, we hadn't found much to criticize—that is, if we didn't compare life in Italy with what we'd known in America!

On the whole, Italy was kind of romantic and the Italians were wonderful to Americans. Well, except for that man in the meat market last week where Laura had ordered two steaks, the best "filetti." A transient lounging around in the doorway watching us made a nasty remark about how these Americans were so rich they lived on beefsteak all the time.

On another day Laura might have ignored him, but that morning the light and gas bill had come and it was a lot higher than usual. After it was paid we'd be down to our last five thousand lire until the end of the month. While that sounds like a lot of money, it was actually about seven dollars and fifty cents at the time.

Laura snapped right back at the man in her best Italian, "Look here, you! Not that it's any concern of yours, but this steak is for our Sunday dinner tomorrow, we're students and we're not rich, and we're sick and tired of being treated as though we were!" On that note she extracted mille lire from the worn black purse we used for our joint house money. "Quanto? How much?" she asked.

The butcher replied, "That will be three hundred and fifty lire, signorina." The butcher liked Americans.

The angry man in the doorway went on, "In the war you Americans sent planes to bomb Milano: you killed my wife!"

The butcher handed Laura her change and the steaks wrapped in thin green paper. The blood had already started soaking through it since it wasn't very good paper. Laura placed it carefully in our wicker shopping basket.

She turned to me and said in English, "That man's impossible!"

As we were leaving she glared at him. "Now let's get this straight," she said. "My cousin was killed in Salerno and I don't like war any more than you do. I'm sorry you lost your wife, but the war's over now! The only thing we can do is forget about it and move on with our lives!"

"Yes," he snarled venomously, "la guerra e finita, but I hate Americans and I won't ever forget!"

The butcher became angry with him then and said, "Va-te ne! Go away!" to the man in a sharp voice and he moved back from the doorway. I noticed he had no overcoat and there was a big patch on the sleeve of his jacket. I felt sorry because it was a very cold winter in Milano that year...

At the vegetable market the padrona's son, Gianni, made the deliveries. Gianni was thirteen and unusually tall for his age, but he still wore short pants which were shiny black and very short, probably because he'd outgrown them. Delivery boys were not allowed to use the elevator at our apartment, so Gianni walked up seven flights of stairs to get to our place, the heavy box of groceries balanced on top of his head.

When Laura opened the door, he gave her a big quivery-lipped smile. "Buon giorno, signorina!" Gianni waited to watch Laura empty the box, his blue eyes like a camera picking up every line of her face and figure. Laura was very attractive...

One day a week or so after this, we were waiting for Gianni to come with the delivery. Laura said, "I think I'll give that poor kid a hundred lire tip today. He's been coming up here for weeks now and we never give him anything." When Gianni came in that day, his hands were raw and red from the cold, but his smile was like a fire on the hearth of his heart.

"Fa freddo. It's cold, Gianni!" Laura said as she closed the door after him. Gianni carried the big box into the kitchen.

"Si, fa molto freddo, signorina! It is very cold." A kid his age ought to be in school, I thought to myself, as I began taking out the fruit and vegetables.

Just then Laura remembered about the tip. "Ecco, Gianni, un piccolo regalo," she said smiling and holding out the pink hundred lire note to him. "Here's a little gift for you!"

For a moment Gianni didn't seem to understand, then his face turned red and the fire in his eyes went out. "Ma no veramente, non lo voglio, truly I don't want it, signorina!"

Laura tucked the money in the pocket of his jacket and said decisively, "Non ne parliamo più: we won't speak of it any more!"

Gianni left without a word, and didn't look at Laura again. After he'd gone she said, "Can you beat that? That's the first time I ever had to coax an Italian to take money!"

I couldn't believe Laura hadn't seen how it was with Gianni. "Well, I'm not surprised!" I said. "It's obvious the little fellow's in love with you! He can't take his eyes off you whenever he's around here."

Laura laughed, "You're kidding: that child? Why he can't be more than twelve: thirteen at the most!"

"That doesn't make any difference: he's got a crush on you."

"That's ridiculous!" Laura retorted.

"Just the same he'd rather have died than take money from you no matter how much it was."

As though trying to make light of the situation Laura said, "That kid ought to be in school. He's too young to be thinking about falling in love!"

"But he isn't, and he has!" I said.

"Well, what am I supposed to do about it?" Laura snapped.

"Nothing, nothing at all," I said. "Just thought I'd mention it, since you don't seem to realize how it is with Gianni."

"So what if I did? I don't have affairs with children!"

EPILOGUE: FORTY YEARS LATER

Times have changed enormously in Italy since those post war days, and most Italians seem to have a lot of money now. Sometimes I think the standard of living in Italy is higher than ours, especially mine here in America! So it's been very amusing to me on various occasions when members of my husband's family were visiting from Italy and still had the impression that Americans have access to unlimited stores of wealth which we obviously possess, but are simply not telling the world about!

Perhaps in many ways some of us are rich, especially when you look at all of this from a higher perspective, which is mostly how I do presently, and not with any particular concern about the wealth and position a lot of other folks have. I've discovered that somewhere along the line in this earthly "schoolhouse" a few people are aware of the futility of hanging onto things, and have begun storing up their "treasure in Heaven." In other words, they're clearing the light within themselves, since this is all that can be taken with us when we leave here.

Just how many "light units" we're able to work with will determine our stay in those invisible dimensions, and not how many homes we own here, or the number of digits on our bank account. Being penniless, though, would for most people be as much of a trap as possessing too much, so somewhere here we bump right into the Buddha and his "Middle Way," whatever the circumstances of our lives are. I've decided that ultimately everything here on Earth is expendable anyway and up for grabs by TIME!

I was once acquainted with a charming woman who was an Italian Princess by marriage. Following her husband's death she became active in a meditation group in New York, being an initiate of the spiritual teacher we both knew. As many people are aware, the initiatory path differs from the outer ritualistic practice observed in most of the world's religions.

Although she ultimately chose to reside in Italy, I don't believe she found a way to interest many people there in the deeper aspects of the spiritual path she'd been involved with. After all, don't Italians have the Pope? Although she was quite advanced spiritually, I do think she was also proud of being a Princess!

In those invisible dimensions where we all go to reside, I don't believe titles, along with wealth, have the same importance we give them here. I read somewhere that although you can't bring your "Rolls Royce" with you when you die, you could take along the knowledge of having owned one, and "zap" out a duplicate for yourself there! Perhaps it's like that with titles as well! Since the clarity of your light is the only I.D. you need in spiritual dimensions, when you begin working with that you're tapping directly into Reality, no matter what path you might have been following, and this could be any of the numerous religions practiced throughout the world.

The late Padre Pio, an Italian priest with the stigmata who lived in a Monastery at San Giovanni Rotondo, demonstrated that his life-long devotion to the Catholic faith could be taken to extraordinary heights of spiritual power and illumination.

After all the years I've spent in meditation and study of the world's religions I've finally come to see that any of these are simply garments the soul is using this time around. I truly don't think all of this matters much on the other side in the Creator's "garden of essence" which includes all souls.

This next little story reveals more about my friend Lucilla and myself in our encounter with a young tenor from Sicily. We were all acquainted with one another, since we studied with the same Maestro there in Milano, and often sang duets together.

Perhaps Lucilla and I were also secretly a little in love with our handsome friend, Roberto, although we certainly wouldn't have admitted it, at least not to one another!

"GHOSTLY" INTERVENTION

Roberto was a tenor, and tenors as everyone knows are a rare and unusual breed of singer. Roberto even had a scholarship with Maestro Montesanto, and it was a known fact that no soprano had ever been granted this boon by the Maestro!

Laura and I thought it very unfair of our teacher to show favoritism in that way, although we had to admit that Roberto did have a thrilling voice. After meeting him a few times in the Maestro's studio we were, along with all the other students, quite captivated by Roberto's charm, especially when we'd learned enough Italian to appreciate how funny he was.

Probably he considered himself the poor man's Caruso, because in a café, or "Tabaccaio," he was known to burst into song with practically no encouragement at all. Laura and I were horrified at first when he lapsed into the intimate "tu" form immediately with everyone, which in the best Italian was strictly taboo and only used by children or foreigners who didn't know how to speak correctly.

But how can you go on being formal with someone who's addressing you with the familiar pronoun "tu" so we slipped quite naturally into using it with Roberto, feeling very naughty and a little bold all the while! In fact, we became great friends almost overnight, although Roberto's intentions toward any pretty girl could never be entirely "friendly!"

It was possible in this instance only because his romantic attachment lay elsewhere in the bed of an over-sexed Signora whose husband made frequent business trips to Rome. Coming from Sicily Roberto was therefore a "terrone" or southerner. In Milano terrones were not thought of too highly and were considered a lazy, worthless lot, while in the south the northerners were called "polenta eaters," a somewhat derogatory expression. Polenta is cornmeal mush. So in spite of the fact that it had never been brought right out in the open and become common knowledge, there existed in Italy a situation verging on kind of a covert "civil war" between the "terrones" and the "polenta eaters!"

But back to Roberto. He was completely terrone, that is, he was lazy, handsome, charming, and possessed of a voracious appetite. Of course like all other terrones, he also had "sangue bolente." The literal translation of this is "boiling blood," which doesn't mean that Roberto had a worse temper than other people do, but that he was passionate and liked to make mad love to just about any female who would respond to him.

That, as we learned, was a very distinct "terrone" characteristic because as Roberto once said, "In Sicily even the dogs have "sangue bolente!" In spite of his torrid origins, however, Roberto was always "un cavaliere" as far as Laura and myself were concerned, calling himself our "papa" and saying he would defend us to the death.

Actually we thought he was so tremendously "simpatico" that now and then we invited him to our apartment for a good home-cooked meal, which Roberto ended up cooking, since he knew more about "home" cooking in Italy than we did! He finally grew bored with his own culinary creations and persuaded us to prepare some American "roba" for him. Roba means stuff.

After that we had a great time watching Roberto grow rhapsodic over a hamburger or southern fried chicken. One day we ran out of ideas and served him a kind of brunch of corn flakes and bananas, followed by pancakes with prosciutto and eggs on the side. Roberto said this was so superb it had never been equaled in all the annals of Italian cookery!

"Caspità, che buono: How good!" was his repeated comment between mouthfuls throughout the entire meal.

After a few weeks we got him to break down and do the dishes, taking turns with us each night, but not until he made us solemnly swear never to let anyone in his family know he'd actually washed dishes! It seems that in Sicily men who are real men don't do dishes, which is strictly woman's work.

We informed him that in our country men did not adhere to this silly idea, and neither did we. Roberto retorted that in Italy it was rumored American cooking was of the worst possible kind, prepared mostly from the contents of tin cans. However, he himself, would now correct this unfortunate impression among his countrymen by speaking out the truth about that.

He also made the magnanimous offer to contribute the sum which he ordinarily spent in "trattorias" for over-cooked spaghetti, etcetera, toward our food budget, therefore feeling free to dine with us at our apartment on a regular basis. It seemed like a perfectly splendid arrangement for us as well, since our Italian began improving dramatically right away. We soon learned, though, that a discreet censorship had to be applied regarding certain expressions Roberto used, such as "A chi se ne fregga?" Translated this means "Who gives a damn?" and was certainly not a very lady-like expression.

Now I wouldn't want to infer that an attack of acute appendicitis could be directly attributed to American cooking, but it was common knowledge that several weeks after Roberto began having dinner with us he was stricken with that precise ailment and rushed to the hospital for an operation!

Needless to say, we both felt a little guilty about that, so when Roberto's landlady stated quite emphatically that she couldn't be burdened with the responsibility for an invalid, what were we to do but take the poor "boy" in to stay with us, following his release from the hospital? Roberto's family lived a poverty stricken life far away in Sicily, and the Maestro showed a remarkable hardness of heart toward his students in matters not directly concerned with their musical education.

So when Roberto's doctor released him, Laura and I brought him home and made him comfortable on our daybed in the den. Roberto was profoundly grateful, declaring that he had the two prettiest nurses in the whole of Italy!

Laura and I both decided, however, that it would be best to keep this entire thing as secret as possible, since even in America such a "Good Samaritan" act might be frowned upon, and in post war Italy would create nothing short of a scandal. Therefore, it became a little alarming to both of us when Roberto's convalescence developed into a lengthy one, due the doctor said to a lazy incision that refused to heal.

Finally our "padrona" learned about it, and sent us a sharp letter in which she strongly expressed her disapproval of the situation, especially since she'd only recently decided not to increase our rent for the apartment.

But worst of all was the fact that Roberto's relationship with Laura was no longer "fatherly" but had become imbued with strong "terrone-sangue-bolente" feelings! Laura, quite fortunately for all concerned, did not reciprocate his affection. It must be stated here, in all fairness that Roberto remained "un cavaliere" to the end, and his "sangue bolente" was kept down to a mere simmer since he truly wanted to continue his friendship with both of us.

One Saturday when Laura and I had gone out together to do the marketing, we decided that recovered or not, Roberto would have to leave, since we certainly didn't want our rent increased.

Laura promised that she would speak to him later without fail, that very day. However, it always proves much more difficult to do a difficult thing than to talk about doing it, so Laura kept putting it off until finally Roberto went to bed, and she still hadn't found a way to tell him of our decision.

Then a very strange thing occurred. Laura said she'd always remember it because it happened at exactly twelve o'clock when everything became as still as a tomb in the apartment, and even the clock seemed to have stopped ticking. I was in bed with my eyes closed in that sort of peaceful limbo preceding sleep, while Laura sat at the dressing table brushing her hair a hundred strokes.

Although the door of our bedroom was kept closed, the large panel in the center was of frosted white glass that you could see hazy images through, and just at twelve o'clock precisely Laura glanced up to see a white figure passing by in the hall. She naturally thought this was Roberto on his way to the bathroom.

A moment later the figure passed again, but this time it paused, came up close to the door and peered in. Laura thought it wasn't very nice of Roberto to do something like that, and decided to tell him so. Then, as she later confided to me, it occurred to her that he might not be feeling well.

She opened the door, went out in the hallway and called, "Roberto, are you ill? Do you need anything?"

There was no response, so she knocked on the door of his room and raised her voice, "Roberto, are you all right?"

Roberto woke up and said in a sleepy voice, "Si, cara. Of course I'm all right! What do you want?"

"Didn't you get up just now and go to the bathroom?"

"Why no," he said, sounding puzzled. "That would be impossible you see, because I was sleeping quite soundly!"

"Then who could that have been?" Laura asked, puzzled also.

"Who could who, have been?" I said, roused out of my pre-sleep reverie by all the commotion.

"Well there must be someone else in this house!"

After Laura's ominous announcement we all went in a body to search through the kitchen, the bath, the dining room and even the closets. No one was there. The outside doors were locked, and the whole apartment was only in its customary disorder.

Then Laura made Roberto wait in our bedroom, along with myself while she showed us exactly what had happened. When she came up close to the glass and peered into the bedroom, it was so suggestive of a real "apparition" that Roberto turned white as a sheet, saying weakly, "Dio mio, che spavento! My God, what a fright!" We had discovered that he was very superstitious, with an absolute horror of anything supernatural.

Since I was also a very down-to-earth person in those days, I immediately concluded that Laura was making all of this up to get Roberto to move back to his own place, so I volunteered some help by saying, "Oh Laura's always seeing things like that!"

Roberto said, "Oh Dio!" again, clutching his incision. None of us got much sleep that night nor the next either, because at midnight we were all anticipating another visit from the "apparition!"

The following morning Roberto admitted that although he certainly didn't want Laura to feel he'd let a little thing like a ghost come between us, he had quite definitely decided it was time he returned to his own place.

As he pointed out, an atmosphere like this wasn't conducive to a speedy convalescence anyway, so the next day he moved back to his own room in a nearby pensione. We both rode with him in the taxi, and got his landlady to promise, a bit reluctantly I must admit to provide Roberto with hot meals for the next week or so until he was better.

At home again I said, laughing, "That was pretty clever of you, Laura, to pull that stunt about the ghost. I didn't know you were such a good actress. I have to tell you that you almost had me believing it was the real thing!"

Laura said, "Why do you think I'd make up something like that?"

"Well didn't you?" I asked.

"No, of course not!" Laura replied, with a horrified look on her face.

"Now wait a minute, Laura. You mean you really saw someone pass by in the hallway?"

"I sure did!" When Laura was serious about something, I noticed she always had a way of looking you straight in the eye with a little frown over her right eyebrow.

And now, even several minutes after she'd stopped talking, I saw her still staring at me with that strange look, and there was an unmistakable frown over her right eyebrow...

EPILOGUE: FORTY YEARS LATER

To the best of my knowledge, after my return to America, the character "Roberto" continued to study singing, but never attained any particular renown as a singer. Maybe that was the "terrone" side of his nature coming to the fore and he just didn't care to commit himself to all the hard work that singing opera requires. Perhaps he's still performing in "tabaccaios" somewhere, or even making a living singing lighter music of some kind.

As I stated previously, Lucilla enjoyed a distinguished operatic and concert career for many years, and in fact as one "fan" has expressed it, she became an operatic legend in Italy, where being a professional in that field is tremendously difficult for anyone. At the time we lived there, almost everyone was an opera "buff" and you couldn't get away with anything. If you were good they knew it, and if you weren't they knew that, too!

Without a "push" from Lucilla, introducing me to the books of Louis Untermeyer, I probably wouldn't have discovered whatever ability I had for writing until much later in life, if at all! But since everything happens as it's supposed to, I can't help feeling that meeting Lucilla and Louis Untermeyer later in New York was all part of my life's plan this time around.

Of course connecting with my husband-to-be on the same ship where I also met Lucilla, was one of the major objectives the hand of destiny extended to me. More than forty years later, I can also report that my marriage to Sal has been notably successful, and although he doesn't write, he has tremendous appreciation for my own work, whether in poetry or prose. Like I said, things happen pretty much as they're supposed to, with certain variables.

I recall having a dream when I was five years old in which I was told that when I grew up I'd become a writer and the author of several books. I do believe this was the "light of prophecy" moving inside my little five-year-old head! But what made me remember the dream so clearly after all this time I really can't say, nor can I explain why I approached my writing career by studying opera for fifteen years. That's another mystery.

However, since we seldom move immediately into a destined direction here in this life of failure and success in "schoolhouse" Earth, that shouldn't be surprising. If we knew how to go right into what we're supposed to do, we wouldn't be taking so long to complete what was projected by spirit to be only a short journey for the soul on this planet, and parlay it into such an extensive one that most of us have now become "prodigal sons."

It would appear that directness, like complete honesty with oneself is a very rare attainment! And speaking of honesty, the account of Roberto's appendix operation was fictionalized somewhat for the foregoing story, since it was actually performed in the doctor's office instead of at the hospital, and without anesthesia, except perhaps a local injection of some kind.

Roberto's finances wouldn't have been adequate for a hospital stay, so he opted to have the surgery on an outpatient basis, accounting for the urgent need of home care. When he later informed us of the horrors he'd gone through during surgery, we found his story almost unbelievable in this age of enlightened surgical practice. He said the pain was so intense when the doctor made the incision into his abdomen and began probing for the appendix, only the tortures in a Nazi prison camp could be at all compared to it.

"I was screaming for God, for my mother, and even for the devil himself to come and get me out of there!" he confessed.

As far as we could tell, this experience was not only debilitating physically for a normally robust man, but it also delivered a tremendous psychological blow, which required several weeks for Roberto to recover from. It's easy to see why pain has become such a "Great Teacher" in spiritual annals, since it often elevates the frequency of the human vehicle to a much higher level. This might be the reason many of those now recognized as Saints, were so willing to endure all kinds of painful experience, from death in the Colosseum to a variety of horrible tortures in the centuries following the crucifixion.

Personally I believe pleasure is an even greater teacher than pain, because no one really wants pain, but for the bulk of humanity holding onto pleasure occupies the number one position of importance! We seldom see that pain and pleasure are like a two-headed goat: what one of them eats nourishes the other! Here I'm not saying it's necessary for anyone to give up pleasure, but only to see the truth that pain becomes the inevitable result of having experienced pleasure…

This next story tells about another adventure with "Laura."

"PASQUALE"

It was my turn to sit down. I'd shifted my weight from the right foot to the left for about the hundredth time before Laura looked up from the postcard she was writing to her sister and said, "I'll be finished in a minute, honey, and then you can sit down.

"Isn't this heat awful?" she complained a few minutes later, running her sweating palm down the skirt of her wine-colored cotton sundress. "My fingers are perspiring so much the pen keeps slipping around and I make all kinds of mistakes!"

"There's a cool breeze now and then off the water," I said, encouragingly as I looked out at the blue Mediterranean surging around the boat. A few moments later I overheard someone say we should arrive at Ischia in another half hour, and I couldn't help exclaiming aloud, "Grazie a Dio! Thank God!"

For the past hour and a half, the sweaty intimacy of the little passenger boat hadn't been especially pleasant, and particularly coming right on the heels of that exhausting train ride from Milano to Naples.

On the train I'd said to Laura, "These European trains may look romantic in a Hitchcock movie, but this is unbelievable! I thought our apartment in Milano was hot, but this darn train has it beat a mile!"

I couldn't help recalling how jubilant we were when our singing teacher, Maestro Montesanto, had informed us that he'd be vacationing on the Island of Ischia for the entire months of July and August, and that any students who wished to continue their training with him would be welcome to join him there for the summer. Well, any students who could afford to spend that much money were free to accompany him!

Laura and I had carefully calculated our finances and decided we'd be two of those making the trip, although as Laura pointed out, "We certainly can't afford to pay those prices at the 'Villa Martinelli' where the Maestro's staying!" So we decided to wait until we got to the Island and then find out if there was a pensione nearby where we could get a room and meals.

After we'd boarded the boat from Naples to Ischia, a handsome young Neapolitan who said his name was "Pasquale" got up and offered his seat to Laura. During our conversation we learned that he lived in "Casamicciola," just where we were headed. He promised to return before we docked and help us with our luggage.

After a few moments, Laura screwed the top back on her fountain pen, sighed and said, "There, that's finished. Now, honey, you can sit down."

I dropped gratefully onto the hard wooden bench, and started staring at the people around us. Just then Laura spotted "Pasquale" in the crowd. "Oh look," she said, "here comes Pasquale!"

At the moment our new friend was "molto occupato," very busy slithering adroitly in and out among the passengers, stepping over numerous pieces of luggage. Now and then he shouted importantly, "Attenzione, attention!" to boisterous children who threatened the safety of three bottles of Coke he was securely clutching. As he came up to us he smiled quite ingratiatingly, showing his amazing white teeth, and the twinkle in those astounding blue eyes, their color borrowed from the sea swirling around the boat. It's said that Neapolitan men are the handsomest in the world, and I could find no argument with that!

Pasquale called out, "Ah, signorine, eccomi! You like Coca cola?" he asked, extending a familiar green bottle first to Laura, and then to myself.

"Oh yes," we both chorused thirstily, accepting his offer, which was better than roses on such a hot, sticky day!

Laura gave him one of her nicest "principessa" smiles bestowed on her adoring public, but usually reserved for people of importance. "How nice of you to do this, Pasquale!"

Pasquale swept off his grimy, once white yachting cap in acknowledgment, and replied in English, "Iz good, hah?"

Laura asked, still maintaining her coy mood, "We'll be arriving at Ischia soon, won't we Pasquale?"

He replied in his picturesque English, "Ah si, Porto d'Ischia coming up veree soon. Dopo, Casamicciola."

I asked, "By the way, Pasquale, do you know of a good pensione there which isn't too expensive? We're students of opera and not tourists you know, so we can't afford to pay too much, since we expect to be on Ischia for a couple of months and have lessons with our teacher several times a week."

Pasquale got the idea right away. "How much you 'tink you can pay?" he asked, his forehead wrinkling with a business-like squint.

"About mille lire a day," I said. "At most fifteen hundred: for room and board that is. It sure would be nice," I added, "if we could live somewhere near the 'Villa Martinelli' where our Maestro will be staying. He's scheduled to arrive in a few days and we'd like to find a place and get settled before he comes."

Pasquale thought deeply for a moment. "Um-m-m, vediamo up po, joosta minuto," he said, giving the impression he was thoroughly unaccustomed to such strenuous activity, but that for us no sacrifice was too great.

"Uno momento," he said, rubbing his chin thoughtfully. "Ah si, yes, I 'tink there iz one. But we see." He patted the empty bulge of his Coke bottle reassuringly. "You joosta leave ev'ryting to Pasquale: I feex for you!"

When we arrived at "Casamicciola," one of several communities on the Island, Pasquale went with us to extract our numerous suitcases from the hodge-podge in the storage compartment. He surveyed the six pieces of luggage, tilted his cap to scratch his head, then announced in a loud voice, "Lotsa valige! You wait here, I go find un facchino, how you say 'porter'?"

Ten minutes later he was back with a young man dressed in faded blue denims, and together they struggled down the pier to the dusty walk in front of the exchange office. I paid the porter, who looked significantly at Pasquale, then left to find someone to watch the suitcases while we went to look at the pensione.

At the time Pasquale forgot to mention the fact, which we learned later, that the "porter" was his uncle, and the young boy he got to watch over the luggage was his younger brother, who somehow always seemed to show up at just the right time!

"Is it far to the pensione?" I asked, looking tiredly up the dusty hillside, where the road wound steeply upward.

"Ah, no, signorina, due passi only!" he said lightly.

As we continued walking, for what seemed half an hour, I began seriously questioning the marvelous Italian gift for exaggeration, wondering what kind of Gargantuan yardstick Pasquale had used to come up with those "due passi" of his, obviously more than two of my steps. Now and then a carriage clattered by on the powdery white road, covering everything with a shower of fine white dust.

Finally we arrived at a villa protected by an impressive wrought-iron gate, and Pasquale "alloed" for the Padrona. As we waited I looked back down the steep hillside, and asked Pasquale, "Are you sure this is close to the 'Villa Martinelli'?"

"Ah si," he replied confidently. "Veree close: sono sicurissimo!" Just then a barefoot maid pattered down to the gate and let us in. As we made our way up the shaded brick-laid walk winding through the garden, we couldn't help showing our surprise and pleasure at the possibility of remaining there for two months.

"Oh, Pasquale, it's a dream!" Laura said ecstatically.

"But doesn't it cost a lot to stay here?" I asked somewhat anxiously.

"You no worry, I feex for you," he said cryptically.

The Signora, obviously the owner of the villa, emerged and stated with freshly ironed silk-shantung finality that her rates were twenty-five hundred lire per person, per day. I looked at Laura dismayed: it was definitely too much.

Pasquale saw that look and concluded the time was ripe to move in on the seemingly immovable Signora. One by one he extracted from his Neapolitan peddler's pack of persuasion, each little charm he possessed.

"You see, Signora," he said, lowering his voice and moving confidentially closer to her, "these signorine are not touristi, but only studenti. And studenti cannot spend so much money like the rich touristi. It is veree hard for them to pay for ev'ryting when the lessons cost so much, too. Especially studenti like these young signorine who are not rich at all!"

He concluded with a dramatic gesture of appeal toward our silent expectant faces staring at the Signora, who was now looking hard at us! She must have been remembering the days when she'd dreamed of becoming a concert pianist, which we learned about later, because she smiled kindly and invited us to come in.

Then she showed us into a cool, green-shuttered room that was obviously not too popular with the "touristi" because one of the twin beds dipped to a depressing hollow right in the middle, and the padrona confessed that it would also be necessary to walk down the terrace, and through the back garden to get to the bath, which was located just outside the kitchen.

So due to these only minor inconveniences which calloused tourists weren't prone to tolerate, she agreed to let us stay for fifteen hundred lire per day each, and this would include all of our meals as well! So suddenly it was all settled and we were almost delirious with joy, which we however decided it was best to conceal for fear the Signora would begin feeling she'd made a mistake in letting us stay for so little!

Shortly after this I returned to the "piazza" below with Pasquale to pick up our suitcases, where the faithful youngster was still on guard, seated with stoic nonchalance on the largest suitcase and making sporadic efforts to pick up a pebble with his bare toes while he waited. His long thin legs looked so ridiculous in those tight short pants, and he was altogether so appealing, a little like Pasquale I thought, that I gave him five hundred lire.

"After all," I reasoned to myself, "what's five hundred lire when we're going to stay at that fabulous villa for fifteen hundred lire a day, meals included!"

Pasquale had disappeared to call a "carozza." The driver as we learned later was his cousin, Antonio, and after much shifting and shuffling, the suitcases were all tucked safely in the back seat with me beside them. Pasquale climbed up front with the driver, and we started the long climb back up to the villa, which was especially hard for the poor horse. The driver urged him on with the intermittent stimulation of his whip, calling out occasionally a cheerful, "Coraggio, coraggio!" to the straining rump. At the steepest point in the road Pasquale leapt nimbly out and walked the rest of the distance. When we arrived at the villa, I felt so sorry for the valiant horse that I gave the driver eight hundred lire when I'd agreed to pay only five.

Pasquale said, with a happy flourish toward the perspiring driver, "Any time you want carriage, signorina, you joosta look for Antonio! I know him long time now, and he take good care of you."

"He make good price for you, too," Pasquale concluded with a wink towards Antonio.

Pasquale brought the suitcases up to our room, while Laura and I tried to decide how much to tip him. Pasquale had really been wonderful to do all of this, so we decided to give him a thousand lire from each of us. Pasquale beamed the biggest "grazie" anyone ever saw and said that any time the "belle signorine" needed a friend just to look for him in the piazza.

"Arrivederci, arrivederci!" he called jubilantly as he disappeared down the garden path. As he went out the gate we heard him whistling the tenor aria from the first act of "La Bohème." We'd discovered that in Italy people knew arias and solos from operas like we do popular tunes here in America.

A few days later we were lounging luxuriously like idle rich tourists in canvas chairs on the terrace, waiting for "cena" to be served. The sun had disappeared over Mount Epomeo, and a cool evening breeze had come in from the sea, bending the white heads of the daisies all one way in rhythmic genuflections, like nuns saying vespers.

The villa was built on a foothill of "Mount Epomeo," and the view was truly magnificent. You could sit for hours under the big Pine tree, looking far away into endless waves of blue that seemed to wash over into the sky. All around, tumbling down the hillside were villas and little farms half hidden among orange and fig trees, with precise rows of grape vines planted in between them.

Laura was ecstatically sipping up the view like a cocktail. "Oh honey," she exulted, "I still can't believe that we could be so lucky!"

Just then the padrona walked past with her big police dog, Arno, and gave us an aloof little nod.

After she'd disappeared toward the back of the villa, Laura giggled, "I guess she's still pretty sore about how it all worked out!"

I agreed laughing. "When she found out we were students of Maestro Montesanto she was fit to be tied! She said that since the Maestro would be living here, too, and by the way he'll be arriving tomorrow, she says he would have brought us here to stay anyway! And she's furious with Pasquale because he tricked her, and then made her pay him for bringing us here!"

"That Pasquale sure is a sly devil!" Laura said. "He knew all along that this was the 'Villa Martinelli' where our Maestro would be staying and he didn't say one word about it!"

Then we both got into a "little-girl" fit of giggling about how it had all turned out. "And he did all right for himself, too! Collecting two thousand lire from us, then five thousand from the Signora: over ten dollars in all. Not bad for an hour's work here in Italy!"

We were still chuckling about all of this when the maid came to call us to dinner...

Personally, though, I'll never forget our handsome and charming Pasquale, with a smile like a cavalier, who had appeared right out of the blue to solve all our problems!

And I'll always remember his extraordinarily beautiful eyes filled with the color of the blue Mediterranean pulsing around the Island far below us each day and all through the night as well, having like a lover a most intimate knowledge of every curving line along the shores it caresses...

EPILOGUE: FORTY YEARS LATER

After Sal and I left the "Island of Ischia" at the end of August, I never saw the "Villa Martinelli" nor Pasquale again except in memory, like so many of the passing scenes in life where as spiritual teachers say, the only reality is the moment of their occurrence. I sometimes wonder, though, if the soul doesn't retain segments of life for its own reality in some private sector of our inner universe where it is possible to visit that "secret garden of our hearts" and relive again some special moment of enchantment whenever we tap into that particular frequency again.

A great scientist of recent times named Einstein, presented something like I'm talking about here in his theory of relativity in which space and time are not absolute, but relative to the observer. So perhaps you along with myself can see the distinct possibility of contacting that "secret garden of the heart" once more, especially when I recall some tremendously joyous experience, and immerse myself in that.

Who can say how many of these timeless moments lie concealed within each soul? Moving backward and forward in Time, grouped together in a kind of "holographic" image, we divide them into the past, the present and the future. Many sages say that when true Reality or the "NOW" reveals itself in our awareness, all three of these divisions disappear and become ONE.

I've read nothing which would indicate that the essence of it disappears, but only that all sense of separation from it is gone! Could this be related to what followers of "zen" define as "satori?" I can definitely see the possibility of that which might account for the effect certain experiences have on us.

I wonder if you've ever been completely absorbed as I often have in watching the movement of the wind blowing over a field of grass, or through the leaves of a tree anywhere, imbued with its own special sentience beyond the power of words to describe? I think poets are especially keyed into this wordless expression concealed in the wind's movement.

I recall reading somewhere in the Bible about the Holy Spirit being like a mighty rushing wind, and I feel sure this is very useful for the purpose of Divine revelation. For writing poetry, though, I prefer gentle breezes blowing, since for me this awakens the song of the soul. I think what I'm talking about now is like the difference between love and lust. For lust anything that can produce orgasm serves its purpose, but for love the experience of the love itself is all that matters and bliss will be present with or without orgasm. Who knows, you might even come up with a poem!

But I already said that in the opening chapter of this book, didn't I! I still feel that it's good to tap into the soul essence, since inside everyone a poet waits to be born. I do believe "he" or "she" is always hiding out in that same intangible essence hoping to reveal the words to express something wordless.

Now and then people get in touch with some former lifetime here on Earth and recall it quite clearly, which leads me to believe that whatever exists in those invisible dimensions remains as part of the "hologram" of our own multi-dimensional awareness, and is still very much alive, separated only by our inability to bring it into conscious focus.

You may wonder what might be accomplished by that. Actually I wasn't thinking about remembering past lives right now, even though I can see the advantage of using such knowledge to resolve something in our present life which might be blocking further development. The late Edgar Cayce did a lot along this line in readings done with many people, and they've been pretty well documented.

What I'm thinking about are soul memories from the past filled with something joyous and ecstatic that live forever in our hearts. I've often wondered how seeing the wind blowing through earthly trees is related to the soul's experience of that on celestial planes, remembered now like a dream is, if remembered at all. Perhaps the essence of that wind blowing through heavenly trees, has its own mysterious connection to something ecstatic here, ultimately transformed into a higher frequency of itself there.

Somehow merging my consciousness with the movement of the wind helps me understand how these different planes of awareness are all united by ONE essence of the soul present on each of them...

This next story reveals another "lesson" Lucilla and I learned that first year in Milano. Actually we shared a lot of lessons like this during the months we were together there, and they weren't all connected to learning to sing...

"OVERCHARGE"

At eight o'clock the portanaia rang the doorbell. "That's probably Angela with the 'Corriere della Sera' and the mail," I thought, as I lurched sleepily toward the door, opened it and peered cautiously through the chained slit.

"Buon giorno, Signorina," Angela said. "Ce la posta. Here's the mail." Angela had the alert look of someone who'd been up for hours already.

"Ah si grazie tante, thank you very much," I said, pleasantly enough, but wondering why she didn't just leave the mail under the door without waking everyone up! Myself in this case, since Laura was still sleeping soundly. I tossed the newspaper with a disgruntled flourish on top of the piano.

My perusal of the mail proved more diverting. There was a letter from home with a five dollar bill tucked inside a piece of carbon paper. I laughed to myself. "Leave it to my Pop to find a way to outwit those mail thieves!"

There was also a bulging thirty-cent airmail letter for Laura from her sister, along with the gas and light bill. I opened it and applied my own system of dollar conversion to the Italian lire, and said aloud to myself, since Laura still hadn't gotten up, "Good heavens, the charge is way too much for this month: over three thousand lire!"

Surely this was sufficient justification for waking Laura! Anyway she had a lesson at eleven and the Maestro wasn't very sympathetic about morning "frogs" in the throat, especially when they were due to the fact that a student had just gotten out of bed and rushed over to the studio without doing enough vocal exercises to warm up the voice.

So to begin the process of waking Laura, I let my new wooden-soled zocoletti "bang" loosely on the marble floor of the hallway, making a tremendous racket. Giving the door of the bedroom a resounding knock, I called, "Lau-oo-ra, want some coffee?"

She replied in a sleepy voice, "Uh-huh, honey, I'll be there in a minute!"

I clattered out to the kitchen where I extracted the grinder from the usual clutter in the cupboard, and filled it with black espresso coffee beans we'd grown to love. I set the tea kettle to boil, then scurried outside into the cold November fog to fetch the bottle of milk from the balcony.

Never in all my life had I appreciated the glory and wonder of an ordinary refrigerator so much as while we were living in Italy and didn't have one! Besides, a person could easily get pneumonia running out in the cold wearing only a thin nylon nightie and sometimes a robe.

As I put the pan of milk on the burner, I thought to myself, "Now when that thing boils over, I can make our café-latte!" I'd discovered that Italian milk had the most amazing propensity to boil over before it ever boiled at all! I sat down with the coffee grinder tucked between my knees, and began the crunchy ritual of grinding the coffee beans. Above the snapping sound of the grinder I whooped out again, "Lau-oo-ra!" who just then pattered into the kitchen. Arranging herself on the high-backed blue chair at the table, she tilted it precariously backward against the wall, then yawned and asked in the middle of it, "Any mail, honey?"

"Uh-huh," I said, clattering off to the den, returning with the mail and the paper.

"Oh goody," Laura said, eagerly opening the envelop from home. "Maybe there's a check in it!"

There wasn't, but that reminded me of our finances. "The light and gas bill came, and it's over three thousand lire!"

"Three thousand lire!" Laura exploded. "We couldn't possibly have used so much. That's ridiculous!" She tilted angrily back in her chair again. "It wouldn't surprise me if the company found out that we're Americans and 'upped' the rates on us just like everyone else does!"

I was busy pouring the fragrant, freshly ground coffee into the top portion of the little "machinetta." Then I screwed on the lid and placed it on top of the lower part of the pot. After filling the top with boiling water, I set the pot on the back of the stove to drip. I'd become quite proficient with that chore.

"I sure think it's awful the way these Italians take advantage of Americans. They all think we're filthy rich!" I said.

I started setting the table for breakfast. "Now take this apartment of ours, Laura. There's nothing extraordinary about it and yet we have to pay a hundred dollars a month rent. Do you think an Italian would be paying that much?" I asked.

"No!" Laura agreed in a loud voice.

Encouraged in my tirade, I went on. "Everyone says that Signora Leone is charging us an exorbitant amount for this apartment and that we should complain about it. Maybe she'd lower the rent."

"I think we should, too. That strega!" Laura said venomously. Strega means "witch" in Italian and one of them must have come by to visit right then because the milk suddenly boiled up in a big balloon, spilling all over the stove.

"Oh darn," I said, leaping up to turn off the gas.

Laura continued our morning tirade, as she set out the sweet rolls and butter. "I'm certain, too, that in the stores they charge us more for everything! When they think they can get away with it, that is!" she added. Laura was a pretty good shopper, and could haggle with the best of them.

"Remember the other day in the 'drogheria' when that clerk tried to charge us ten lire more for the soap?" I reminded her. "Of course he might have made a mistake, but I don't think so!"

At this point I filled the oversize coffee cups half full of steaming hot black coffee, adding the boiled milk until they threatened to overflow, and then sat down. Laura stirred three heaping teaspoons of sugar into her cup, and spread a roll with a huge pat of butter.

I thought to myself, "No wonder she's gaining weight!" but decided not to make any comment about that, considering how bad we already felt. Nobody wants to be reminded about their weight, anyhow, especially when they've gained.

Laura said in between voracious bites of her roll, "I just love this café-latte don't you, honey?"

"I sure do," I said, but without much enthusiasm. "I wanted to get my hair done today, but I don't think I'll go back to Anna. She overcharged me last time, remember? Signora Leone told me that the bill should be around seven hundred lire, but Anna charged me a thousand!"

"And speaking of overcharging," Laura said, "I forgot to tell you that after my lesson on Friday, I was talking to that new American tenor, Frank Richards, who lives at the 'Casa Albergo' and he told me he had heard that our Maestro doesn't charge everyone the same price for lessons. The American students pay him twice as much as the Italians do!"

"He also said that Roberto, that tenor from Sicily doesn't pay anything for his lessons, since he has a scholarship with the Maestro! Can you believe that?"

I exploded quietly, "I think it's mean of the Maestro to show favoritism like that, especially when a lot of his students are having a hard time paying him for their lessons!"

"That's the truth!" Laura jumped up, banging her knee on the table, and almost falling off her chair. "The Maestro!" she exclaimed. Good grief, we've been talking for hours and it's almost time for my lesson! And I'm not even dressed yet!"

In a few minutes she came out of her room and declared in a loud voice, "And what's more I don't even feel like singing this morning either"…

A few weeks later in January, Laura got a terrible cold and then a pain in her chest. I became so worried about her that I called the doctor

Signora Leone had recommended to us. Dottore Lombardi was a paunchy little man about fifty with grayish hair, and an unattractive but kindly face. After he'd examined Laura thoroughly, he said she had pneumonia and prescribed injections of penicillin, along with ter-ramycin tablets. He informed us that the drugs would be expensive, and that we'd have to pay a nurse to come in and give her the injections of penicillin twice a day.

Although Laura's eyes opened wide, she didn't even inquire how much all of that would cost. Dottore Lombardi knew how it was with students, though, and he asked. "Come va il denaro? How are your finances? If you need money," he said, "I could loan you ten thousand lire today and more later if you need it."

"Oh, no, no thank you, Dottore!" Laura said quickly. "We can manage"...

During the following weeks the doctor came almost every day or so to see Laura, and she slowly recovered. One day she asked, "Dottore, we've been expecting you to send us your bill. I don't know how much it will be, but we've saved fifteen thousand lire to pay part of my account with you."

Dottore Lombardi touched Laura's arm lightly, looking for the illusive vein to take the blood test he wanted. He found it and deftly inserted the needle.

"Now tell me, he said if you begin to feel dizzy, and we'll go a little slower." When he'd finished drawing the blood, he removed the needle with a quick tug, placed a piece of alcohol-soaked cotton on it, and bent Laura's arm so it wouldn't bleed. "Now keep your finger pressed tightly over it."

After a moment of silence he said, "Last week my wife and I saw an American film in which that actress, Ginger Rogers, was preparing a special kind of sandwich. We'd like very much to try some American food like that."

"You can try it right here!" I said. "As soon as Laura's better we'll be delighted to have you both as our guests. But what was the name of that sandwich, Dottore: do you remember?"

For a moment his mind traveled back to the movie they'd seen. "I think it was," and he probed his memory for the strange word, "I think it was 'Hahm—boorg—oors'!"

We all laughed at his funny pronunciation of the familiar American sandwich, and Laura told him, "We'll fix you the best hamburgers we've ever cooked in our whole lives. You'll never find their equal again in all of Italy!"

Suddenly the doctor picked up his case, looked at his watch, and exclaimed: "Oh Dio, I'll be late at the hospital! And now, about your bill."

Laura and I both grew noticeably tense, wondering how in the world we were going to get enough money together to pay the good doctor for all the house calls he'd made.

"Some weeks ago," Dottore Lombardi said, "I discussed this with my wife, and we decided not to charge you for my services. Things are going well for us now and we can afford to forget about this one!" he added, looking at the dumbfounded look on our faces with the sweetest smile, and a very knowing twinkle in his eyes...

EPILOGUE: FORTY YEARS LATER

There's a saying in Italy which I've grown to love: "Tutto il mondo e un paese!" Paese means village, but translated with a broader, more expanded meaning it becomes, "The whole world is one country!" As I continue with my inner investigation, more and more of the hidden truth in these words is revealed to me.

Throughout this world so filled with conflict and separation, what is actually ONE? In their suffering, and in their pain people are one, since suffering speaks no tongue yet every language, and at one time or another we've all known joy, making the world ONE in that as well. So suffering and joy create both sides of the coin of life, which we must all experience until we learn to truly love one another as human beings.

In those invisible realms, love is the "oneness" that speaks the language of the heart, and when we learn this language we'll find it's the only one which can make the whole world ONE country in spirit. In post-war Italy we saw both suffering and immense joy in the hearts of the people. Each day in early morning I recall listening to horse-drawn vehicles rumbling by, loaded with fresh fruit and vegetables for delivery to the little local markets. What haunts my memory is how the drivers of these carts would be singing some popular "canzone," or even a favorite aria from an opera, a sound that will remain forever in my heart.

Music springs from the very soul anywhere people are singing in this world, and whether inspired by sorrow or joy, both rise from the depths of the heart, making the world one in its listening also. Now and then on a frosty night we'd wake up, hearing in the distance the strains of music rising all the way up to our seventh floor apartment from a

"Tabaccaio" on Via degli Scipione, the street where we lived. Of course these were the voices of men who were inebriated, but thoroughly enjoying themselves singing various popular "canzoni" or now and then some ensemble from an opera.

Perhaps the Italian language, filled with so many open vowel sounds, accounts for the beauty of their singing, quite remarkable if you happened to be awake and listening in the night. It's said that there are more naturally beautiful voices in Italy than anywhere else in the world. This would indicate, to me anyway, since I lived there for almost two years, that the soul of Italy is still alive and well...

Although Lucilla and I would spend an occasional morning bitching about finances, as in the foregoing story, we were both open to the lesson "Dottore Lombardi" clearly demonstrated to us. Knowing him softened our hearts, and we started looking on our surroundings with a fresh view, and a whole new feeling.

After spending more than forty years of investigation into the inner levels of my own awareness, I've discovered that life is truly the best teacher of itself. I've also found that Mother Nature is the first and last "Great Teacher" on this planet and when we learn to listen to her, she speaks directly to our hearts...

DEATH ON ISCHIA

Laura and I had both decided over a year ago in America to continue our study of opera in Italy, which as you may know has been the Mecca for students of singing for decades. My decision was made in Hollywood, and Laura had been more or less pushed into hers by friends on the east coast while performing on Broadway.

In America we'd been fascinated by recordings of many great singers from the past. Laura was drawn to the famous diva, Rosa Ponsel, which her own voice resembled in many ways, while I doted on singers with lighter voices: Galli Curci, and Rosa del Monte, a soprano who was once famous in Italy.

Strangely enough the teacher Laura and I both ultimately studied with in Milano, had decided to vacation on the "Island of Ischia" that first summer, devoting part of his time to teaching students who wished to accompany him there and continue their lessons for the months of July and August. We found this prospect tremendously exciting, since Ischia is famed for its breathtaking scenic beauty as well as renowned for its natural mineral and mud baths, boasting each year a number of seemingly miraculous cures by many suffering from rheumatism, arthritis and other related ailments. Hundreds of pain-ridden people find relief in its layers of oozing grey mud and hot mineral baths, said to be radio-active also. After a few weeks of treatment many literally "take up their beds and walk"…

One day in August we returned to the villa, after having lunch in town with friends from Naples, to find a new resident had just arrived from Milano. Her name was "Signora Dellapina" and she'd come presumably to take the "cure." She was without doubt, as we both agreed, the dearest little old lady we'd ever met anywhere. At first she seemed so frail and quiet in her manner you almost forgot she was there.

Her quietness, though, was something like that of a flame. Each time she made the climb up the sloping walk leading to the villa, she would lean breathlessly on her cane, her thin lips writhing from the pain in her legs. The baths really did wonders for her circulation, though, and after a couple of weeks she didn't even have to use her cane any more.

She would call in greeting, "Buon giorno!" as brightly as a child, stopping to talk to us for a few moments where we sat studying under the huge Pine tree in the garden. She grew quite fond of us and expressed a desire to hear us sing.

One day as we watched her walk proudly, with a glowing smile up the steps to the villa, Laura said, "Poor thing, I suppose our lives must seem very glamorous to her, since we're from America and all that!"

"Uh-huh," I agreed, closing my score of Rigoletto. "I wonder what her husband's like? Funny he'd let her go off alone to stay on the Island."

"Oh, he was probably too busy to come with her. She says he's a big attorney in Milano." Laura closed her score of Tosca, also, and we both gazed dreamily down at the blue shimmer of the Mediterranean, where a passenger boat from Naples sketched a deep arc in the water as it maneuvered to pull into the harbor. A hot breeze moved with desultory whispers through the Pine tree, sending a few pungent dry needles raining down on top of our heads and into our laps.

Suddenly Laura asked, "Honey, did you ever notice the look on the Signora's face when she talks about her husband? Her eyes just glow when she says his name, and her smile is sweet as an angel's. When she says 'Luciano' it's sort of like her lips kissed each vowel."

"Oh yes," I said, wishing Laura would be quiet so I could take a nap. "You can see she's crazy about him."

That evening at dinner Signora Dellapina was in rare good spirits. She confided to Laura, "You know, when I was a girl about your age I studied singing, too. Oh, I thought my career was everything until I met

Luciano!" On her lips the "EE" met the "AH" and caressed it, just as Laura had pointed out.

"After our marriage he didn't want me to go on with my career any more so I gave it up." She made that appalling confession with the blissful smile of someone who had just exchanged a ten-cent trinket for a pearl the size of a baseball.

The Signora continued speaking, the same happy lilt in her voice. "I haven't touched the piano for months, but tonight I'd like to play and have you girls sing for me! Would you?" she asked, a little shyly.

Of course we said yes, so that evening, after dinner, which was really "supper" at the villa, she played for us on the old relic of a piano in the drawing room and we sang for her. While I was singing "Caro Nome," Laura told me later that the Signora's lips were silently following the words. When I finished singing, she said, "Brava!" and meant it.

After Laura had sung something from "Tosca," she was also praised lavishly, and we all went outside to sit in the little pergola in the garden. It had gotten so hot and stuffy inside the villa, making the Signora strangely out of breath.

Now and then the wind passed through the climbing ivy sounding like a taffeta skirt going by, while down below the villa, the powdery white ribbon of the road spun far away in the moonlight, soft as the echo of a muted violin...

The Signora started talking first. "Both of you girls have lovely voices, as so many young singers do." She was silent for a moment listening to the flowing tide of laughter and revelry drifting up from the piazza far below. "But," and here she hesitated for a moment, "you're not yet in love with singing: you're only infatuated with it!"

She patted Laura's hand with a kindly gesture. "You must fall in love with singing, like I love Luciano." Her breath again became like a kiss as she spoke his name.

"For a love like that," and here she repeated her words with slow emphasis, "for a love like that, no sacrifice is too great, and no disillusionment too hard to bear. Each sacrifice will be like closing a door to be alone with your 'Beloved' and any disillusionment a window opening into the depths of your heart."

Hardly breathing, we waited for her to go on speaking, while the wind stirred the ivy again and a lemon fell with a thud like a drumbeat in a nearby grove. "But now, my dear ones, it's long past my bedtime," she said, standing up to leave, seeming only a shadow in the moonlight as we walked silently up the steps to the villa. Before entering, she turned to us.

"Thank you both for singing tonight: it was truly a great pleasure for me. Buona notte!"

"Buona notte, good night," we chorused in the darkness that had fallen around the villa, now lit only by the moon.

Later in our own room, we lay listening to the rhythmic chirping of the crickets through the open shutters. "Funny," Laura said, "how they seem to pick up the rhythm of any melody you might have in your mind as you listen."

"I've noticed that, too. You know, Laura, I've been thinking about what the Signora said. Maybe she really gave up her career because her voice wasn't good enough. That happens to a lot of singers doesn't it?"

"I suppose," Laura agreed. "Or maybe," she said thoughtfully, "she was just too much in love with her Luciano to be in love with singing any more, the way she said we have to be"... Her voice trailed off.

"What do you think about that, Laura? I mean what she said tonight about being in love with singing?"

"I think...Oh it was so beautiful the way she said it that I wanted to cry!"

"Me, too." I said, falling silent. There was just something so poignant about the Signora, something fragile as an angel's wings floating by in the dusk and touching each heart as they passed...

The next day some American friends of Laura's came over from Capri and we were kept busy showing them around Ischia. During that time we didn't see much of the Signora, except at "colazione" before we left. She seemed unusually quiet and pale. In answer to Laura's inquiry about her health, she said she hadn't been feeling very well and the doctor had advised postponement of the baths until she was better.

The next morning the maid, Norina, told us the Signora had been taken ill in the night and the doctor would be coming to see her that afternoon. Laura said right away, "Honey, let's go up and talk to her. Maybe there's something we can do for her."

When we tiptoed into her darkened room, the Signora was pleased as a child to see us, and we smiled, too, just to show her that we thought she looked fine, although the change in her appearance was shocking! Her skin had taken on an alarming pallor, and her eyes looked strange, too, like windows at night when the lights have been turned out.

After a few minutes, the Signora told Laura her feet were freezing, and that a hot water bottle would be wonderful.

I said immediately, "I'll go down and get mine for you right away, Signora." Laura volunteered to stay for a while and read something in her best Italian, which was pretty good if I do say so! The Signora was so pleased with this that Laura spent every available moment after that at her bedside. A couple of days later it became apparent that the Signora was critically ill with a serious heart condition, and the padrona of the villa decided to send a wire to the Signora's husband in Milano right away.

The following day at dinner, Laura had just come down from the Signora's room and said anxiously, "She just seems to be getting worse all the time. It's terrible to see her suffer so!"

"Can't that old fogy of a doctor do something for her?" I asked, somewhat indignant and frustrated by the whole thing.

"I suppose he's doing all he can, giving her some kind of injections for her circulation and her heart." Laura had been peeling a plump green fig still warm from the sun. They were so plentiful on the island we enjoyed them with almost every meal. I knew Laura loved them, but now she put it down untouched.

"Oh honey," she said almost in tears, "she keeps asking for Luciano. Why doesn't that darn man get here!"

Later that night, about three in the morning, Laura came into our room and woke me. She was crying and saying over and over again, "Oh, the poor little thing."

I must confess that I was a little annoyed with being awakened from a pleasant dream. I'd discovered that sometimes Laura was a little too emotional for my nature, but in spite of all that I put my arms around her as she lay on the bed, and attempted to soothe my sobbing friend. After a few minutes she decided to tell me about what had happened.

"Oh honey, it was awful. Her husband didn't get here in time, and I just couldn't leave her. I was frightened out of my wits, but I simply couldn't go. She held my hand and begged to see Luciano. When she got a little delirious at the end, she thought I was Luciano."

Laura started sobbing again. "Oh God, she loved that man more than anything in this world, and he didn't come. Now she's dead!"

Later that afternoon Signore Dellapina arrived. He was stunned and seemingly stricken with grief, but we concluded that as far as we were concerned he was really quite ordinary. In fact we found it difficult to understand why the Signora had loved him so much! He decided that the funeral and burial Mass would take place right there on the Island the next day.

In Italy there were no morticians then and the body was usually prepared for burial by the family and friends of the deceased. In this case the maid, Norina, and the padrona of the villa performed this function for the Signora.

Norina, apparently a practiced "ghoul" in the art, conveyed graphic reports to us. She said the Signora's heart had burst when she died leaving the mattress of her bed soaked clear through with blood, so it would have to be buried, too. She added that the mattress had been one of the padrona's finest: worth at least fifty thousand lire!

The following day Laura got sick to her stomach when Norina described how the Signora's body had become so swollen from the heat that it was a terrible struggle just to get it in the coffin! At noon the funeral was held in the nearby church. During the service the flies kept buzzing in and out through the open windows and around the wooden casket, settling finally on the blue hand-painted basin that had been placed beneath it. It was already half-filled with her blood...

The air was stifling, heavy with the sweaty, unwashed smell of humanity and the sickening fetor of death. Laura turned suddenly white and crept shamefaced out of the church. After a moment so it wouldn't be too noticeable, I joined her, and we huddled like two naughty children on the marble steps of the church. Although I closed my eyes to forget what was going on inside, it didn't help.

Then I started staring at the unbelievable crimson of a bougainvillea vine gone riot on a nearby wall. Across the road was a garden filled with fig trees, heavy with hot green figs lolling plumply beneath the broad green umbrellas of their leaves.

All along the way, where the road wound past the church, the hillside held up pink and white bouquets of oleander in bloom, and a bird aroused from its afternoon nap scolded truculently from the depths of an orange tree.

Far below, the sky met the sea in a long cool sweep of blue that moved on and on past seeing, while little white clouds went reeling by, drunken in the blue. All around us the Earth was alive and sparkling with beauty.

As we sat there on the steps, the wind began playing games like a mischievous boy, skipping around to peek under the leaves, sliding down the hill on the tops of the trees, then teetering on the long fence rows of grape vines. A wandering minstrel breeze blew down out of the shadow of "Mount Epomeo" singing with the fragrance of ripening grapes. It entered the open windows of the church and emerged dissonant with the smell of death, and all of the grapes gone rotten.

The sickening sweet smell of the corpse made Laura feel faint. She got up with a sigh and took my arm. "Come on, honey, let's get away from here and go for a walk." Then arm in arm we made our way down the powdery descent of the road, silently for a long time, while the choir continued chanting the "Libera Me" for the dead. As we walked, the sound of the singing grew fainter in the distance until at last it faded away…

At last we came to the familiar "piazza" where we sat down at a little table outside and ordered two cappuccinos. As we sipped our favorite refreshment Laura said wonderingly, "Just before the Mass, Norina told me something so wonderful about the Signora I still can't get over it! Do you know who she was, before she married Luciano I mean?"

"Probably a singer like us who decided to get married instead of going on with her career!" I said.

"Oh no, it wasn't like that at all! She was a famous singer at La Scala! What fools we were not to have guessed it!"

"Well come on, Laura," I asked, "who was she anyway?"

"Rosa del Monte, that soprano on your recording: the one you loved to listen to before you came to Italy!"

EPILOGUE: FORTY YEARS LATER

More than forty years have passed since this story unfolded, and in the interim I've drawn closer to the threshold for my own departure. I've also come to see the truth that birth and death are the great "levelers" of existence here on this Earth, two states that must be shared by all of us. At the same time, they provide the "leavening" for the unfoldment of life here in all its multiple expressions, since through birth and death all things are balanced and made new.

Each end brings a new beginning, just as that beginning moves toward its own inevitable end. Throughout our lives and the death that follows, the soul remains the only connecting link that endures eternally. I've often asked myself how many of us have realized that awareness itself is the "cord" which binds life and death together. I've also seen that only in the rarest of cases are we conscious of its activity!

Until the time comes for this, we're flying blind, and the process simply unfolds itself, seemingly beyond our knowing or our control, no matter how hard we try. The truth is, we can become aware of the soul and learn to take responsibility for our lives. While the unfolding of events is rarely changed, they too are affected by our inner response until we ultimately enter a state of balance where joy comes to replace the sorrow that's been our experience for millennia. I've discovered that only spiritual joy makes all things new each moment, and as this understanding opens in our hearts the sting of death passes away...

Here I must confess that I took certain liberties with the story about the Signora, who was actually our Maestro's wife. She'd come to join her husband on the Island for a few weeks before returning to Milano and as fate would have it the Maestro had to leave not long after she arrived to take care of some urgent business matters in Milano. In the interim the Signora was taken mortally ill with a chronic heart condition and died before her beloved husband could get back to her.

She had indeed been a famous singer at one time and done many performances at "La Scala." Both Lucilla and myself also deeply appreciated her evaluation of our own musical progress in the work we did with her husband, the Maestro.

Her death on Ischia only added to the strange feelings I had about the Island. From the moment I set foot on Ischia that summer I sensed a remarkable connection with something I now find difficult to express in words, poetically or otherwise. Since as a rule I don't recall the past lives I've spent in many places on this Earth, I can't attribute the peculiar sense of euphoria I experienced on Ischia to any such recall. Whether that prior life had been pleasant or turbulent I really can't say, since usually our lives partake of both anyway.

I do vividly recall the night a strange "dry storm" hovered over the Island for a long time, remembered now like a dream is, seemingly real and yet unreal. It appears that the greater part of our human existence, or existences here on this Earth, falls into the fabric of a dream, once we've experienced them.

In the first section of this book about Italy, there's a poem in which I attempted to capture the feeling I had during that "Dry Storm" on Ischia, and if you've gotten this far in my "Affair of the Heart" you've probably read it, since it was one of those I'd shown Louis Untermeyer when we first met.

This next story goes back to the time when Lucilla and I first arrived in Milano and were trying to decide where to live and whether that would be alone or together. I think our choice to remain together was one of those wonderful little serendipitys life sometimes bestows. Maybe it was also part of the "plan" the Lord had in mind for me when I'd first asked for his help so long ago in Los Angeles…

IT'S BEEN DONE!

After our arrival in Milano, Laura and I decided to share a room at the "Grand Hotel." The manager liked us so much he offered to give us a reasonable monthly rate if we wanted to stay. He even agreed to move a piano into our room so we could do our practicing during the day.

We considered this for a while, but then I said to Laura, "I do think it would be ever so much better if we found a small apartment somewhere that we could afford."

"It would be a lot more work, too, don't forget that!" Laura reminded me, but I could see she was interested.

"So what?" I replied. "We can't sing all the time, and besides I think we'd get awfully tired of the menu here in the hotel restaurant, even though it's pretty good."

Laura looked thoughtful. She had a deep and abiding respect for good food. "That's true," she agreed, "and what with doing the marketing and all, our Italian should improve tremendously."

"Hah," I scoffed, "my Italian, you mean: You already speak like a native!"

Laura laughed, pleased with the compliment. "If you knew how to speak better, dear Carciofino, you'd know how many mistakes I make!" she said laughing.

"Carciofino" was a pet name Laura had coined for me, because as she said, that was what I looked like when I had my hair up in pin curls. In Italian carciofino means "little artichoke." I really didn't mind. You could call me anything as long as you did it with love, even a "Wop" which I'm not, because I'm Irish with not one speck of Italian in me.

When Laura came back from her lesson that afternoon, she brought a "Corriere della Sera" paper with her and began browsing through the Italian equivalent of a want-ad section. "Ah-ha, here's one," she said. "Agensia, agensia: the Maestro said we'd find something quicker if we went to a rental agency," she explained.

"This one's on Via Fatebenefratelli," she said.

"The Via what?" I asked.

"Fatebenefratelli: it means 'make good brothers'!"

"Well that's a good sign anyway," I said, "once I learn to say it. Let's go."

The girl at the agency sent us to an address on "Via Degli Scipione." We found the place, situated right on the corner of busy "Piazza Maria Adelaida" with trams coming and going from all directions. "It sure will be noisy here!" I said.

"But the girl at the agency said the apartment we're to look at is on the seventh floor, and from there we won't hear much of the noise down below!" Laura said, counting balconies up to the seventh floor from where we stood.

The concierge, or portanaia was very nice to us, and after she'd rung the bell to let "Signora Leone" know we were coming up, she went and opened the elevator for us with her key. Everything seemed to be under lock and key in post war Italy.

"The Signora's name is on the door," she said.

We liked our padrona right away. She was diminutive as a Venetian figurine, and in general one of the dearest people you might hope to meet in Italy, or America. I couldn't really say if she was old or young, since she was somewhere around fifty but still looked barely forty, or younger.

The apartment, as it turned out, was just what we wanted, and after Laura had gone through the customary haggling and gotten a slight adjustment in the terms, we agreed to take it for three months. We made arrangements to return the following morning with the money, and

Signora Leone told us we could move in at any time since she lived with her sister in the big apartment house on the other side of the piazza. She pointed it out to us from the window.

In a few weeks we were so comfortably settled in our new apartment that we couldn't imagine ever having considered living in a pensione, or even a hotel. The Signora had been very kind, also, giving us a lot of advice on housekeeping and shopping in Italy, which to put it mildly, was "different" from the way things were done in America!

Now and then we invited the Signora over for tea. Once we went to have dinner with her, and a week later asked her to have dinner with us. We could see that she enjoyed "mothering" us and didn't act like a typical "padrona" at all. Our lessons were going fine, too, and I was beginning to learn some Italian, much to the patient amusement of storekeepers and clerks in the neighborhood. Laura spent a lot of time just gossiping and collecting various recipes for native Italian dishes like risotto Milanese, which is a delicious steamed rice cooked with onion, chicken broth, parmesan cheese, olive oil and saffron.

She also learned how to cook "ossi buchi." Translated this means "bones with holes" and doesn't sound very appetizing until you see that the bones are filled with marrow, surrounded by succulent veal and all cooked in a delectable sauce. We tried all kinds of things, and even talked of making lasagna sometime. One day Laura came in carrying a bulging market basket. It had been her turn to shop that day and my turn to cook.

"Where were you? It's been over two hours." I knew that as usual Laura had stopped to talk to someone in the neighborhood.

"Oh, you know how long it takes to go to all these little stores!" she said. "Then I stopped to chat with Angela for a few minutes." Angela, as you may recall, was the portanaia in our apartment and liked us a lot. I mean in spite of the fact that we gave her a fairly big tip each month.

"Guess what Angela told me?" Laura asked in that teasing voice of hers, deliberately meant to whet the appetite of my curiosity. When she was saving some particularly juicy tid-bit to tell me she always threw me a cue that way. Now I picked it up.

"I'd never guess in a million years, Laura, so tell me!"

"Well, Angela said that Signora Leone's husband isn't dead at all like we thought he was, but that he ran off to live with another woman!"

"And how would Angela know that?"

"Don't be silly: portanaias know everything!"

I laughed, "Oh yes, I forgot. And when did all of this happen? Recently?"

"Oh no, over six years ago. He went off with Tina Colabrese: you know, the movie actress. It seems she was his mistress for a while, and then he just took off with her: left the Signora flat and she doesn't even know where he is."

"The swine!" I said. "He wouldn't get away with that in America. She could get a divorce and force him to support her."

"I guess she doesn't want a divorce anyway," Laura said. She had a very tender heart and an equally romantic outlook on life. "Speaking of that, I wonder what she lives on?"

"Well, she owns this apartment, and there's the rent we pay her," I pointed out.

"That's so: I forgot about that. And she may have inherited money from her family, too."

Laura went back to playing her game. "And do you want to know something else?"

"Uh-huh. What else?"

"The Signora still believes her husband will come back to her some day!"

"What!" I exclaimed incredulously. "You mean to say that she'd take him back after what he's done?"

"That's what Angela told me, and just as though nothing had ever happened. I guess she must love him a lot."

"Well that's the height of something or other!" I said.

"Maybe it's the height of love," Laura said.

"But you know as well as I do that he won't be back. I've heard about his kind before." I started unpacking the groceries Laura had bought.

"Oh, I don't know about that." Laura was chewing on a tidbit of Bel Paese cheese. "He might turn up again some day."

"Don't be silly, Laura!" I said with a laugh.

Laura went on. "That's the trouble with you, Carciofino. You don't have any faith. You're too pessimistic about life!"

"Only realistic, Laura! I face facts and it isn't difficult to see how Italians feel about marriage. Look at the young girls we've met here for instance. They don't have any of the freedom we do, and their parents guard them with everything but chastity belts. Yet their one consuming thought is to get married as soon as possible! Why? because after that anything goes! The daily life of a married couple in Italy sounds like an excerpt from the Decameron."

Boccaccio's Decameron was one of the books Laura had brought along with her in that big trunk. She laughed at my remark, "Well, I don't think it's quite that bad!"

"No?" I snapped back. "How about Signora Lombardi who gave the party where we sang last week? Why Maestro himself says she left her husband and baby to go live with the man she's with now, just because he has a lot of money. And that tenor who studies with the Maestro: Oh, what is his name?" I said, trying to remember it.

"Oh, you mean Roberto."

"Yes, Roberto. Well he brags openly to everyone about being her lover!"

"Maybe he'd like to be," Laura said. "You hear all kinds of stuff like that."

"But this is true!" I said. "I could tell just by the way they looked at one another."

Laura got up and started breaking eggs into a bowl. "Let's fix something to eat," she said. "I'm starving!"

"So am I." I washed the grapes and the flower-like red and green leaves of lettuce for the salad. The red lettuce was called "radicchio" and had a slightly bitter taste, something like that of ciccoria, or chicory, which resembles dandelion greens. There was also some arugala, another favorite. Even the very popular aperitive, called "Compari," or "Cenar," or something like that had the same bitter taste Italians seem to relish.

While Laura fixed the omelette, I set out the piece of marvelous "Bel Paese" cheese she'd brought and the big round loaf of freshly baked bread. Laura loved to cook and even when it was my turn I didn't mind having her take over! When the omelette was done, she cut it into two steaming portions and we sat down.

"This is marvelous," I said, "and not too dry. Just the way I like it!" Suddenly Laura started laughing like an idiot.

"What's so funny?" I asked.

"Oh, just the thought of being so concerned about the amorous affairs of the Italians, and here we sit as dateless as a couple of nuns!" I didn't think that was so funny and decided to talk about it.

"Well, we did go out a few times! Remember?" I said pointedly. "And we found out that these hot-blooded Latins get to the 'all or nothing at all' stage right after the first date, and then it isn't a date anymore: it's an 'appuntamento' at some hotel!"

Laura laughed and said, "Coraggio, honey. Anyway don't you enjoy my companionship, dahling?"

"Sure, but not like that! Oh go fly a kite, you expatriate from Broadway!"

Laura laughed again. She must have been born laughing. "I heard that the Maestro has a couple of American students coming soon, a tenor and a baritone. Maybe they'll take us out! That would be nice. I'll take the tenor and we'll sing duets."

"If you were a man on the loose in Italy would you be dating an American girl? These women are as hot-blooded as the men!"

"Maybe they'll be the shy type and choose us!" Laura said laughing again. "But from what I remember about American men, they have the same basic ideas as Italians. 'Tutto il mondo e un paese' you know. That's what the Italians say!" Laura reminded me.

"I know," I said, "and although the world may be just one big country when it comes to love, the Americans take longer getting around to 'IT'"…

One night a couple of weeks after that Laura and I were on our way home from a neighborhood movie. Our wiles had so far aroused an interested, but still "dateless" response from the two American students we'd met at the Maestro's studio. Laura figured that they didn't have enough money for dates, but I said, "Nonsense, they're playing the Italian field."

As we approached the "Tabaccaio" on the corner, Laura said, "It's early yet. Let's stop in for a cappuccino."

"All right." I agreed. After we sat down, we decided to let our figures go to the devil and have some pastry, too. Then we just sat there talking. In Italy it's easy to fall into this leisurely way of life since just about everyone does it. The owner of the place, Rolando, was absolutely crazy about Americans, and whenever he could he'd slip over to our table for a few minutes to talk, mostly about America.

I never saw anyone so crazy about America! If his wife wasn't around he'd sit at our table and order a drink for us on the house. One night we drank a whole bottle of champagne…

That evening we were debating the financial folly of ordering two more cappuccinos when Rolando came by, beaming as usual. Rolando was an energetic little Neapolitan who told us once that Neapolitans were interested in only three things in life: making love, dancing and eating. In that order!

Now he made an almost imperceptible little bow, and said, "Buona sera, signorine, belle signorine Americane! Come va? How are things going?"

We told him "fine" and then of course got into the usual discussion about America and how much he wanted to go there to live. After this he said that he had a new American recording he wanted to play for us. Rolando loved American popular music. He must have had dozens of records by American bands and singers. But before he got away we ordered two more cappuccinos.

"You know, he reminds me of us before we came over here," I said. "Remember how we used to get absolutely rhapsodic over Neapolitan 'canzoni' when we were in America?"

"I still do!" Laura said. She loved singing "Avuchella" and could reach out and grab me every time she did. She sang it with a Neapolitan accent, too, and the Italians loved it.

"I remember, too, Laura, but it's different now that I know something about the country. And don't think for a minute that if Rolando could realize his dream and go to America he wouldn't soon feel the same way we do!"

"Feel what way?" Laura asked, somewhat puzzled by the cynical attitude I'd had lately.

"Well, not disappointed exactly, but like we'd awakened from a dream of what we thought Italy would be like, into the reality of what it really is!"

Laura thought about that for a minute.

"That's true, Carciofino, but I bet if you fell in love, Italy would suddenly seem like the paradise you dreamed it was!"

The juke box suddenly began playing a "Nat King Cole" recording and Rolando looked over at us, smiling broadly as usual while listening to American music. I think that juke box was his most prized possession.

"It does seem good to hear American music again, doesn't it?" I said to Laura, with almost a maudlin sense of pride. "I couldn't stand this stuff in America, but now I love it! Maybe I'm beginning to get homesick!"

The waitress brought our cappuccinos, while I glanced over at a young man and a girl sitting close together at a table in the corner. They were obviously lovers because they sat always with some part of their bodies touching, just laughing and saying foolish things. I couldn't help feeling a little envious.

"Speaking of lovers," I said, lowering my voice, "look at those two over there in the corner. Don't they look like a devoted pair of 'fidan-zati'?" I asked.

"Well, maybe they are," Laura said.

"Of course they're not! They're both wearing wedding bands!"

"So what!" Laura retorted. "Maybe they're newly-weds."

"Don't be naive! What would they be doing here at this time of night? They're married all right, but to someone else: otherwise why would they be sitting back there in the corner away from the window? My guess is that they don't want to be seen from the street!"

"They probably want to be alone: newly-weds always want to be alone don't they?" Laura asked.

"How would I know? But I'll bet a dollar to a doughnut that they're meeting here to keep an 'appuntamento' together. Look at how his eyes keep moving around the room to see if anyone he knows has come in?"

"It could be a nervous habit. A lot of people do that!" Laura flung at me defensively. I gave her a disgusted look without saying anything more until Rolando came and joined us at our table.

He asked how we liked his new record, especially the song by Nat King Cole. We told him we liked it a lot and then I asked, "Rolando, who's that young couple sitting over there in the corner?"

"Non lo so, I don't know," he replied with a shrug. "They don't come from around here because I never saw them before."

"There, you see!" I said to Laura in English. "It has to be an 'appunta-mento' or they wouldn't have come to a strange section of the city like this!"

"Well, they could be from somewhere else. Maybe they're here for their honeymoon!" she said.

"Milano," I said incredulously, "for a honeymoon! Milano has one of the worst climates in the world." Rolando understood a few words of English and asked what a 'honeymoon' was.

"That's a 'luna di miele'" Laura explained, glancing at the young couple. Rolando followed her gaze.

"Credo di no. E già troppo vecchia, quella li: I don't think so, the girl is too old. In Italy a girl marries while she's still very young."

He'd heard me say, "appuntamento" in Italian as Laura and I were talking, so now he looked at me with a sly little wink and said "appuntamento" while we all laughed. After that we settled up the "conto" and said good night to our friend.

I knew Laura couldn't quite forgive me for being right about that couple, and when we were crossing the piazza, she said, "I get so disgusted with you sometimes, Carciofino. You always expect the worst of everybody. I don't think you have any faith at all!"

"I wouldn't go so far as to say that!" I said by way of making amends. "I just don't believe in miracles sometimes."

"Well, I do!" Laura said, "and I hope I never get over it! I'll bet that if you'd been right there on the spot and seen the appearance of our Lady of Fatima you'd have called it an optical illusion!" Laura was a devout Catholic and "The Miracle At Fatima," was the movie we'd been to see that night.

"No," I said. "That was probably mass hysteria!"

"You're hopeless," Laura snapped, as she got out her key to unlock the wrought-iron gate which was always kept locked after ten at night...

The next day it was Laura's turn to do the shopping. The rent was due, also, and she said, "I'll just run over to see Signora Leone and pay the rent."

"Don't get talking and stay too long," I reminded her. "Remember, you have a lesson at three."

But Laura was gone a long time, and when she came in her face was glowing like a neon light flashing a smile for a toothpaste ad. "You'll just never guess what happened!"

"You got another check from home!" I said.

"Oh you'll just never guess this one!" Laura's voice was as exultant as a little girl who just had a talk with Santa Claus.

"Well, I guess I won't so why don't you just go ahead and tell me?" I said, still somewhat disinterested at that point.

"O.K." Laura was too impatient to keep up the game any longer. "Here, sit down and get set for some big news!" She led me toward the armchair in the den so we could talk. "Well, here it is!" she announced dramatically. "The Signora's husband has come back, and he's home to stay!"

I was totally dumbfounded. "When did all of this happen?"

"Last night. And you should see them. They're acting like a couple of sposini!"

For once I had nothing to say. "Her husband is awfully nice really: talks like he's only been away on a business trip or something. And the Signora looks years younger, just years!" Laura got up and twirled excitedly around the parquet floor.

"Now do you believe in miracles?" she asked. "Because this is, at least sort of a minor one."

"In this case I certainly do! Only this miracle will probably send us apartment hunting again since we're living in Signora Leone's own place."

"Not very far!" Laura said, "because the Signora told me, that around the first of the month there will be a vacancy here on the fifth floor, and she's sure the padrona will let us have that. She promised to speak to her personally about it and see that we get a good deal."

"Meno male!" I said, relieved about that. "Meno male" is a wonderful expression in Italian that has all kinds of hidden meanings, but in

English it translates to "less bad." Laura was still tacking along on her cloud of triumph.

"Oh, isn't it wonderful," she sighed, whirling over to the piano and playing a few bars of "Anema e core," a beautiful love song about young lovers.

"It really is!" I agreed, and meant it.

Still playing, Laura said, "I think it's the most beautiful love story I've ever heard, and if I were a writer I'd write a story about it, that's what I'd do!"

"You're an incurable romantic," I said, dismissing the subject once and for all.

But Laura wouldn't let it go at that. "Maybe you're being so mean because you wish it were happening to you," she said, with a final flourish over the piano keys.

"Maybe it's because that story's already been written, Laura," I said, "And has just been done again…right here!"

EPILOGUE: FORTY YEARS LATER

I also took a lot of liberties with this story, since our "Padrona" was a different type altogether. She was middle aged and somewhat grouchy, showing up unexpectedly on a trip from nearby Genoa to see that everything was all right in her apartment. Now and then she cooked some delicacy for us such as her "ragu" made from the intestines of chicken. This was an economical dish since it was prepared from the "innards" of the chicken, left inside it when you bought it. Either you threw that part out or made "ragu."

"Ragu" was a lot of work to prepare, though, snipping the squiggly grey intestines open with scissors, cleaning them and then soaking them in salt water for a while. It looked like miles and miles of intestines while the Signora was preparing them. Later before making the "ragu" she would snip them into bite-size fragments. Maybe she wondered why I closed my eyes when I took my first taste of her sauce which had taken so long to prepare, but Lucilla wasn't so squeamish and said it tasted something like tough hamburger meat.

But enough about that. As you know, I'd met the "love of my life" on our voyage to Italy, but until he came looking for me in Milano a few months later, I was more or less biding my time and learning to sing. I also discovered in the interim a gift for writing poetry, spending many leisure moments developing that art, along with my singing.

This signaled the "beginning of the rest of my life," and I've never really ceased writing since that time. My friend, Lucilla, who was directly responsible for revealing this new direction for my creative energies, was as surprised as I was when Sal, the man I'd met on the ship, put in an unannounced appearance in Milano and phoned me, having gotten the number from "Madame Carmen Melis," the teacher I was studying with at the time. Following this, our romance unfolded and Italy became the most glorious place in the world! My heart truly overflowed with love, completely transforming life around me until Italy became Heaven on Earth.

I've discovered that love, both human and Divine is the force that illumines this world, then helps us transcend it by providing a glimpse of those invisible dimensions on the other side, even while we're still residing in this troublesome body, our "cage of flesh and bones," as I frequently call it!

If there's a miracle worker, or a dispenser of magical potions in this world, it's love. When love expands into what has been defined as "unconditional" then the Christ who dwells within each heart produces miracles such as "Fatima" and "Lourdes," reflecting the ecstasy of Saints and revealing the glory of the human soul.

Sometimes, though, it brings just a personal little miracle into our lives that no one else knows about, something I've experienced many times throughout my life...

ALL SORTS OF THINGS
HAPPEN ON BALCONIES!

Balconies. I love balconies! Even in America I was always drawn to a house with a balcony, especially one large enough so you could sit outside and watch the world flowing by… Maybe that's one of the reasons I liked Italy so much: Italy was full of balconies! I noticed them right away on that bus ride from Messina up to Taormina, a side trip we'd taken in Sicily before disembarking at Genoa and boarding the train for Milano.

After that I could just picture myself leaning over a balcony somewhere, and being serenaded by a handsome, Valentino-type lover! When Lucilla and I decided to take an apartment together in Milano, it was way up on the seventh floor, and I could see how that would present difficulties! The building was also located on the corner of a busy piazza with trams clattering by at all hours of the day and night. All the same though, it was still pleasant to imagine a tenor with a stentorian voice, or maybe wearing a microphone, coming by to serenade me of an evening.

I should make it clear right at the start of this chapter that in Italy we encountered two types of balconies: front balconies, and back balconies. The front balconies were, as you might surmise, more for "show" while the back balconies were reserved for strictly utilitarian purposes, which as it turned out were legion at that time. We lived in Italy during the difficult post-war years, and along with the Italians, experienced together many of the resultant hardships. Most of these back balconies looked out on a courtyard, completely enclosed by a half dozen or so apartment buildings. It was here, as you'll soon see, that a large portion of the daily ritual in Italian family life, could be observed at close range.

Since in Italy the refrigerator was a luxury few families could afford then, the balcony became a sort of open-air icebox, where in crudely constructed screened-in cupboards, or some other battered receptacle, many semi-perishable foods were stored. In the winter, the cold damp air provided its own frigid temperature, and in the summer a small icebox preserved necessities like milk and cheese. With such primitive refrigeration methods it's quite evident why shopping became a daily chore for most people, which Laura and I divided between us on a very amicable basis.

The "spazzatura" or garbage disposal chute, was also located outside on the balcony. This was a narrow vent descending into some obscure nadir region below the building, and it seems almost superfluous to mention here that it was always getting plugged up!

I used to stand outside on our back balcony in Milano on any pleasant day around noon, just enjoying all the smells while preparations for the mid-day "pranzo" were in progress. It was gastronomically exhilarating just to sniff the delectable sapore of cooking "sugo," or sauce for the pasta, frying garlic, and the saffron odor of steaming risotto Milanese. Most pungent of all was the fragrant, caramelized smell of the black Italian coffee.

This mid-day meal was actually dinner for most Italians, followed by a long rest period before they returned to work. What we'd consider our big meal of the day in the evening, was in Italy only a light supper, consumed rather late in the day or early evening. Throughout their preparations for the noonday "pranzo" the women were continually running in and out to get something from their outdoor iceboxes, or to throw refuse into the "spazzatura" followed by the clatter of their wooden-soled zocoletti. We found that shoes like these protected your feet from the icy chill of the marble floors, so commonly used throughout Italy.

When the doors were open, as they usually were all spring and summer, we could see the women bustling around in their miniature marble-floored kitchens, from stove-to-table-to-sink-to-cupboard-to-stove-to-balcony-to-table again, in an endless concatenation of preparatory steps for the meal...

Almost any day seemed to be wash day in Italy, although as I recall there was a decided preference for "Lunedi," or Monday, just as it was in America. Since there were no handy washing machines, I often thought of how the maids and housewives must have dreaded the laundering of those oversize sheets used on the huge matrimonial beds, which most married couples started out with as part of their dowry when they were married. Although we didn't have one of those beds in our apartment, the maid who came to clean and wash for us must certainly have had a few problems doing our laundry in the bathtub, then hanging it to dry on the balcony!

On any pleasant day, those adorable Italian children could be seen running around on the balcony, or just looking wistfully through the iron grating when there was nothing more exciting to do. On the top floor of the building, just opposite ours in the courtyard, was an apartment that was for us the epitome of apartment house luxury with its walled-in terrace, bright splashes of potted plants and climbing vines on a trellis. In the springtime we watched enviously as life began creeping upward again into the plants and vines, putting forth new green leaves on the dried winter foliage.

Even after we'd been living in Milano for six months or so, I still dreamed of that dark-haired, soulful and sexy Italian tenor coming to serenade me, and although I was by then aware that such a thing was quite unlikely, there were times when I could almost hear him strumming on his mandolin, or guitar, I didn't care which, and singing one of those haunting melodies, like "Torna Sorrento," "Non Ti Scordar di Me," or "Avuchella."

Of course, I visualized how later that night in our moonlit library, my friend, Lucilla, having fortuitously departed for a three day engagement in Switzerland, or Spain, or anywhere else but home, HE would gather me fiercely to his passionate Italian chest, murmuring tenderly various phrases I'd heard in Italian movies: "Oh bella, gioia, ti amo! Darling I love you!" Or perhaps he'd whisper "Ti voglio bene, I wish you well," which oddly enough translates to I love you in a very serious way!

Then finally he might say, "Non posso vivere senza di te! I can't live without you!" All just blah, blah, blah of course, at this point, since I must regretfully report that I was never serenaded under a balcony in Italy or anywhere else! The only romantic overtures I ever heard of taking place at the apartment where we lived, via the balcony that is, were made to a tenor by a girl who lived on the floor above him. He told us she used to put love notes in her shoes and throw them down from her balcony to his, but he just tossed the shoes back up again because he wasn't interested. He called her "La Fantasma." The translation of that, as implied here, would be "The phantom!"

We never used our front balcony much except for "looking." It was diverting sometimes to gaze down at all the trams converging in the piazza, and the tiny automobiles: topolinos they called them, which means "mouse," or the myriad bicycles and lambrettas whizzing by. Early in the morning there were always those horse-drawn carts and wagons from the country, loaded with big crates of fresh vegetables and fruit, brought to the city daily to stock the local markets.

On the corner was an open-air flower stand with its colorful blossoms looking like vandalistic brush strokes in technicolor on the drab chiaroscuro of Milano's streets. I was appalled at the almost complete absence of color in Northern Italy, where I'd always thought that people of such fiery temperament would dress and surround themselves with equally incandescent colors.

Actually, it was as though they deliberately chose to wear a mask of drabness, mirrored in ultra conservative hues confined to black and grey, or navy blue! But fiery temperaments they certainly had! Why just down the street from where we lived a "cornuto," which is a deceived husband, strangled his wife and then threw her body off the balcony.

Like I said, all sorts of things can, and do happen on balconies! Now and then on a moonlit night I'd go out on our balcony and just look at the moon, composing poetry and keeping an expectant ear open for that long-awaited serenade, but all I ever heard was the neighbor's radio! I think that probably the most vivid memory I have of Italian balconies is the familiar cacophony of sounds heard from my own bed, which invariably awakened me every morning at about eight o'clock.

That was the hour when the women began beating their rugs and draperies, cushions, blankets and clothing: just about anything that could be hung outside. Everything they owned it seemed had to be taken out and beaten, where the whacking of the beaters was interspersed with laughter and calling, "Buon giorno, ha dormito bene? Good morning, and did you sleep well?" The Italians always asked you that.

And in between the incessant beating, the portanaia's daughter would start singing an old canzone: "Luna rossa ne parla 'e te" accompanied by an off-beat whack, whack, whack. Now and then a mother could be heard calling to her child, "Antonio, che fai? What are you doing? Non tocare! Don't touch!"

One morning long before we arrived in Milano, a scream had been heard piercing the air, as a woman fell to her death on the cobbled walk in the courtyard below, all other sounds frozen in her cry of horror. That scream had been forgotten when we lived there, except in the memory of those who had heard it. Now and then from the piazza I'd hear the clackety-clack of horses' hooves, or the intermittent clang of trams, their roaring and zinging electrical snap drowning out the ceaseless medley of sounds floating up from all the balconies in the courtyard.

Often I heard on the floor above, a bed that moved with muted, soft flesh beats of love, or maybe it was only "lust!" and I thought, "My God, that's the way a life is conceived, this is how life begins so early in the morning here in the heart of Italy amid all its passion, joy and sorrow, while women beat their rugs and sing 'canzoni' as they work."

Yes, I suppose one of the reasons I loved Italy so much, even though I was never serenaded on one, was because it had all those balconies, and like I said, all sorts of things can and do happen on balconies!

EPILOGUE: FORTY YEARS LATER

Well, to tell the truth I've never gotten over my attraction to balconies! Whenever we stay in a hotel, or even a motel with a balcony I always go out to explore it and "sit for a spell!" Most private homes don't boast a balcony here in America, but a lot of condos have them, and some apartments.

Across the street from us there's a lovely apartment with potted plants and a barbecue on the balcony. The tenant who once lived there walked around naked in his room with a python curled around his shoulders, but later we heard he'd died of "AIDS." I don't think he caught it from the python. So that's what we're dealing with today in many parts of America. Probably in Italy, too, although I wouldn't know about that.

Like I said somewhere earlier, "Tutto il mondo e un paese!" Since this whole world is one country, we share many radical changes taking place presently, right along with a lot of incredible new ideas which are setting us up for the coming new Millennium. Whether we'll have homes with balconies at that time, I really can't say, but if we do, and I happen to be here again doing my own thing, I'll more than likely be happy to be serenaded while standing on one of them…

Juliet lives forever in my heart, and spirit has become my Romeo! Spirit always is, but we externalize it and name it Charlie, or Rolando, Kristina or Heather, then fall in love with it and probably out again, seldom knowing the true "Beloved" has been serenading our hearts, disguised in all of these forms…

"MONTE VERGINE"

About thirty miles from Naples there's a mountain called "Monte Vergine," which would bear a remarkable resemblance to other mountains in the "Irpina Range" were it not for the fact that on the eastern side of it there's a monastery built by the Dominican monks. This monastery is situated perhaps a hundred feet from the summit, looming staunchly upward from a sheer cascade of rock.

On the very spot where it's said the Virgin appeared in a vision to the monk who founded the Monastery, is built the "Cappella dell'Apparizione." Directly below the Monastery, at the base of "Monte Vergine" is the little village of "Capedaletto," notable chiefly for its new and completely modern Sanitarium for tuberculars situated on the outskirts. To the right of "Capedaletto," fanning out into the valley, there's the province of "Avellino" and a few little villages: "Atripalda," and "Monteforte." However, it's from "Capedaletto" that access to the Monastery is gained.

During the festival, which reaches its height in the latter part of September, the little village rouses herself, like an indolent woman to prepare for the hordes of visitors, pilgrims, tourists, and even opportunists who arrive to throng her streets.

Throughout the village brightly decorated little stalls sell souvenirs, relics, curios and handicrafts from all the outlying districts. Every day, and especially on weekends, big touring cars arrive from Naples, filled with happy celebrants wearing festival costumes, each group decked out in the whimsical colors it has chosen. One gets the impression that flocks of tropical birds have come to display their exotic plumage. A particular group might choose to wear black trousers, or skirts, yellow blouses and red leis, while others are dressed in an incredible indigo blue, crowned with amazing white hats.

The big touring cars, covered with masses of bright flowers, have become "floats" gliding through the streets of "Capedaletto" while the occupants flutter about, cooing and crying like birds on their flowering perches.

From "Capedaletto" they turn onto the sinuous road leading to the Monastery, as the demented drivers plunge and careen around the sharp "S" curves, creating an effect completely wild and filled with exhilaration like a sacred "kirtan" in India! When they reach the large piazza, the cars are parked and the pilgrims get off to tour the Monastery and the grounds surrounding it. There's a surprisingly up-to-date observatory and restaurant run by the monks for the convenience of visitors who stay to sample their simple fare, fortified by a good red wine made by the monks.

There's another road leading to the Monastery, the "one less traveled by" since it must be made on foot. This path, rough and strewn with stones, winds upward from "Capedaletto" to the Monastery, about five or six miles in all. Now and then little groups of peasants who've come to make this difficult pilgrimage, perhaps twenty-five or thirty in each one, have walked a long way on foot, sometimes as much as a hundred miles. In itself this isn't so astonishing, except that they've walked the whole distance in their bare feet, and must now make the steep, torturous ascent to the Monastery. Already their feet are sore and bruised, and some are bleeding from cuts on the sharp stones. There are a few men in the group, but it's mostly made up of women, some with nursing babies in their arms, or older children crying and tugging at the dusty skirts of their mothers. All the while they continue praying, or singing little songs to the Virgin.

At the final phase of the arduous climb, there are crude steps built to mark the fourteen "Stations of the Cross." Here the pilgrims kneel and finish the pilgrimage on their knees! At each "station" there's a painting, or bas-relief in stone, set against the mountainside, depicting that particular event of the Christ's walk to Calvary, and at each "Station" the pilgrims pause to pray and meditate.

Here the path has been cut into the mountainside, and is almost completely shaded by green shrubs meeting in an arch overhead. The wind stirring through the leaves is like an echo of the whispered prayers rising upward from below, and the light that filters downward to touch the heads of the praying pilgrims is green and cool. On they move, crawling painfully from the "Station" where the condemnation of Jesus takes place to where he receives the cross and sets out for Calvary.

Then comes the first fall and he meets his mother. Simon Cyrene takes the cross and bears it for him, while Veronica wipes his face. Moving onward to the second fall Jesus speaks to the women of Jerusalem, and then to the third where he's stripped of his garments, is crucified and dies. Finally his body is taken down from the cross and laid in the tomb... From "Station" to "Station" the pilgrims move still on their aching, wounded knees until they reach the end of the "Via Dolorosa," ultimately arriving at the Monastery, where every year many miraculous healings have been known to occur.

At the beginning of the path, and all along the way, crippled beggars and mendicants of all kinds are selling post cards, or some other trifle. During the last weekend of the festival, a young medical student had come to visit a distant relative in "Avellino." He first went to inspect the Sanitarium near "Capedaletto" and was greatly impressed with its modern facilities. Afterwards he decided to explore the footpath leading to the Monastery.

Stationed beside the way was a tattered cripple, begging. At first glance he appeared to have lost both legs, since he kept the stump of one leg laid out piteously on the knee of his good leg. All the while he was calling, "Aiuto, per carità, per l'amor di Dio aiuto un povero disgraziato: have pity, help a poor unfortunate one for the love of God!" When a group of pilgrims went by, many paused to give small amounts, but most of them were poor also.

With the well-to-do tourists and sightseers, the cripple fared better. Although the young medical student wasn't rich either, he said, "All right, a hundred lire won't break me!"

As he stooped to place money in his basket, the cripple murmured gratefully, "Dio vi benedica! God bless you!" The student turned and continued up the path. However, it wasn't long before he grew tired of his solitary walk, and decided to go back, noting the cripple still stationed at his post. A little further up the way a young red-haired boy, perhaps ten years old, was trying to sell bunches of dispirited, unidentifiable flowers. They looked as though they'd been picked at least a week before that and at the moment, the boy was attempting to make a sale to a pretty auburn-haired young woman.

"You buy some flowers, lady? One hundred lire."

"No," she said, walking on.

"Seventy lire maybe?" he asked following her.

"No," she repeated, her voice adamant.

"Fifty lire: half," the youngster bargained, trotting behind her on the path.

She still shook her head "No" but now she smiled.

"Lady," the boy persisted, undaunted, "you are such a pretty lady. Your husband must love you very much!"

She turned, smiled and then walked on. "Lady, if you bring these flowers home I think he will love you more!"

She walked onward, not looking back and the youngster, beaten but cheerful, spun around to walk back down the path. However, he turned to call loudly after her, his parting shot: "But lady, you have such pretty red hair, just like mine!" That got her. Her smile stretched into a grin, then broke into a laugh.

"All right, you win!" she called. "Here's your hundred lire, you little red-headed rascal: and keep the flowers!" The young medical student had been watching this whole episode, not because he had any particular interest in what took place, but because he thought the auburn haired girl was the most beautiful girl he'd ever seen. He walked quickly in order to come up beside her.

"Mi scusi," he said, "but could you tell me where I can get a bus to the Monastery? It seems a bit far to walk!" Actually he hadn't intended to go to the Monastery at all, but that seemed the most logical thing to say at the moment!

She laughed and said, "Well, no, you see, I don't live around here either and I was just thinking the same thing."

After that they walked on together. As they came abreast of the crippled beggar he called again to the young medical student, "Aiuto, per l'mor di Dio!" having apparently forgotten that the young man had already given him money, or on seeing him in the presence of a young girl, hoped to wrest another donation from him. However, the young couple continued on their way, oblivious to his entreaties...

The cripple called after them, "Mascalzone, pecatore, disgraziato: scoundrel, sinner, disgraced one!"

But the young couple only laughed as they passed him, looking for the bus that would take them up to the Monastery. At the Monastery they saw everything, and yet you might say they really saw very little because they'd become so engrossed in finding out about each other! Obviously they were quite successful, because later in a secluded spot beneath a thick-foliaged tree the young medical student kissed the red-haired girl, and held her in his arms for a while as they talked.

While they were thus occupied, another couple emerged from the restaurant, where with other members of their group they'd been having a rather belated dinner. They wore festival costumes and the casual manner of those who had been married for a long time. They were followed by a solicitous white-clad monk.

The young husband stepped back a few paces to snap pictures of everything in sight, particularly the white robed brother who was attempting to appear oblivious to the magical clicking of the camera. However, the young photographer made such a point of photographing him again and again, seeking for new angles, that the good brother couldn't restrain himself from assuming a picturesque profile now and then, just to please such an ardent camera enthusiast.

The young man's wife, who wore red flowers in her hair, whispered to her husband, "But Antonio, why are you making all of these pictures when you know well there's no film in the camera!"

He answered quickly with a furtive smile at the monk, "Of course, cara, I know that, but don't you see how happy we've made the good brother? Perhaps he is so happy he'll give us a big discount on the bill: capisci?"

Just then a "litter" passed by on which an emaciated man with gnarled and swollen legs was borne into the Chapel. Although his eyes were filled with a certain incredulity, they also mirrored hope. "I believe, Oh Lord, help thou mine unbelief!"

After this a little group of pilgrims approached, still climbing painfully on their knees up the long flight of steps, their lips moving incessantly. Now and then someone would bend down, and reverently kiss the marble steps, revealing not only humility but reverence in their eyes...

EPILOGUE: FORTY YEARS LATER

Twenty-five years or so after the foregoing "vignette" was written our family made a trip to Italy for the canonization of Mother Elizabeth Seton, the first American-born Saint. During our five-week stay we drove up the Mediterranean coast, then back down on the Adriatic side, seeing whatever we could along the way. As part of our itinerary we made a special trip to "Monte Vergine," the setting for the foregoing "vignette."

Although I'd never seen it personally, my husband had often spoken of it, since it was located near his family home in "Avellino." When he read the story I'd written in New York about a place I'd never seen, and with such realism, he was completely astounded.

"Honey, it almost seems like you were there!" he said. "Are you sure you weren't?"

Perhaps I was, on some other plane of awareness. I've always had this peculiar ability to picture some particular place in my mind's eye until it seems I'm actually experiencing it. Maybe this story of "Monte Vergine" grew out of something like that… In another chapter of this book, entitled "Death On Ischia," I left the Island early in the morning on the day the Signora died, knowing nothing about it until weeks later in Paris when word of her death finally reached me. After I'd written an account of it in poetic form, my friend, Lucilla, who was on the Island through all that took place, said her hair literally stood on end as she read my poem.

"How could you have known about the blue hand-painted basin they placed under the casket?" she later asked me. Although she knew for a fact that I hadn't been present physically that day, she said, "You must have been there in some part of your spirit!"

In spirit... I think the whole key to so many things in life lies right there in those words, because in spirit there's no separation, although throughout time we've created multiple divisions of here and there: you and me, we and they, one country versus another, and even my religion as opposed to yours.

As we cease maintaining the separation, the oneness appears, and in that oneness we can be in two places at once, and even more! When that time comes, this world may truly become one country in spirit, bringing our conflict with one another to an end...

When we toured the Monastery at "Monte Vergine" I was astounded to see in the Chapel the miraculously preserved body of one of the brothers who had died there in the fifteenth century, looking as though he'd just fallen asleep in death and would awaken one day to resume his life in the world he'd left behind.

Perhaps this is how it will be when we return home to the source from which we came. On opening our eyes to the glory of those invisible worlds, will all of the past we've spent on Earth seem to have been but a prolonged sleep of forgetfulness?

Maybe then we'll see that what we called life, was only death's long sleep from which we've awakened as from a dream, now over and gone at last...

AFTERWORD
FROM THE AUTHOR

If you liked the mystical-spiritual ideas that were expressed in this book, particularly in Section Four entitled "Forty Years Later," then you may be interested in reading some of my other work in a group of books called "Conversations With My Son," in which Evan and I get into many discussions about life and this human existence, seen through the eyes of youth and my own maturity. Evan frequently reminds me that his name means, "Speaker of Truth," and that I should listen to what he has to say. I do!

There's also a group of eight books, or journeys to invisible dimensions on the other side, in the form of a "feline fantasy" called "The Butch Books."

Many volumes of nature poetry will be available as well, mostly in "tanka" form with a running commentary in prose, books such as "What the Moon Sees," also mentioned here in my "Affair of the Heart." You may recall reading a poem from that which I've included in this volume, entitled "Moon Drinkers."

About the Author

Mildred Marshall Maiorino, orphaned at an early age, always found a way to devote energy to the study of various creative arts. While in Italy to further her operatic career, she read the anthologies of Louis Untermeyer and discovered her love for writing. Returning periodically to her singing career, she discovered an interest in oil painting, but enjoyed her writing most of all. Presently she has written more than one hundred yet to be published books.